Social Anxiety and Social Phobia in Youth

Characteristics, Assessment, and Psychological Treatment

SERIES IN ANXIETY AND RELATED DISORDERS

Series Editor: **Martin M. Antony,** *Anxiety Treatment and Research Centre, St. Joseph's Hospital, Hamilton, Ontario, Canada*

SOCIAL ANXIETY AND SOCIAL PHOBIA IN YOUTH
Characteristics, Assessment, and Psychological Treatment
Christopher A. Kearney

A Continuation Order Plan is available for this series. A continuation order will bring delivery of each new volume immediately upon publication. Volumes are billed only upon actual shipment. For further information please contact the publisher.

Social Anxiety and Social Phobia in Youth

Characteristics, Assessment, and Psychological Treatment

Christopher A. Kearney

University of Nevada
Las Veges, Nevada

 Springer

Library of Congress Cataloging-in-Publication Data

Library of Congress Cataloging-in-Publication Data

A C.I.P. Catalogue record for this book is available from the Library of Congress.

ISBN 0-387-22591-9   e-ISBN 0-387-22592-7   Printed on acid-free paper.

© 2005 Springer Science+Business Media, Inc.

Printed in the United States of America

9 8 7 6 5 4 3 2 1

springeronline.com

For Derek and Claire —
May your lives be social ones (but a little careful too).

PREFACE

A great benefit of being a clinical child psychologist is the opportunity to conduct and review research on fascinating areas of human, youthful behavior. And perhaps no behavior is as central to human existence as *social* behavior, and the lack thereof. In writing this book, therefore, I have been doubly blessed with the chance to examine seminal works on behaviors that are so critical to the development and quality of life of children.

This book covers the major historical aspects, characteristics, assessment strategies, and psychological treatment techniques for youths with social anxiety and social phobia. Chapter 1 provides an introduction to the related constructs and history of social phobia. Chapters 2 and 3 provide a summary of the characteristics and etiological variables that pertain most to youths with social anxiety and social phobia. Chapters 4 and 5 provide an overview of research- and clinically-based assessment strategies and recommendations for this population. Chapters 6–9 provide a description of treatment techniques that are most relevant and empirically supported for youths with social anxiety and social phobia. Chapter 10 covers issues regarding general and relapse prevention as well as difficult cases and future directions.

This book is intended for a wide array of audiences, including clinical and counseling psychologists, school and educational psychologists, social workers, psychiatrists, pediatricians, guidance counselors, principals, teachers, and other relevant professionals. In general, though, the book is meant for those who simply wish to gain a better knowledge of youths with social anxiety and social phobia. The literature in this area is growing fast, and keeping up with the technologies that have been developed to measure and address this important population is crucial.

This book is also a testament to the research pioneers in the area of childhood social anxiety and phobia, including Deborah Beidel, Annette La Greca, Anne Marie Albano, Jerome Kagan, Cynthia Last, Philip Kendall, and Wendy Silverman, among many others. The book is also testament to those adult social anxiety and phobia researchers who have contributed so much to the foundation of childhood assessment and treatment technologies in this area, including Richard Heimberg, Samuel Turner, Philip Zimbardo, David Barlow, and Murray Stein, among many others.

I would like to thank Marty Antony, the series editor, and the good people of Kluwer/Academic Plenum for the opportunity to publish this book. I specifically thank Ms. Sharon Panulla at Kluwer/Academic Plenum for her invaluable assistance. In addition, I must give an *enormous* thank you to Amie Lemos, my tireless graduate student who spent months and months tracking down for me hundreds of articles and books. I thank my other graduate students as well for their patience, including Kelly Drake, Lisa Linning, Jennifer Vecchio, and Krisann Alvarez. As always, I thank Charles Rasmussen of the University of Nevada, Las Vegas for his support and successful efforts to secure a comfortable work environment. Finally, I thank my wife, Kimberlie, and our two children, Derek and Claire, for their wonderful emotional support and patience as well. They continue to be my best friends and teachers.

CONTENTS

CHAPTER 1

DEFINITION AND HISTORY OF SOCIAL PHOBIA AND RELATED CONCEPTS IN YOUTH

"Amber is a 15 year old girl who is often described by her friends as reserved, quiet, thoughtful, and sometimes a bit passive."

"Parker is a 7 year old boy who is socially withdrawn from his classmates at school and who is described as worrisome and interpersonally awkward by his teachers."

"Tamatha is a 4 year old girl who usually cries when around new people or situations or when asked to leave her mother's side."

"Alex is a 5 year old boy who, despite being liked by his peers, often keeps to himself at preschool and seems to prefer solitary activities."

"Tyanna is a 12 year old girl who has just entered middle school and is feeling moody and anxious about meeting new people."

"Daniel is a 13 year old boy who is fearful and anxious when socializing with unknown peers, and often refuses school to avoid strangers, tests, and physical education and English classes."

Of all the expectations we have regarding our children, a basic one is that they will enjoy being with other people. For example, we hope our children will be generally popular and well-liked by classmates, happy to speak to relatives, respectful of others, compliant to adult requests, willing and able to have friends, enthusiastic about attending soccer games and birthday parties and other social events, and cheery and confident with peers. As such, we spend a great deal of time talking to our children, encouraging them to play with others, enrolling them in various activities, and asking them about their friends. For most children, social experiences are positive, pleasant ones that build interactive skills and facilitate individuation and independence.

For other children, however, social experiences may be troublesome, upsetting, or even painful. Indeed, some children struggle in social interactions to the point that they cannot engage in even basic activities such as going to school, sleeping at a friend's house, or talking to unfamiliar people. These children have been described historically in many ways, and some are thought to have social phobia. *Social phobia* can be generally defined as a severe, irrational fear and avoidance of social interactions and/or situations that involve performance before others, evaluation by others, and possible negative consequences such as embarrassment (American Psychiatric Association, 2000).

Social phobia is the main topic of this book, but children with difficulty in social relationships have also been described in many other, related ways. In this chapter, concepts are introduced that have been used historically to describe people who are reticent about interacting with, and performing before, others. In addition to social phobia, these concepts most often include *introversion, shyness, social withdrawal, behavioral inhibition,* and *social and performance anxiety*. All of these concepts overlap to some extent with each other and with social phobia, and may seem indistinguishable in some children. A good example is introversion, which is discussed next.

INTROVERSION

Trait theorists have long argued that human personalities can be distilled into several main factors or categories (e.g., Allport & Odbert, 1936), and some of these seem particularly relevant to social phobia. One trait in particular has been *introversion*. For example, Jung conceptualized humans as having several basic attitudes or predispositions to act in certain ways (Jung, 1921/1971). Introversion was one such attitude, and was characterized by aloofness, inhibition, and a focus toward inner experience and away from others. Conversely, *extraversion* was an attitude characterized by a need for social contact and attention and enthusiasm for cultivating friendships.

The concept of introversion-extraversion was greatly expanded by Eysenck, who thought this dimension intersected with a second continuum: *instability-stability* (Eysenck & Eysenck, 1963) (see Figure 1.1). Like Jung, extraversion was characterized by a generally sociable and gregarious nature, but in Eysenck's approach one that could range from restlessness, aggressiveness, anger, and impulsivity (unstable) to confidence,

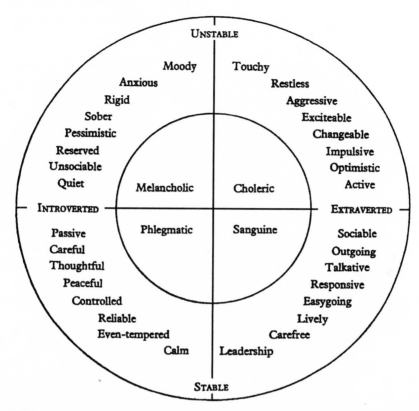

FIGURE 1.1. Diagram showing approximate position of various traits in two-dimensional factor space. Also shown are the four classical 'temperaments' or 'humours', corresponding to the four quadrants. (Used with permission).

optimism, and liveliness (stable). Conversely, introversion was characterized by a generally quiet and reserved nature that could range from rigidity, anxious depressiveness, and extensive social withdrawal (unstable) to stoicism, thoughtfulness, and temperance (stable). Amber, described above, might best be characterized as introverted. A trait related to introversion, *neuroticism*, involves a combination of unstable, introverted characteristics with dysphoria, nervousness, low self-esteem, perfectionism, guilt, and pessimism (John & Srivastava, 1999; McCrae & Costa, 1999). A combination of introversion and neuroticism might be closely related to social phobia.

Personality trait theorists have, of course, expanded Eysenck's ideas about introversion-extraversion and stability-instability by suggesting dimensions of openness, agreeableness, conscientiousness, and many others

(Cattell, 1966; Guastello, 1993; Kroger & Wood, 1993; McCrae & Costa, 1986). However, introversion and extraversion remain powerful descriptors of personality today, and their seemingly innate nature spawned the study of related characteristics, such as shyness, which is discussed next.

SHYNESS

Shyness is often conceptualized as a general tendency toward social withdrawal or intense individuation motivated by concerns or worry about evaluations from others (Rubin & Asendorpf, 1993; Zimbardo, 1982). As such, shyness is often associated with behavioral, cognitive, and emotional features. The construct is sometimes seen as a type of temperament or trait that is similar in ways to introversion (Buss & Plomin, 1984; Cattell, 1973). Indeed, shyness and introversion share characteristics such as social reticence, retreat, and disconnectedness.

Shyness, however, may refer more specifically to an approach-avoidance conflict (should I stay or should I go?) and worry about social evaluation, whereas introversion may refer more generally to a quiet and reserved nature (Henderson & Zimbardo, 2001a; Lewinsky, 1941). Furthermore, measures of shyness and introversion correlate only moderately at best (Cheek & Briggs, 1990). However, one could be both introverted *and* shy. In fact, shyness is sometimes viewed not as a trait but rather a process, emotion, or state of being that fluctuates depending upon one's situation (Leary, 2001). One could thus be generally introverted and occasionally shy.

Different subtypes of shyness have been proposed in the literature. Primary examples include the following:

- Eysenck conceptualized shyness as *introverted*, where a person simply preferred to be alone but could be with others, and *neurotic*, where a person was self-conscious around others, worried about possible negative consequences of social interactions, and inhibited socially (Eysenck & Eysenck, 1969).
- Pilkonis differentiated shy people into those who are *privately shy* or *publicly shy*. Privately shy individuals were described as socially skilled but full of self-doubt, whereas publicly shy individuals were described as less skilled, more inhibited, and very distressed in social situations (Pilkonis, 1977).
- Zimbardo characterized shy people as *shy introverts* or *shy extraverts*, depending on their level of sociability with others. Shy introverts were thought to have poorer social skills, less willingness to approach others, and fewer dating opportunities than shy extraverts

(Zimbardo, 1977). Subsequent studies have found physiological and social skills differences between shy people who are willing or less willing to be sociable (Schmidt, 1999; Schmidt & Fox, 1994).

- Buss differentiated shy people into those who are *fearful* or *self-conscious*. Shy, fearful people were characterized by an early-developing fear of new situations, autonomic reactivity (i.e., somatic anxiety symptoms), and low self-esteem, whereas shy, self-conscious people were characterized by later-developing concerns about oneself in social or public situations (Buss, 1986). Fearful shyness may be closely related to behavioral inhibition (see later section), whereas self-conscious shyness may be considered more of a cognitive phenomenon (Oakman, Farvolden, van Ameringen, & Mancini, 2000).
- Asendorpf (1990a; Asendorpf & Meier, 1993) viewed shyness along a social approach-social avoidance conflict spectrum. In this conceptualization, shy, *socially reticent* children want to engage in social interactions with peers but are unsuccessful at doing so, perhaps because of high social anxiety about negative evaluation. On the other hand, shy, *socially avoidant* children want to withdraw from social interactions and may even be depressed. These children may also be thought of as *conflicted* (i.e., high approach-high avoidance) and *avoidant* (i.e., low approach-high avoidance), respectively (Schmidt & Fox, 1999).
- Cheek and Krasnoperova (1999) differentiated shy people into those who are *withdrawn* or *dependent*. Shy, withdrawn people were characterized by a need for autonomy and independent interpersonal orientation, whereas shy, dependent people were characterized by a greater need for affiliation and emotional support from others. The latter subtype has been described as more anxious in social and assertive situations (e.g., Bruch, Rivet, Heimberg, Hunt, & McIntosh, 1999).

A common theme of these subtypes is that some shy people seem more socially adept, engaging, confident, and comfortable with their shyness, whereas other shy people seem to lack social skills, develop considerable worry and anxiety in social situations, and withdraw more. Parker, the boy described earlier, may resemble this latter subtype. The former group may have features that resemble a personality disorder (see later sections), whereas the latter group may have features that resemble social phobia (Turner, Beidel, & Townsley, 1990). However, enormous variability and heterogeneity is seen among people who are shy.

The heterogeneity of shyness is further demonstrated by the fact that the construct is often viewed as nonproblematic and possibly even adaptive in some people (Chen, Rubin, Li, & Li, 1999; Schneier & Welkowitz, 1996). Indeed, shyness is often considered nonpathological and seems to be present in a large sample of the population, perhaps as many as 40–50% (Henderson & Zimbardo, 2001b; Zimbardo, 1977). In addition, shyness may be related to several *positive* features in children, such as kindness, compliance, diligence, and absence of impulsivity and behavior problems (Schmidt & Tasker, 2000).

For other people, however, especially those who are quite self-conscious and anxious, shyness can interfere with attempts to function adequately in social relationships. McNeil (2001) conceptualized shyness along a spectrum that ranges from fearlessness to normality to excessive shyness or an anxiety disorder, the latter representing a maladaptive level of shyness. Excessive shyness and resulting problems in peer relations can also lead to low self-esteem and various other emotional and behavioral disorders (Bruch & Cheek, 1995; Heiser, Turner, & Beidel, 2003).

BEHAVIORAL INHIBITION

Another type of temperament that is related to introversion, shyness, and social phobia is behavioral inhibition. *Behavioral inhibition* generally refers to a pattern of fearfulness, timidity, avoidance, and guardedness surrounding new stimuli such as strangers or novel objects or events (Kagan, Reznick, & Snidman, 1988). Behavioral inhibition was characteristic of Tamatha, the young girl described earlier. This predisposition, which is present in about 15–20% of youths, has been linked to some of the constructs described in this chapter (Albano & Detweiler, 2001; Kagan & Snidman, 1999). Recall from above, for example, that fear-based shyness may be most closely related to behavioral inhibition (Buss, 1986). In addition, behavioral inhibition seems predictive of social withdrawal (see next section) and social phobia in some youths (Hayward, Killen, Kraemer, & Taylor, 1998; Mick & Telch, 1998; Schwartz, Snidman, & Kagan, 1999) (see also Chapters 2 and 3). Behavioral inhibition, along with certain forms of shyness, social withdrawal, and social fear, likely has some genetic predisposition and/or familial connection as well (Plomin & Daniels, 1986; Plomin et al., 1993; Rose & Ditto, 1983; Rubin, Burgess, Kennedy, & Stewart, 2003).

Although behavioral inhibition, shyness, and social phobia seem to have overlapping features, there may be important differences between them. Shyness, for example, may be a bit narrower construct than behavioral inhibition in that shyness tends to relate more specifically to social situations and resulting discomfort (Rothbart & Mauro, 1990; Saudino, 2001). Behavioral inhibition, however, relates more broadly to many different kinds of new situations and does not necessarily involve withdrawal from many *social* situations. Others, however, see behavioral inhibition as a *subtype* of shyness (Beidel & Turner, 1999). Finally, not all youths with behavioral inhibition necessarily develop social phobia, and many youths with social phobia are not behaviorally inhibited (Biederman, Hirshfeld-Becker, et al., 2001; Schwartz et al., 1999).

As an aside, behavioral inhibition may also be differentiated from *stranger anxiety*, a normal developmental phenomenon in many 7–12-month old children (Emde, Gaensbauer, & Harmon, 1976). Stranger anxiety at this age is often manifested by crying and turning or pulling away when encountering unfamiliar people, and is likely the result of biological predispositions and improved cognitive development (e.g., an enhanced ability to discriminate faces). The phenomenon is not present in all children and may depend heavily on context, or the strangeness of the overall environment. For example, many babies are particularly distressed if a stranger approaches them suddenly in an unfamiliar setting or in the absence of their primary caretaker (e.g., Smith, Eaton, & Hindmarch, 1982). Unlike behavioral inhibition, however, which tends to be stable, stranger anxiety generally declines during a child's toddler years.

SOCIAL WITHDRAWAL

Another construct pertinent to those described so far is *social withdrawal*, which may be defined as contact with peers at less than a normal rate or time alone at more than a normal rate (Rubin et al., 2003). Indeed, social solitude does seem characteristic of introversion, shyness, and behavioral inhibition. However, social withdrawal in children often occurs from both familiar *and* unfamiliar peers, whereas people who are introverted, shy, and/or behaviorally inhibited are generally more wary of unfamiliar stimuli (Burgess, Rubin, Cheah, & Nelson, 2001). Social withdrawal should also be distinguished from *social isolation*, whereby peers actively *reject* a child (e.g., due to aggression) and his or her attempts to interact with them (Rubin, Burgess, & Coplan, 2002). In addition, a child could be *socially neglected*, receiving few positive endorsements from peers, but not necessarily socially withdrawn (Rubin & Asendorpf, 1993).

Children may be socially withdrawn for many reasons, such as introversion, shyness, behavioral inhibition, or mental disorders involving depression, anxiety, or other maladaptive behaviors. For example, behavioral inhibition does seem predictive of social withdrawal in later childhood and adolescent years, and a main aspect of internalizing disorders in youths is avoidance and withdrawal from social situations (Rubin &

Asendorpf, 1993; APA, 2000). In addition, children may withdraw from peers because they have not developed appropriate social skills due to anger, overactivity, impulsivity, inattention, or other maladaptive behavioral characteristics (Barkley, 1998; Gresham & Evans, 1987). On the other hand, many children, like Alex described earlier, are socially withdrawn simply because they prefer to be alone (i.e., low approach motivation), and do not necessarily avoid others (i.e., high avoidant motivation) or have a mental disorder (Asendorpf, 1990b).

Social withdrawal in childhood tends to be stable and can be associated with many negative consequences. Chief among these include insecurity, low self-esteem, dependency, peer rejection and victimization, later anxiety and depression, and difficulty maintaining social relationships (Rubin et al., 2003). In addition, the negative consequences of social withdrawal seem to compound as a child ages. Long-term effects are likely mediated by certain parenting styles, family attachments and stressors, temperamental qualities, and behavior problems (Rubin, Burgess, & Hastings, 2002).

SOCIAL AND PERFORMANCE ANXIETY

Yet another construct that seems to overlap with introversion, shyness, behavioral inhibition, and perhaps social withdrawal is *social and performance anxiety*. Social and performance anxiety may be defined as adverse physiological arousal in social or performance situations that involve possible evaluation by others, with accompanying worry or fear of psychological harm and a desire to escape or avoid these situations (Schlenker & Leary, 1982). In children, social and performance anxiety is often similarly conceptualized as fear of negative evaluation, social distress, and social avoidance (La Greca & Stone, 1993). As such, social and performance anxiety is commonly thought to comprise a wide variety of physiological, cognitive, and behavioral components (Lang, 1968), some of which are listed in Table 1.1. Common social situations include starting and maintaining conversations, playing and cooperating with others, expressing affection, and negotiating solutions to problems, among others. Common performance situations include tests, recitals, games, presentations, and athletic demonstrations, among others.

Social and performance anxiety is considered to be a normal human reaction in many situations. For example, some such anxiety is usually present when meeting someone for the first time (perhaps on a blind date), interviewing for a job, taking an important test, or playing a musical instrument before others. Tyanna, described earlier, experienced normal levels of social and performance anxiety as she entered middle school and met

TABLE 1.1. Common Components of Social and Performance Anxiety in Youth

Physiological	Cognitive	Behavioral
Increased heart rate	Worry about harm to self	Avoidance
Trembling/shaking	Thoughts of being scared	Escape
Shortness of breath	Thoughts of appearing foolish	Reassurance-seeking
Muscle tension	Self-deprecatory thoughts	Lack of eye contact
Frequent urination	Thoughts of inadequacy	Temper tantrums/crying
Nausea/vomiting	Thoughts of incompetence	Shaky voice
Headache/stomachache	Trouble concentrating	Freezing
Dizziness	Thoughts of negative evaluation	Clinging to adults
Sweating	Thoughts of negative consequences	Rituals
Diarrhea	Thoughts of lack of friends	Withdrawal

certain peers for the first time. Social and performance anxiety is often mild to moderate in situations like these, and therefore nonproblematic. Even in therapeutic settings, the goal of treatment is not to eradicate social and performance anxiety but to reduce it to manageable proportions without avoidance (e.g., Hope, Heimberg, Juster, & Turk, 2000). In addition, most people cope with social and performance anxiety in appropriate ways, such as calming themselves or "putting aside" or "working through" anxiety to focus on a particular task (e.g., test). Furthermore, some social and performance anxiety could be adaptive in nature, as when inappropriate behavior is inhibited or alertness is increased in key situations (Kearney & Drake, 2002).

Other people, however, experience very severe levels or extreme forms of social and performance anxiety. Often these levels occur to such an extent that avoidance, escape, overdependence on familiar others, acting-out behavior problems, and other inappropriate coping strategies are present. In addition, such levels of anxiety are obviously quite distressing and usually interfere with one's ability to enjoy a regular social life or even go to school or work. People at this extreme end of the social and performance anxiety spectrum are often considered to have social phobia, a diagnostic condition. The diagnostic description of social phobia and related disorders will therefore comprise the rest of this chapter.

SOCIAL PHOBIA AND RELATED DISORDERS

All of the constructs described so far (introversion, shyness, behavioral inhibition, social withdrawal, social and performance anxiety) represent characteristics that *could* lead to substantial difficulties in social relationships and performance before others. However, these constructs usually represent *nonclinical* populations, or people who still function adequately in their daily life. Furthermore, some of the constructs can be conceptualized as socially acceptable traits or cardinal features of one's personality (introversion, shyness), whereas others may represent developmental processes (social withdrawal, behavioral inhibition, social and performance anxiety) that are expected to vary among normal youths (Masia & Morris, 1998).

In contrast, *social phobia* is a term that represents a *clinical* population because its characteristics are excessive, developmentally inappropriate, avolitional, persistent, resistant to reasonable contrarious arguments, and linked to avoidance or maladaptive interference in various areas of daily life functioning (Albano, 1995; Silverman & Rabian, 1993). For example, children with *social and performance anxiety* often become somewhat nervous when confronting a new evaluative situation, eventually become accustomed to social and evaluative situations with repeated exposures to them, and typically attend social events, albeit with some trepidation. However, children with *social phobia* experience debilitating and developmentally inappropriate panic attacks and other symptoms in social and performance situations, fail to become accustomed to these situations even with repeated exposures, excessively avoid these situations, and subsequently become impaired in key areas such as academic and social development (Albano & Detweiler, 2001).

As such, social phobia is not so much a trait as it is a *mental condition*. The other constructs described in this chapter could help predispose a child toward social phobia, but do not represent a formal diagnostic state as does social phobia. Social phobia has been described in different ways from a diagnostic perspective, and the historical evolution of social phobia and related constructs from this perspective is presented next.

DSM-I

The concepts of emotional instability and social anxiety were present in the initial version of the Diagnostic and Statistical Manual of Mental Disorders (DSM-I) (American Psychiatric Association, 1952). Under the general category of "personality trait disturbance," for example, an "emotionally unstable personality" involved cases where a person "reacts with excitability and ineffectiveness when confronted by minor stress," and his or her "relationship to other people is continuously fraught with fluctuating emotional attitudes" (p. 36). Although people with social anxiety could theoretically be categorized under this distinction, another possibility involved the psychoneurotic disorders, which included problems such as "anxiety reaction" and "phobic reaction" (pp. 32, 33). An anxiety reaction was considered "diffuse and not restricted to definite situations or objects," and may have included vaguely defined social situations. Another diagnostic classification, "psychoneurotic reaction, other" (p. 34), could have applied to people with social anxiety as well.

With specific respect to children, very few diagnostic categories were available in DSM-I. For children with severe social anxiety, the diagnosis perhaps most applicable might have been "adjustment reaction of childhood" with "neurotic traits" (pp. 41, 42). This particular diagnosis involved "transient symptomatic reactions of children to some immediate situation or internal emotional conflict" (p. 41). The neurotic traits subtype of this diagnosis included unspecified phobias. Although heavily based on psychodynamic theory and with poor empirical basis and coverage, the DSM-I did at least provide a starting point for considering neuroticism and related mental disorders in children.

DSM-II

Psychoneurotic disorders were expanded a bit in DSM-II (American Psychiatric Association, 1968), but still did not include a specific mention of social fears. Instead, the most relevant diagnoses were anxiety neurosis and phobic neurosis, both of which involved fear and panic-like symptoms in conjunction with different objects or situations. Personality disorders were described as well that involved deficits in social functioning.

A new section on "behavior disorders of childhood and adolescence" also included "withdrawing reaction of childhood (or adolescence)" and "overanxious reaction of childhood (or adolescence)" (p. 50, APA, 1968). The former referred to "seclusiveness, detachment, sensitivity, shyness, timidity, and general inability to form close interpersonal relationships" (p. 50). As such, a common personality trait (shyness) was considered part of a mental disorder. Overanxious reaction of childhood (or adolescence) referred to "chronic anxiety, excessive and unrealistic fears, sleeplessness, nightmares, and exaggerated autonomic responses" (p. 50). This disorder was also marked by self-consciousness, poor self-confidence, overly conforming behavior, and apprehensiveness in new or unfamiliar situations. Both disorders, though psychometrically unsound, could thus be applied to some extent to children with extensive social and performance anxiety.

DSM-III

The advent of DSM-III in 1980 revolutionized the study of childhood anxiety (and clinical child psychology in general) by including a wide

TABLE 1.2. Diagnostic Criteria for DSM-III Avoidant Disorder of Childhood
or Adolescence

A.	Persistent and excessive shrinking from contact with strangers.
B.	Desire for affection and acceptance, and generally warm and satisfying relations with family members and other familiar figures.
C.	Avoidant behavior sufficiently severe to interfere with social functioning in peer relationships.
D.	Age at least 2 1/2. If 18 or older, does not meet the criteria for Avoidant Personality Disorder.
E.	Duration of the disturbance of at least six months.

(Used with permission).

array of separate childhood diagnoses that included "anxiety disorders of childhood and adolescence" (American Psychiatric Association, 1980). Indeed, much of the research literature that is cited and discussed in this book was published after 1980. The DSM-III contained two diagnoses that were highly applicable to socially anxious children: avoidant disorder of childhood and adolescence, and social phobia.

The diagnosis of *avoidant disorder of childhood and adolescence* was applicable only to youths (see Table 1.2) and primarily involved a "persistent and excessive shrinking from contact with strangers of sufficient severity so as to interfere with social functioning in peer relationships, coupled with a clear desire for affection and acceptance, and relationships with family members and other familiar figures that are warm and satisfying" (pp. 53–54). The diagnosis was analogous to conceptualizations of social withdrawal, described earlier, but key differences were present. In particular, the diagnosis had to last at least six months, significantly interfere with social functioning (e.g., difficulty making or keeping friends), and involve *strangers* (i.e., not familiar people as more general social withdrawal could).

The diagnosis of *social phobia* was largely applicable to adults but could be extended and given to youths if criteria were met. Social phobia (see Table 1.3) primarily involved a "persistent, irrational fear of, and

TABLE 1.3. Diagnostic Criteria for DSM-III Social Phobia

A.	A persistent, irrational fear of, and compelling desire to avoid, a situation in which the individual is exposed to possible scrutiny by others and fears that he or she may act in a way that will be humiliating or embarrassing.
B.	Significant distress because of the disturbance and recognition by the individual that his or her fear is excessive or unreasonable.
C.	Not due to another mental disorder, such as Major Depression or Avoidant Personality Disorder.

(Used with permission).

TABLE 1.4. Diagnostic Criteria for DSM-III-R Avoidant Disorder of Childhood or Adolescence

A.	Excessive shrinking from contact with unfamiliar people, for a period of six months or longer, sufficiently severe to interfere with social functioning in peer relationships.
B.	Desire for social involvement with familiar people (family members and peers the person knows well), and generally warm and satisfying relations with family members and other figures.
C.	Age at least 2 1/2 years.
D.	The disturbance is not sufficiently pervasive and persistent to warrant the diagnosis of Avoidant Personality Disorder.

(Used with permission).

compelling desire to avoid, situations in which the individual may be exposed to scrutiny by others" (p. 227). In particular, a person with social phobia avoided situations that could involve negative evaluation and consequences, experienced distress from the disorder, and understood that his or her fear was unreasonable. Whether the latter two symptoms could accurately apply to younger children or to those with limited cognitive development, however, was debatable.

DSM-III-R

Avoidant disorder of childhood and adolescence and social phobia were retained in the revised version of DSM-III (DSM-III-R) (American Psychiatric Association, 1987). Few changes were made with respect to avoidant disorder (see Table 1.4), although the symptoms were more specifically ordered to reflect a child's reaction to both unfamiliar *and* familiar people (i.e., shrinking versus desire for social involvement). Again, the diagnosis was somewhat but not completely analogous to the construct of social withdrawal. Despite the revision, however, the validity of the diagnosis remained highly questionable. In fact, in the research literature, little difference was seen between children with avoidant disorder and children with social phobia, except that children with avoidant disorder tended to be younger than children with social phobia (Francis, Last, & Strauss, 1992). These latter authors contended that their finding may have been due to simple developmental differences, as fear of strangers tends to emerge before concerns about social performance and evaluation from others.

A larger overhaul in DSM-III-R occurred with respect to the diagnosis of social phobia (see Table 1.5). Specific examples of socially phobic situations and exclusionary diagnoses were provided, and the diagnosis called for an "immediate anxiety response" in concert with exposure to a socially phobic situation. In addition, the earlier "compelling desire to avoid" was

TABLE 1.5. Diagnostic Criteria for DSM-III-R Social Phobia

A.	A persistent fear of one or more situations (the social phobic situations) in which the person is exposed to possible scrutiny by others and fears that he or she may do something or act in a way that will be humiliating or embarrassing. Examples include: being unable to continue talking while speaking in public, choking on food when eating in front of others, being unable to urinate in a public lavatory, hand-trembling when writing in the presence of others, and saying foolish things or not being able to answer questions in social situations.
B.	If an Axis III or another Axis I disorder is present, the fear in A is unrelated to it, e.g., the fear is not of having a panic attack (Panic Disorder), stuttering (Stuttering), trembling (Parkinson's disease), or exhibiting abnormal eating behavior (Anorexia Nervosa or Bulimia Nervosa).
C.	During some phase of the disturbance, exposure to the specific phobic stimulus (or stimuli) almost invariably provokes an immediate anxiety response.
D.	The phobic situation(s) is avoided, or is endured with intense anxiety.
E.	The avoidant behavior interferes with occupational functioning or with usual social activities or relationships with others, or there is marked distress about having the fear.
F.	The person recognizes that his or her fear is excessive or unreasonable.
G.	If the person is under 18, the disturbance does not meet the criteria for Avoidant Disorder of Childhood or Adolescence.

Specify generalized type if the phobic situation includes most social situations, and also consider the additional diagnosis of Avoidant Personality Disorder.

(Used with permission).

replaced with "is avoided," and the option of enduring a socially phobic situation with intense anxiety was provided. Avoidant behavior was also expected to have interfered with social functioning. The DSM-III-R also contained a subtype of social phobia, *generalized type*, that supposedly included people with social phobia who avoided or dreaded most social situations, as opposed to one or two specific ones (e.g., public speaking only). A consideration of avoidant personality disorder in this instance (see below) was recommended as well.

With respect to children, a significant change in DSM-III-R criteria for social phobia was the provision that youths could not simultaneously meet criteria for both avoidant disorder and social phobia. This suggested that avoidant disorder covered the symptoms of social phobia but may have included other forms of social withdrawal as well. For example, some youths may withdraw from some social situations for reasons other than anxiety (see earlier discussion). However, as mentioned above, little empirical evidence was available to clearly differentiate avoidant disorder and social phobia.

For historical purposes, one should note that the DSM-III and/or DSM-III-R contained other childhood mental disorders that could have overlapped with avoidant disorder and social phobia. For example, the initial essential feature of *overanxious disorder of childhood and adolescence* was "excessive worrying and fearful behavior" that may have included worry about future and past events, injury, personal competence, peer group activities, and meeting the expectations of others (APA, 1980, p. 55). In DSM-III-R, the essential feature of this disorder was altered to "excessive or unrealistic anxiety or worry" (APA, 1987, p. 63). In both versions, however, marked self-consciousness and susceptibility to embarrassment or humiliation (p. 57) were also part of the disorder. Overanxious disorder was found to be highly comorbid with other childhood anxiety disorders, including social phobia, and was criticized for its poor clinical value and low reliability (Beidel, 1991; Kashani & Orvaschel, 1990; Klein & Last, 1989; Silverman & Eisen, 1993). The disorder was later integrated with generalized anxiety disorder, which also involves general, uncontrollable worry about many situations and events (see below).

Furthermore, the essential feature of *schizoid disorder of childhood or adolescence* in DSM-III was a "defect in the capacity to form social relationships" (APA, 1980, p. 60) and lack of interest in friendships. This disorder was distinguished from avoidant disorder in that children of the latter group were interested in social participation but "inhibited by anxiety from forming social contacts" (p. 61). Schizoid disorder of childhood or adolescence was eliminated in DSM-III-R and essentially integrated into schizoid personality and pervasive developmental disorders.

DSM-IV AND DSM-IV-TR: AVOIDANT DISORDER OF CHILDHOOD AND ADOLESCENCE

Avoidant disorder of childhood and adolescence was deleted in updated versions of the DSM (DSM-IV and DSM-IV-TR) (American Psychiatric Association, 1994, 2000) and essentially integrated into the diagnosis of social phobia. Perhaps this was in reaction to the lack of differentiation found between avoidant disorder and social phobia, but the deletion may have had important ramifications for clinicians. Though the criteria for avoidant disorder were indeed problematic, a key principle of the diagnosis was that children often withdrew from social situations for reasons other than clinical levels of anxiety (Vasey, 1995). For example, as noted earlier, many youths withdraw from peers due to anger, sadness, or even introversion or shyness (or subclinical levels of social and performance anxiety). The deletion of avoidant disorder leaves these children without a diagnostic "home," and may promote the use of a social phobia diagnosis in cases where the criteria do not adequately apply.

TABLE 1.6. Diagnostic Criteria for DSM-IV-TR Social Phobia
(Social Anxiety Disorder)

A.	A marked and persistent fear of one or more social or performance situations in which the person is exposed to unfamiliar people or to possible scrutiny by others. The individual fears that he or she will act in a way (or show anxiety symptoms) that will be humiliating or embarrassing. **Note:** In children, there must be evidence of the capacity for age-appropriate social relationships with familiar people and the anxiety must occur in peer settings, not just in interactions with adults.
B.	Exposure to the feared social situation almost invariably provokes anxiety, which may take the form of a situationally bound or situationally predisposed panic attack. **Note:** In children, the anxiety may be expressed by crying, tantrums, freezing, or shrinking from social situations with unfamiliar people.
C.	The person recognizes that the fear is excessive or unreasonable. **Note:** In children, this feature may be absent.
D.	The feared social or performance situations are avoided or else are endured with intense anxiety or distress.
E.	The avoidance, anxious anticipation, or distress in the feared social or performance situation(s) interferes significantly with the person's normal routine, occupational (academic) functioning, or social activities or relationships, or there is marked distress about having the phobia.
F.	In individuals under age 18 years, the duration is at least six months.
G.	The fear or avoidance is not due to the direct physiological effects of a substance (e.g., a drug of abuse, a medication) or a general medical condition and is not better accounted for by another mental disorder (e.g., Panic Disorder With or Without Agoraphobia, Separation Anxiety Disorder, Body Dysmorphic Disorder, a Pervasive Developmental Disorder, or Schizoid Personality Disorder).
H.	If a general medical condition or another mental disorder is present, the fear in Criterion A is unrelated to it, e.g., the fear is not of Stuttering, trembling in Parkinson's disease, or exhibiting abnormal eating behavior in Anorexia Nervosa or Bulimia Nervosa.

Specify if:
   Generalized: if the fears include most social situations (also consider the additional diagnosis of Avoidant Personality Disorder)

(Used with permission).

DSM-IV AND DSM-IV-TR: SOCIAL PHOBIA

The diagnosis of social phobia (also referred to as social anxiety disorder) was retained in DSM-IV and substantially overhauled again (see Table 1.6). Criteria for the disorder were changed to refer to marked and persistent fear of social and performance situations as well as concern about negative evaluation and consequences. In addition, the "immediate anxiety response" of DSM-III-R was replaced with the presence of specific panic attacks in social and performance situations. *Situationally bound panic attacks* refer to attacks that occur only in specific and predictable situations. For example, one may have a panic attack when about to engage in public speaking, but never at any other time. *Situationally predisposed panic attacks* refer to attacks that are somewhat but not completely predictable or necessarily linked to a specific stimulus (APA, 1994, 2000). For example, one may have panic attacks in social- and performance-based situations more so than in other situations, though not necessarily always. Greater exclusionary criteria for diagnosing social phobia were added as well in DSM-IV, and the generalized subtype was retained.

Another key feature of DSM-IV criteria for social phobia was its greater attention to developmental differences by limiting the presence of some symptoms in children. For children to be diagnosed with social phobia, for example, insight into the fact that the symptoms are excessive, and the presence of formal panic attacks, are not necessary. Anxiety in social and performance situations must still occur, but such anxiety may be expressed in various ways, including behaviors that are sometimes considered immature or even externalizing in nature (i.e., crying, tantrums). In addition, the six-month criterion for social phobia now applies only to youths, children must show the capacity for normal social relationships with familiar people, and social and performance anxiety must occur around peers and not simply around adults. Many children, for example, are naturally content with peers but quite nervous around adults. These children would not generally qualify for a diagnosis of social phobia.

DSM-IV and DSM-IV-TR: Problems With the Diagnosis of Social Phobia for Youths

Despite its widespread use, the diagnostic definition of social phobia for youths remains somewhat problematic. First, many of the criteria are vaguely defined and left to considerable clinical judgment. Key phrases left ambiguous, for example, include "marked and persistent fear," endurance of situations with "intense anxiety and distress," and "interferes significantly with the person's normal routine" (APA, 2000, p. 456). Second, four of the most important aspects of the disorder (i.e., relationships with others, expression of anxiety, insight, duration) are presented quite differently for adults and children, suggesting that social phobia in youths may eventually require an independent definition. In related fashion, the presence of panic attacks in children, though less so in adolescents, remains highly controversial (Kearney & Silverman, 1992; Ollendick, 1998). Including formal panic attacks for diagnosing social phobia makes questionable the applicability of the diagnosis to younger children.

Third, the psychometric strength of the diagnosis for youths has not yet been fully explored (see Chapter 4). Fourth, little guidance is given for differentiating social phobia in children from other mental disorders (see next section for example) and from other constructs such as those described in this chapter. Although the DSM definition of social phobia is popular among clinicians and researchers, and is emphasized in this book, the definition is imperfect with respect to youths and caution should be exercised when administering the diagnosis. Finally, some have argued that the term "social anxiety disorder" should be used instead of "social phobia" because the former conveys a greater sense of "pervasiveness and impairment" and is more easily distinguished from specific phobia (Liebowitz, Heimberg, Fresco, Travers, & Stein, 2000, p. 192). However, use of the term "social phobia" remains dominant in literature involving youths and so is employed in this book.

DSM-IV and DSM-IV-TR: Other Relevant Diagnoses

Certain DSM-based personality disorders also involve withdrawal from social contact and could be applied to youth. Avoidant personality disorder (APD), for example, refers to a "pervasive pattern of social inhibition, feelings of inadequacy, and hypersensitivity to negative evaluation" (APA, 2000, p. 721). The distinction between APD and generalized social anxiety disorder remains unclear, however, as the DSM-IV-TR stipulates that the two disorders show "a great deal of overlap" and may be "alternative conceptualizations of the same or similar conditions" (p. 720). Both disorders, for example, are associated with avoidance of school-based and extracurricular activities that involve extensive social interaction. In fact, some have argued that having APD and generalized social phobia in one diagnostic system is not yet warranted (e.g., Heimberg, Holt, Schneier, Spitzer, & Liebowitz, 1993; Widiger, 1992).

Some criteria for APD are not listed for generalized social anxiety disorder, however, including low self-esteem, lack of risk-taking behavior, and sense of inadequacy. In addition, Kernberg, Weiner, and Bardenstein (2000) distinguished APD and generalized social anxiety disorder in children, stating that those with APD tend more to need strong proof that significant others will be supportive and noncritical before engaging in social interactions. In addition, those with APD do not generally display fear or panic attacks in social situations, but rather substantial vigilance for criticism and rejection by others. The ongoing search for cues and evidence that one will be disapproved or disfavored is paramount to fear of social situations. Those with APD are also generally deficient in social skills, inhibited with respect to emotional expression, and highly apprehensive about approaching unfamiliar stimuli (Kernberg et al., 2000).

Other mental disorders could also involve aspects of social avoidance and dysfunction. *Schizoid personality disorder* involves a "pervasive pattern of detachment from social relationships and a restricted range of expression of emotions in interpersonal settings" (APA, 2000, p. 697). Those with schizoid personality disorder do not generally exhibit social anxiety but rather a simple disinterest in human relationships and emotion. Still, the extensive social withdrawal evident in this disorder could overlap with those with social anxiety or avoidant personality disorders. *Generalized anxiety disorder* involves "excessive anxiety and worry," and in children is often focused toward "performance or competence at school or in sporting events" (APA, 2000, pp. 472, 473). Obviously such concerns could intersect with worries about negative evaluation from others and interfere with social functioning. In addition, the traditional, albeit flawed notion of *school phobia* sometimes refers to a child's irrational fear of stimuli related to a school setting, which could include social/evaluative stimuli (Kearney, 2001). In the DSM, a diagnosis of *specific phobia of school* could thus apply (APA, 2000).

Other relevant diagnoses include *paranoid* (i.e., reluctance to confide in others), *schizotypal* (i.e., lack of close friends or confidants), and *obsessive-compulsive* (i.e., overcontrol and inhibition of expression) personality disorders. In addition, *selective mutism* (e.g., unwillingness to speak publicly), *depression* (e.g., diminished interest in social activities), *schizophrenia* (i.e., negative dimension), and *sexual dysfunctions* (e.g., avoidance of sexual contact with a partner) may involve severe social deficits and anxiety. Of course, many mental disorders also involve impairment in social functioning.

ICD-10: DCR-10

In addition to the DSM, versions of the International Classification of Diseases (ICD) and its Diagnostic Criteria for Research (DCR) have been published over the last several decades. The most recent version includes a specific diagnostic category of *social anxiety disorder of childhood* (SADC) (see Table 1.7). The essential feature of SADC involves "wariness of strangers and social apprehension or anxiety when encountering new, strange or socially threatening situations" (World Health Organisation, 1994, p. 306). Such anxiety should be generally much more severe than is typical for a child and should greatly interfere with his or her social functioning.

Also in ICD-10, under "childhood emotional disorder, unspecified," are "other childhood disorders of social functioning" (pp. 310, 314). These problems include "common abnormalities in social functioning" (p. 310) that may involve behaviors related to SADC, such as general withdrawal from peer groups for reasons other than anxiety. This ICD distinction could be somewhat analogous to avoidant disorder discussed earlier.

TABLE 1.7. Diagnostic Criteria for ICD-10 Social Anxiety Disorder of Childhood

A.	Persistent anxiety in social situations in which the child is exposed to unfamiliar people, including peers, is manifested by socially avoidant behaviour.
B.	The child exhibits self-consciousness, embarrassment or overconcern about the appropriateness of his or her behaviour when interacting with unfamiliar figures.
C.	There is significant interference with social (including peer) relationships, which are consequently restricted; when new or forced social situations are experienced, they cause marked distress and discomfort as manifested by crying, lack of spontaneous speech or withdrawal from the social situation.
D.	The child has satisfying social relationships with familiar figures (family members or peers that he or she knows well).
E.	Onset of the disorder usually coincides with a developmental phase where these anxiety reactions are considered appropriate. The abnormal degree, persistence over time and associated impairment must be manifest before the age of 6 years.
F.	The criteria for generalized anxiety disorder of childhood are not met.
G.	The disorder does not occur as part of broader disturbances of emotions, conduct or personality, or of a pervasive developmental disorder, psychotic disorder or psychoactive substance use disorder.
H.	Duration of the disorder is at least 4 weeks.

(Used with permission).

ORGANIZING THE SOCIAL
ANXIETY-RELATED DIAGNOSES

McNeil (2001) proposed a continuum that may be helpful for organizing the social anxiety-related diagnoses that are available. Recall that such disorders would be located at the far end of a shyness spectrum (see Figure 1.2). One aspect of this continuum would include people with one specific type of phobia in a social and/or evaluative situation. Many people, for example, are terrified of public speaking but have few problems socializing with people outside of this one situation. Further along the continuum would be people with social phobia of the nongeneralized type, or those who experience maladaptive anxiety in a few social and/or evaluative situations. Nongeneralized social phobia is sometimes referred to as specific, performance-based, limited, circumscribed, or discrete social phobia as well. Symptoms are often transitory with low general interference or avoidance (Lang & Stein, 2001).

A more severe group would include people with generalized social phobia, or those who chronically experience most social and/or evaluative situations as highly anxiety-provoking and thus avoid them. Finally, those with avoidant personality disorder (or related personality disorders) would represent the extreme end of the continuum. People in this latter group perhaps experience generalized social phobia, pervasive

Continuum of Social Anxiety

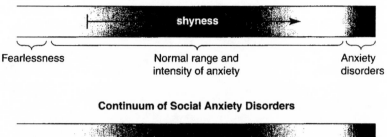

| Fearlessness | Normal range and intensity of anxiety | Anxiety disorders |

Continuum of Social Anxiety Disorders

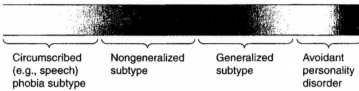

| Circumscribed (e.g., speech) phobia subtype | Nongeneralized subtype | Generalized subtype | Avoidant personality disorder |

FIGURE 1.2. Proposed model of the continua of social anxiety (top) and social anxiety disorders (bottom). (Used with permission).

deficits in social relationships, and very extensive problems with respect to sensitivity, anxiety, self-esteem, and inhibition. Of course, related behavior problems such as depression or psychoses should also be considered when placing groups along this continuum.

FINAL COMMENTS

The diagnosis of childhood social phobia is certainly linked with many historical constructs, such as introversion, shyness, behavioral inhibition, social withdrawal, and social and performance anxiety. Key aspects of the mental disorder, however, seem to be excessive levels of anxiety and worry in social and performance situations and significant interference in daily life functioning. However, like shyness and the other constructs, social phobia is manifested heterogeneously in children. The diverse characteristics of children with social phobia are described in Chapter 2.

MAJOR CHARACTERISTICS OF YOUTHS WITH SOCIAL ANXIETY AND SOCIAL PHOBIA

As mentioned in Chapter 1, youths with social anxiety and social phobia have varied and heterogeneous characteristics. The purpose of this chapter is to summarize the research literature regarding the major child-based characteristics of this population. In particular, this chapter will cover social concerns in nonclinical and clinical children, epidemiology and demographic characteristics, symptomatology, diagnostic comorbidity, general impairment and avoidance, peer relationships, other child characteristics, subtypes, and course and outcome. Some child-based variables pertinent to etiology that also characterize this population, including behavioral inhibition and cognition, are summarized here but presented in more depth in Chapter 3. A good starting place for understanding social phobia in children is to examine what children worry about in general. As one might suppose, these worries often include social and evaluative phenomena.

WHAT ARE CHILDREN IN GENERAL CONCERNED ABOUT?

As children develop cognitively, their concerns about their surrounding environment become increasingly abstract and complicated (Gullone & King, 1997; Vasey, Crnic, & Carter, 1994). In particular, maturing children differentiate complex stimuli (e.g., familiar and unfamiliar faces), become more curious as they move about, understand cause-effect relationships, anticipate negative outcomes, and compare themselves to ideal parameters (Muris & Merckelbach, 2001). As such, specific concerns in younger children about such things as monsters, darkness, and big dogs often give way to more general concerns in older children and adolescents about personal harm, family, friends, and school (e.g., Muris, Merckelbach, Gadet, & Moulaert, 2000).

General concerns of older children and adolescents often involve social and evaluative phenomena as well. With specific respect to children, for example, Silverman, La Greca, and Wasserstein (1995) evaluated second- to sixth-graders and found that two of the four most frequently reported *categories* of worry involved school (64.1%) and performance (53.5%) situations. In fact, school-based performance was a very frequently reported concern (81.5%) along with concerns about teachers, being called on in class, and performance in sports, music, and dance. This was especially true for girls more so than boys. Other frequently reported social worries included minor events (e.g., worry about anothers' feelings; 70.3%) and being betrayed (62.1%), teased (48.9%), or ignored (24.4%) by friends or others. Bell-Dolan, Last, and Strauss (1990) also found that many nonclinical youths reportedly withdraw from others (14.5%) and have fears of public speaking (21.7%), dressing before others (14.5%), and blushing (10.7%). Others have found as well that worries about school, being teased, making mistakes, and one's appearance are not uncommon in children (Muris, Meesters, Merckelbach, Sermon, & Zwakhalen, 1998).

With specific respect to adolescents, researchers have noted that many endorse social anxiety items on questionnaires (e.g., Boyd, Ginsburg, Lambert, Cooley, & Campbell, 2003). In addition, Essau and colleagues (1999) found that nearly half (47.2%) of nonclinical German youths aged 12–17 years reportedly had social fears, with girls (50.8%) testifying so more than boys (42.0%). Prevalent social fears included:

- performing before others or taking tests (31.1%)
- speaking in public (19.7%)
- conversing with others (9.2%)
- eating or drinking in public (8.3%)
- participating in social events (7.0%)
- writing before others (2.9%)

Social-related concerns are thus quite prevalent among youths in general, meaning that some will naturally have such concerns at a severe level. Such children may qualify for a diagnosis of social phobia (Essau et al., 1999), and are discussed next.

WHAT ARE CHILDREN WITH SOCIAL PHOBIA CONCERNED ABOUT?

Regarding children with social phobia, or those with more severe fears, similar concerns are often expressed. For example, Strauss and Last (1993) found that youths with social phobia aged 4–17 years tend to fear school (64%), public speaking (57%), blushing (25%), crowds (21%), eating or drinking before others (18%), dressing before others (14%), and using public restrooms (7%). In a more extensive analysis, Beidel, Turner, and Morris (1999) examined the specific targets of fears in 50 children with social phobia aged 7–13 years. Situations feared most by these children, as reported from interview, usually involved performances before others (e.g., reading, playing a musical instrument, writing) and everyday social interactions (e.g., starting a conversation, talking on the telephone, playing with other children) (see Table 2.1).

TABLE 2.1. Types of Social Situations Feared by Children With Social Phobia ($n = 50$)

Situation	% Endorsing at least moderate distress
Reading aloud in front of the class	71
Musical or athletic performances	61
Joining in on a conversation	59
Speaking to adults	59
Starting a conversation	58
Writing on the blackboard	51
Ordering food in a restaurant	50
Attending dances or activity nights	50
Taking tests	48
Parties	47
Answering a question in class	46
Working or playing with other children	45
Asking the teacher for help	44
Physical education class	37
Group or team meetings	36
Having picture taken	32
Using school or public bathrooms	24
Inviting a friend to get together	24
Eating in the school cafeteria	23
Walking in the hallway/hanging out at the lockers	16
Answering or talking on the telephone	13
Eating in front of others	10
Dating	NA

Note: NA = not applicable. (Used with permission).

Most youths endorsed many situations as distressing, leading the authors to conclude that generalized social phobia is highly characteristic of this clinical population. From daily diary data, similar concerns were evident, especially with respect to unstructured social interactions, performance before others, having to respond to others, and doing something (e.g., eating, using the restroom) in a public place. In fact, youths with social phobia reportedly experienced nearly five distressing events per week. Of course, some of these situations may overlap. For example, a child could encounter school-based situations involving several stressors at once, as when he or she must answer a question in class when giving an oral presentation. Indeed, many adolescents with social phobia fear situations involving informal and formal interactions with others, assertion, and observation by others (Hofmann et al., 1999).

In my experience, many children with social anxiety or social phobia also dread situations that likely require them to encounter the presence of others, such as entering a classroom, hallway, cafeteria, locker room, physical education class, or group activity. In addition, adolescents with social anxiety or social phobia often fear situations like dating, church retreats, job interviews, and driving tests, among others. Some youths with social phobia are also reluctant to engage in family-oriented activities such as gatherings, meeting family friends, answering the door or telephone, or ordering their own meal during a family dinner at a restaurant (Albano, Chorpita, & Barlow, 2003). In many cases, these youths fear excess attention from others and being judged in a harsh, negative manner.

EPIDEMIOLOGY

Although social fears are common among youths, the exact prevalence of childhood *social phobia* is unclear. This is partly so because many available studies on the topic employed older DSM-III-R diagnostic criteria, grouped children with social phobia with children with avoidant disorder or other anxiety/phobic disorders, and/or assigned children with fears of public speaking (now social phobia) to simple phobia groups. As such, older epidemiological studies covering many childhood behavior disorders reveal a wide range of prevalence of DSM-III/DSM-III-R childhood social phobia (0.7–15.1%), with most figures around 1–4% (Anderson, Williams, McGee, & Silva, 1987; Benjamin, Costello, & Warren, 1990; Costello, 1989; Costello et al., 1988; Fergusson, Horwood, & Lynskey, 1993; Kashani & Orvaschel, 1990; Lewinsohn, Hops, Roberts, Seeley, & Andrews, 1993; McGee et al., 1990; Shaffer et al., 1996; Verhulst, van der Ende, Ferdinand, & Kasius, 1997). These earlier figures generally mirrored those found for adults but assessment limitations may have suppressed true prevalence rates (Wittchen & Fehm, 2001).

Prevalence rates for DSM-IV-based childhood social phobia are sparse but seem to parallel earlier estimates. For example, Essau and colleagues (1999, 2000) found the prevalence of social phobia among adolescents to be 1.6%. In addition, Wittchen, Stein, and Kessler (1999) found the prevalence of social phobia in 14–17-year-olds to be 2.7% for males and 5.5% for females (4.0% total). Rates of non generalized (2.9%) and generalized (1.2%) social phobia were reported as well. In a sample of 14–24-year-olds, lifetime and 12-month prevalence rates for social phobia were reported as 3.5% and 2.6%, respectively (Wittchen, Nelson, & Lachner, 1998). Rates were slightly higher for females (lifetime and 12-month prevalence: 4.8%, 3.7%) than for males (lifetime and 12-month prevalence: 2.2%, 1.5%). Inclusion of subthreshold cases increased overall lifetime and 12-month prevalence rates to 7.3% and 5.2%, respectively.

Higher prevalence rates have been reported in other studies. For example, Sonntag and colleagues (2000) found an overall prevalence rate of social phobia to be 7.2% among 14–24-year-olds. Nelson and colleagues (2000) also reported a lifetime prevalence rate for social phobia to be 16.3% in adolescent twins, but the circumscribed nature of the sample limits the external validity of this figure. In comparison, prevalence rates for DSM-IV-based adult social phobia reportedly range from 2.7–13.7% (DeWit, Ogborne, Offord, & MacDonald, 1999; Wittchen & Fehm, 2001), and the DSM-IV-TR reported prevalence range for all persons with social phobia is 3–13% (APA, 2000).

Prevalence rates for childhood social phobia may increase with time (Rodriguez, Caballo, Garcia-Lopez, Alcazar, & Lopez-Gollenet, 2003). Indeed, Kendall and Warman (1996) found that diagnoses of childhood social phobia via parent report increased significantly when switching from DSM-III-R (18% of sample) to DSM-IV (40% of sample) criteria. Prevalence rates may increase as childhood social phobia becomes more well-known and as diagnostic criteria evolve to become more sensitive to children. Some have argued as well that DSM-III-R social phobia and DSM-III-R avoidant disorder may be combined to derive a general estimate of DSM-IV social phobia in youths (Stein, Chavira, & Jang, 2001). The deletion of avoidant disorder in DSM-IV likely means that some children with social interaction difficulties will be shoehorned into a diagnosis of social phobia, which will naturally increase the latter's prevalence.

Although the exact prevalence of childhood social phobia remains unknown, the problem is a very common reason for referral to specialized childhood anxiety disorder clinics (Last, Francis et al., 1987; Last, Perrin, Hersen, & Kazdin, 1992; Kendall and Warman, 1996; Velting and Albano

2001). In addition, enough evidence exists to suggest that the frequency of the disorder is at least comparable to other major childhood behavior disorders (Ford, Goodman, & Meltzer, 2003; Costello, Mustillo, Erkanli, Keeler, & Angold, 2003).

DEMOGRAPHIC CHARACTERISTICS

GENDER

A large majority of psychometric studies of child self-report measures indicate that girls report significantly more social *anxiety* than boys, especially with respect to fear of negative evaluation (Beidel, Turner, & Morris, 2000a; La Greca, 1998, 2001) (see also Chapter 4). In addition, several studies indicate that social *phobia* is somewhat more prevalent among girls than boys. Among studies with larger samples of identifiable youths with social phobia, for example, 59.0% were female (180/305 participants) (Beidel, 1991; Beidel et al., 1999; Essau et al., 1999; Francis et al., 1992; Hofmann et al., 1999; Last et al., 1992; Spence, Donovan, & Brechman-Toussaint, 1999; Strauss & Last, 1993; Wittchen et al., 1999).

One should note, however, that most of these data involved either child self-report or samples referred to specialized clinics, leaving open the possibility that boys are less likely to volunteer true answers about their social anxiety or be referred for social anxiety problems. On the other hand, some have found that boys with social anxiety are more likely to be referred for treatment than girls, even though girls generally have higher levels of social anxiety (Compton, Nelson, & March, 2000). For some boys, the stigma of social anxiety may hasten treatment.

Certain kinds of social fears and related constructs also seem more prevalent among girls than boys. Essau and colleagues (1999), for example, found that girls more often reported fears of performance and test situations than boys, though no gender differences were found with respect to eating or drinking in public, writing before others, participating in social events, public speaking, conversing with others, or avoidant behavior. In addition, the authors found that girls, more so than boys, had fears of embarrassment, being judged as stupid or weak or crazy, having a panic attack, experiencing confusion or shame, vomiting, and turning red.

Girls with social phobia have also been found to have more parent-reported internalizing problems, neuroticism, and social distress than boys with social phobia (Beidel et al., 1999), though this has not always been replicated (Beidel, Turner, Hamlin, & Morris, 2000). In addition, high social anxiety in girls but not boys with anxiety disorders has been shown to be related to problematic self-worth and social skills (Ginsburg, La Greca, &

Silverman, 1998). Finally, Dell'Osso and colleagues (2002) examined hundreds of 18-year-old Italian high schoolers and found that social anxiety was substantially higher in the young women than men. This difference included areas of interpersonal sensitivity (e.g., hypersensitivity to criticism), behavior inhibition and somatic symptoms, and specific anxiety and phobic features (e.g., of body image, oral examination) (pp. 228–229).

AGE OF DIAGNOSIS, REFERRAL, AND ONSET

Assigning a diagnosis of social phobia to youths seems much more likely to occur in older childhood and adolescence than in young childhood (Beidel, 1998; Essau et al., 1999; Last et al., 1992; Strauss & Last, 1993; Velting & Albano, 2001). Indeed, entry into middle school is a very common time for childhood social phobia referrals (Albano et al., 2003; Kearney, 2001). However, researchers have also described many younger children with social phobia (i.e., 7–13 years) (Beidel, 1991; Beidel et al., 1999), and younger children tend to report more social anxiety than older children (Compton et al., 2000; La Greca, 2001).

One possible reason for this difference is that childhood social phobia has a bimodal distribution with respect to age of onset: very early in life and early adolescence (Stein, Chavira, & Jang, 2001). Another possibility is that many children with social phobia are not referred for treatment until the disorder has developed considerably. For example, Strauss and Last (1993) reported a mean age of onset of 12.3 years and a mean age of referral of 14.9 years among youths with social phobia. Parents sometimes wait until a serious disruptive problem (e.g., noncompliance, school refusal behavior) develops before pursuing treatment for their child (see also Last et al., 1992). Indeed, in one study, only 23.5% of youths diagnosed with social phobia and 14.5% of youths with social fears had utilized mental health services (Essau et al., 1999). In other studies, only 21.5–43.0% of 14–24-year-olds with social phobia had sought treatment (Wittchen et al., 1998; Wittchen et al., 1999).

Retrospective studies of adults with social phobia also indicate a common onset around mid-adolescence (i.e., age 15–16 years) (Schneier, Johnson, Hornig, Liebowitz, & Weissman, 1992; Thyer, Parrish, Curtis, Nesse, & Cameron, 1985; Wittchen, Essau, von Zerssen, Krieg, & Zaudig, 1992), though sometimes younger (i.e., age 12.7 years) (DeWit et al., 1999). In addition, people with generalized social phobia may have an earlier mean age of onset than those with nongeneralized social phobia (i.e., age 10.9–12.5 years versus 14.0–16.9 years) (Mannuzza et al., 1995; Wittchen et al., 1999). As with many forms of psychopathology, the younger the age of onset of social phobia, the more severe the disorder seems to be.

SOCIOECONOMIC STATUS

Studies of youths with social phobia indicate a wide range of socioeconomic statuses (SES) (Beidel et al., 1999; Francis et al., 1992; Strauss & Last, 1993). In addition, one examination of social anxiety within children with anxiety disorders indicated no family income differences (Ginsburg et al., 1998). On the other hand, test anxiety has been found to be more severe among children of low-income families (Guida & Ludlow, 1989), and Last and colleagues (1992) found that 45.9% of their sample of youths with social phobia came from families of low SES. These samples generally represent families referred to specialized clinics, however, and little evidence exists to suggest strong socioeconomic tendencies in one direction or another regarding this population.

RACE AND CULTURE

Race may or may not be a key aspect of childhood social anxiety or phobia. The research literature indicates (1) *a higher prevalence of Caucasians* (e.g., Beidel, 1991; Beidel et al., 1999; Francis et al., 1992; Last et al., 1992; Strauss & Last, 1993), (2) *a lack of racial differences* (Ferrell, Beidel, & Turner, 2004; Ginsburg et al., 1998; Last & Perrin, 1993; Pina & Silverman, 2004; Treadwell, Flannery-Schroeder, & Kendall, 1995), or even (3) *a higher prevalence of African-Americans* (Compton et al., 2000). However, these samples may simply reflect youths referred to specialized clinics and not those of the general population. Indeed, Compton and colleagues (2000) found that *community-based* Caucasian children were more likely to endorse symptoms of social phobia and not social anxiety, whereas African-American children were more likely to endorse symptoms of social anxiety and not social phobia.

A key drawback of many studies of childhood anxiety in general and social phobia in particular has been a lack of specific attention to race. In addition, the few studies that have examined race have pooled youths with diverse anxiety diagnoses. For example, Ginsburg and Silverman (1996) examined 242 Caucasian and Hispanic youths with various anxiety disorders, 29 of whom had social phobia. Very few differences were found between the racial groups, with exceptions being higher rates of separation anxiety disorder and overall fear among Hispanics. In addition, Beidel, Turner, and Trager (1994) compared high test-anxious Caucasian and African-American children and found the latter group to be more likely diagnosed with social phobia. Conversely, though, African-American youths with social phobia have been found to report less social distress than

Caucasian youths with social phobia (Beidel et al., 1999; Beidel, Turner, Hamlin, & Morris, 2000). Finally, Chilean students have been found to have higher test anxiety compared to North American students (Guida & Ludlow, 1989).

The cross-cultural aspects of social phobia may be examined from clinical, anthropological, and synthetic perspectives (Stein & Matsunaga, 2001). A *clinical* scientific approach focuses on strict methodology and has led to the development of criteria, assessments, and treatments for social phobia. An *anthropological* scientific approach focuses on understanding a phenomenon such as social phobia within its cultural context. For example, shyness, social anxiety, and internalizing behaviors are seen in many cultures as highly positive characteristics (Chen et al., 1999; Weisz et al., 1987). In addition, the perspective allows for the possibility that social anxiety and phobia may be differentially presented across cultures. A commonly cited example is *taijin kyofusho*, a Japanese form of social phobia that is characterized more by poor insight and fear of offending *others* than Western-based fear of personal embarrassment (Kashara, 1988; Tseng, Asai, Kitanishi, McLaughlin, & Kyomen, 1992).

Finally, a *synthetic* approach that combines clinical and anthropological aspects focuses on the universality and similarities of social anxiety while accounting for some cultural differences. In fact, fears of failure and criticism are commonly seen in children across many different cultures (Dong, Yang, & Ollendick, 1994; Ollendick, Yang, King, Dong, & Akande, 1996; Payne, 1988; Yang, Ollendick, Dong, Xia, & Lin, 1995). However, much more work is needed with respect to racial and cultural variables and childhood social phobia.

SYMPTOMATOLOGY

Children with social phobia have been found to display various symptoms. These often include somatic complaints, general fearfulness and anxiety, depression and suicide, selective mutism, externalizing behavior problems, substance use, and school refusel behavior. These sets of symptoms are described next.

SOMATIC COMPLAINTS

Children with anxiety disorders often have somatic complaints, and a diagnosis of social phobia mandates the presence of key somatic symptoms (APA, 2000; Last, 1991) (see Chapter 1). Children with social phobia and/or high test anxiety often have somatic complaints that include heart palpitations, shortness of breath, trembling or shaking, blushing, sweating, and nervousness or "butterflies" in the stomach (Beidel, 1998; Beidel, Christ, & Long, 1991; Essau et al., 1999). Complaints of illness, stomachaches, unsteady voice, and associated clinging and crying are common to this population as well (Albano et al., 2003). Children with social phobia *and* other kinds of problems (e.g., school refusal behavior) often have a myriad of somatic complaints that also include breathing problems, pain, motor difficulties, nausea/vomiting, lightheadedness, and menstruation symptoms, among others (Bernstein et al., 1997; Kearney, 2001).

GENERAL FEARFULNESS AND ANXIETY

As mentioned earlier, youths with social phobia fear many specific social and/or evaluative situations. In addition, however, youths with social phobia tend to have higher levels of general fearfulness and anxiety compared to youths with other anxiety disorders and to normal controls (Last, Francis, & Strauss, 1989; Peleg-Popko & Dar, 2001; Spence et al., 1999; Strauss & Last, 1993). This is especially so with respect to fears of failure, criticism, going to school, injury, danger, and those stimuli noted earlier. Beidel and colleagues (1999) found that *nonsocial* fears among children with social anxiety disorder often include injections (51%), blood tests (35%), high places (30%), seeing blood (28%), darkness (23%), bees/insects (21%), thunderstorms/lightning (21%), and doctors/dentists (21%), among others.

Beidel and colleagues (1999) similarly found that children with social phobia, compared to controls, have higher levels of social distress and tend to be rated as more anxious and less skilled in read-aloud and social interaction tasks. In addition, children with social phobia took longer to speak in social interactions, which led the authors to link behavioral inhibition and childhood social phobia (see later section and Chapters 1 and 3). Children with social phobia may not necessarily show more general, test, or physiological anxiety compared to youths of other anxiety disorders, but do seem to have comparatively more negative reactions and negative coping behaviors when faced with performance-based situations (Beidel, 1991). Children with high test anxiety, compared to controls, also have more fearfulness, worries, depressive mood states, and trait anxiety (Beidel & Turner, 1988). Finally, youths with social worries or phobia may have elevated levels of anxiety sensitivity, or overconcern about one's internal physical sensations, as well as frequent panic attacks (Kearney, Albano, Eisen, Allen, & Barlow, 1997; Silverman & Weems, 1999). However, more research is needed regarding these latter variables.

DEPRESSION AND SUICIDE

Youths with social phobia typically rate themselves as more depressed compared to controls (Beidel et al., 1999; Francis et al., 1992; Strauss & Last, 1993), and may have significant rates of negative affect (i.e., combined anxiety and depression) (Inderbitzen-Nolan & Walters, 2000) (see also Chapter 3). In fact, parents and teachers tend to rate youths with social phobia as having more internalizing problems, including depression, compared to controls (Beidel et al., 1999). Furthermore, moderate comorbidity exists between childhood social phobia and depression (see below), and children with social phobia often have negative thoughts of oneself (Albano et al., 2003). However, youths with social phobia may not be necessarily more depressed than youths with other anxiety disorders (Francis & Radka, 1995).

Beidel and colleagues (1999) suggested that childhood social phobia often precedes dysphoric mood, the latter sometimes strong enough to become a secondary disorder. This contention is supported by the fact that (1) general childhood anxiety disorder and symptoms seem to precede depression in many cases (Brady & Kendall, 1992; Kovacs, Gatsonis, Paulauskas, & Richards, 1989), (2) socially anxious children have been found to be younger than youths with dysphoria (Epkins, 1996a), and (3) social phobia was found to precede depression 81.6–100.0% of the time in adolescents and young adults with social phobia (Essau et al., 2000; Wittchen et al., 1999). Children with social phobia and children with depression likely share many characteristics such as negative affect, low self-esteem, cognitive distortions, avoidance and withdrawal, and some somatic symptoms.

Some people with social phobia also seem to be at greater risk for suicidal behavior compared to controls (Davidson, Hughes, George, & Blazer, 1993). Among female adolescent twins with social phobia and depression, Nelson and colleagues (2000) found substantially increased risk for suicidal ideation, suicide plan, and suicide attempt. On the other hand, Strauss and colleagues (2000) found no significant difference in rate of social phobia diagnosis among youths who were nonsuicidal (1.4%), suicide ideators (2.1%), or suicide attempters (1.9%). Similarly, Pawlak and colleagues (1999) examined female adolescents and young adults and found that social phobia per se was not associated with elevated risk for suicide.

Despite the conflicting evidence, researchers have urged greater attention to the issue of suicide among youths with anxiety disorders (e.g., Albano et al., 2003). In addition, good clinical sense would seem to dictate that many youths under enormous social and evaluative stress may consider suicide. When addressing this population, therefore, erring on the side of caution and carefully assessing for depression and risk for suicide is recommended.

SELECTIVE MUTISM

Selective mutism refers to a "persistent failure to speak in social situations (e.g., school, with playmates) where speaking is expected" (APA, 2000, p. 125). The reasons for selective mutism have been debated for decades, although many researchers conclude that selective mutism is often tempermentally- and anxiety-based in general and perhaps linked to social phobia in particular (Dow, Sonies, Scheib, Moss, & Leonard, 1995). For example, selective mutism is often linked to shyness and general anxiety (Ford, Sladeczek, Carlson, & Kratochwill, 1998; Steinhausen & Juzi, 1996), researchers have reported very high rates of social anxiety and social phobia among samples of youths with selective mutism (Black & Uhde, 1995; Dummit et al., 1997; Elizur & Perednik, 2003; Vecchio & Kearney, 2005), and few differences are seen between youths with social phobia and those with selective mutism (Yeganeh, Beidel, Turner, Pina, & Silverman, 2003).

On the other hand, the large majority of youths with social phobia do not have selective mutism (see below), and etiological factors other than social anxiety are related to selective mutism. Indeed, the prevalence of childhood social phobia (see above) is much greater than for selective mutism (0.71%) (Bergman, Piacentini, & McCracken, 2002). Persistent failure to speak to others and to develop appropriate peer relationships does seem to facilitate the development or diagnosis of social phobia. However, for most youths with social phobia, factors other than selective mutism are obviously influential as well.

EXTERNALIZING BEHAVIOR PROBLEMS

Internalizing behavior problems are clearly associated with many cases of social phobia in children. Of greater controversy is the extent to which externalizing behavior problems are associated with childhood social phobia. Adults with social phobia, compared to controls, do report significantly higher rates of past misbehavior, stealing, lying, poor grades, fighting, running away, and property destruction (Davidson, Hughes, et al., 1993). Among youths with social phobia, Beidel and colleagues (1999) found that externalizing behavior problems were rated higher than norms but were not extensive in nature. In addition, youths with social phobia do not generally meet criteria for externalizing behavior disorders (e.g., attention deficit hyperactivity disorder, conduct disorder) (see diagnostic comorbidity section below).

Although social phobia and externalizing behavior disorders are not often linked in the literature, Albano and Detweiler (2001) outlined ways in which the two categories can be associated. For example, children with social phobia and children with externalizing behavior disorders often experience or have:

- inappropriate or maladaptive interpersonal styles
- inaccurate perceptions of social cues from others
- inaccurate estimations of threat by others, even in ambiguous situations
- difficulty making or keeping friends
- peer rejection
- familial reinforcement of inappropriate social behavior
- impaired social problem-solving skills
- cognitive distortions

Albano and Detweiler (2001) noted that more extensive research is necessary to explore these similarities, and developmental psychopathology investigations are sorely needed in this area. Still, clinicians who address youths with social phobia or externalizing behavior problems may wish to explore whether overlapping symptoms and sequelae are occurring.

Substance Use

Adolescents with anxiety disorders, particularly those with multiple anxiety disorders, are generally at risk over time for developing illegal drug dependence (Woodward & Ferguson, 2001). With respect to social phobia, Sonntag and colleagues (2000) found that dependent smoking was prevalent in 31.5% of youths with social phobia, 26.1% of youths with a social fear but not social phobia, and 15.4% in youths with neither social fear nor social phobia. In addition, the authors found that most youths began cigarette use *after* the onset of social fears or phobias. On the other hand, Johnson and colleagues (2000) found that adolescent cigarette smoking was *unrelated* to increased risk for social phobia in young adulthood. In addition, smoking and social phobia seem unrelated in adults (Baker-Morissette, Gulliver, Wiegel, & Barlow, 2004).

Nelson and colleagues (2000) also reported that social phobia and depression in youths was associated with elevated risk for alcohol use disorder. Wittchen and colleagues (1999) reported as well that social phobia preceded substance use disorder 85.2% of the time among their sample of 14–24-year olds. Some shy youths also engage in significant substance use (Zimbardo & Radl, 1981). Researchers have contended that many adolescents self-medicate their symptoms of anxiety, and some do so to such an extent that drug abuse and dependence occur (Albano & Detweiler, 2001).

School Refusal Behavior

School refusal behavior refers to a child-motivated refusal to attend school and/or difficulties remaining in classes for an entire day (Kearney, 2003). Youths refuse to attend school for many reasons, some of which are anxiety-based (e.g., separation, social, general anxiety or worry) and some of which are based on desires for reinforcement outside of school (e.g., attention or tangible rewards). Anxiety-based school refusal behavior is sometimes referred to in the literature as school phobia, school refusal, or even separation anxiety (Kearney & Silverman, 1996). Diagnoses of childhood social phobia have been examined in anxiety-based and more general samples of youths with school refusal behavior.

Adults with social phobia do report, compared to controls, that they were often more truant and more likely to be expelled from school (Davidson, Hughes, et al., 1993). With respect to children, Kearney (2001) summarized anxiety-related diagnoses from four diagnostic studies of anxiety-based school refusal behavior (i.e., Bernstein et al., 1997; Last, Francis, et al., 1987; Last & Strauss, 1990; Last, Strauss, & Francis, 1987). Across these samples, social phobia was present in 33.6% of youths and was the most common anxiety disorder following the antiquated diagnosis of overanxious disorder (36.5%).

Others have reported more restricted rates, however. For example, Beidel and colleagues (1999) found that 10% of their sample of youths with social phobia refused to regularly attend school. Egger and colleagues (2003) reported the prevalence of social phobia among youths classified as pure anxious school refusers (3.2%), pure truants (0.2%), mixed school refusers (0.0%), and non-school refusers (0.5%). For these four groups respectively, prevalence rates for social anxiety (8.5%, 1.8%, 14.2%, 3.6%), performance anxiety (6.7%, 0.8%, 1.4%, 1.5%), and shyness with peers (28.2%, 10.3%, 6.7%, 11.8%) were also reported. Across 143 youths with primary school refusal behavior, including those who refused school for reasons other than anxiety, Kearney and Albano (2004) found that 3.5% had a primary diagnosis of social phobia and that 4.2% had a secondary diagnosis of social phobia. In addition, as expected, diagnoses of social phobia were most associated with youths who refused school to avoid stimuli that provoked negative affectivity or to escape aversive social and/or evaluative situations.

The relationship between social phobia and school refusal behavior is perhaps not surprising given that many youths worry about school-based social interactions, tests, peer evaluations, and performance expectations (see earlier sections). As a result, one might expect that some youths will experience particularly high levels of worry and anxiety regarding school, especially social and evaluative situations there, and attempt to avoid or escape those situations by missing school. Indeed, many parents refer a child with social phobia for treatment after he or she has strongly resisted attending school.

DIAGNOSTIC COMORBIDITY

As one might expect given the discussion so far, children with social phobia are often described as having a wide swath of comorbid diagnoses. Empirical evidence for this comes from two types of diagnostic studies: those focusing on youths with various anxiety disorders and those focusing more specifically on youths with social phobia.

YOUTHS WITH VARIOUS ANXIETY DISORDERS

Because the area of childhood anxiety disorders has substantially evolved only recently, many initial studies in this area evaluated comorbidity within general samples of youths with anxiety disorders or various mental disorders. A general finding across these earlier studies was that youths with anxiety disorders (including social phobia) also met criteria for many other mental disorders, especially other anxiety disorders and depression (Brady & Kendall, 1992; Kashani & Orvaschel, 1990; Last & Strauss, 1990; Last, Strauss, & Francis, 1987). Studies of more specific anxiety (e.g., test anxiety, panic disorder) or depressive clinical child samples often revealed some comorbidity with social phobia as well (e.g., Beidel & Turner, 1988; Kearney et al., 1997; Lewinsohn et al., 1993). Children of various anxiety disorders, including social phobia, may also have comorbid externalizing behavior disorders (Russo & Beidel, 1994), but this association is not strong (Lewinsohn, Zinbarg, Seeley, Lewinsohn, & Sack, 1997).

YOUTHS WITH SOCIAL PHOBIA

Some researchers have specifically evaluated youths with high social anxiety or social phobia with respect to diagnostic comorbidity, although many employed DSM-III-R criteria. For example, Francis and colleagues (1992) found that youths with social phobia often met criteria for another anxiety (90.9%) or an affective disorder (24.2%). More specifically, Last and colleagues (1992) found that many youths with social phobia also met criteria for overanxious disorder (47.5%), simple phobia (41.0%), separation anxiety disorder (26.2%), avoidant disorder (21.3%), obsessive-compulsive disorder (13.1%), and panic disorder (8.2%). Strauss and Last (1993)

similarly found that many youths with social phobia also met criteria for
overanxious (41.4%), avoidant (20.7%), separation anxiety (17.2%), and affective disorders (17.2%), the latter usually depression (10.3%). Similarly,
Wittchen and colleagues (1999) found that 14–24-year-olds with social phobia often had comorbid substance use, depressive, eating, and other anxiety
disorders (see also Verduin & Kendall, 2003).

Using DSM-IV criteria, Beidel and colleagues (1999) evaluated
50 youths with social phobia and found that 60.0% had concurrent diagnoses. Comorbid diagnoses included:

- generalized anxiety disorder (10.0%)
- attention-deficit/hyperactivity disorder (10.0%)
- simple (specific) phobia (10.0%)
- selective mutism (8.0%)
- separation anxiety disorder (6.0%)
- obsessive-compulsive disorder (6.0%)
- depression (6.0%)
- panic disorder (2.0%)
- adjustment disorder with anxious and depressed mood (2.0%).

Velting and Albano (2001), citing earlier data, reported that 41 children
with social phobia received zero (29%), one (26%), two (26%), or three or
more (19%) comorbid diagnoses. Of those receiving comorbid diagnoses,
the most common were overanxious disorder (43%), simple phobia (26%),
and mood disorder (19%). In a more limited sample of 17 youths with social
phobia, Essau and colleagues (1999) found that many also met additional
criteria for a somatoform (41.2%), depressive (29.4%), or substance use disorder (23.5%) as well as agoraphobia (23.5%). Essau and colleagues (2000)
also reported substantial comorbidity between childhood social phobia
and obsessive-compulsive disorder (15.3%). Data thus generally indicate
that children with social phobia often meet criteria for other anxiety disorders as well as depression, and that the prevalence of externalizing behavior problems is considerably lower than for internalizing problems.
Interestingly, however, data also indicate that many children with social
phobia have *no* other mental condition.

GENERAL IMPAIRMENT AND AVOIDANCE

Adult studies indicate that social phobia is associated with decreased
quality of life as well as school dropout, unemployment and reduced work
productivity, alcohol abuse, depression and suicidal behavior, other anxiety disorders, restricted social interaction and satisfaction, and various

other occupational, academic, and social impairments (Davidson, Hughes, et al., 1993; Kessler, Foster, Saunders, & Stang, 1995; Quilty, Van Ameringen, Mancini, Oakman, & Farvolden, 2003; Wittchen & Beloch, 1996; Wittchen, Fuetsch, Sonntag, Muller, & Liebowitz, 2000). Similar findings have been reported for adolescents or young adults with social phobia, as many experience broad, severe impairments in social, academic, and occupational functioning, perhaps even more so than youths with other anxiety disorders (Albano & Detweiler, 2001; Beidel, 1991; Essau et al., 1999, 2000; Wittchen et al., 1999). In many cases, these impairments result from the associated problems of social phobia described in this chapter (e.g., cognitive distortions, depression, poor social networks). However, impairments from social phobia are derived as well from pervasive avoidant behavior.

Youths with social anxiety, compared to controls, have significantly more negative coping behaviors in response to anxiety-provoking events (Beidel, 1991). Such negative coping often comes in the form of *avoidance*. For example, Essau and colleagues (1999) found that many boys and girls with social fears often or always avoid the target of their fear (17.0% and 16.1%, respectively, for gender), feel that their anxiety or avoidant behavior is excessive or unreasonable (38.9% and 47.3%, respectively), and report that their anxiety or avoidance has lasted for months or years (26.6% and 31.2%, respectively). More specifically, Beidel and colleagues (1999) found that approximately 35% of youths with social phobia display a wide range of avoidant strategies when encountering socially distressing stimuli. These strategies most commonly included pretending to be sick, crying, noncompliance/refusal to go somewhere, hiding one's eyes so as not to be called on, pretending not to hear someone speak to them, and waiting to use a restroom until home.

Pervasive avoidant behavior may generally cause youths to fail to meet key developmental challenges in adolescence (Albano et al., 2003). These challenges include dating, working outside of school, completing school and college, becoming more socially independent and assertive, developing social support networks, and learning about the world in general, among others. Coupled with the other problems discussed in this chapter, social phobia in adolescents and young adults can thus be readily seen as a potentially crippling form of mental disorder.

PEER RELATIONSHIPS

In addition to avoidance, impairment from social phobia often comes in the form of disrupted peer relationships. Social anxiety can hinder peer relationships in various ways: inhibiting the development of new friendships, facilitating ridicule and exclusion from peer groups, generating poor perceptions of one's social qualities, and impeding the development of adequate social skills. These hindrances are discussed next.

INHIBITING THE DEVELOPMENT OF NEW FRIENDSHIPS

Vernberg and colleagues (1992) examined nonclinical adolescents who had recently relocated and found that their social anxiety significantly influenced the development of companionship and intimacy in their new friendships. The authors also noted, however, that *types* of social anxiety can change over time depending on the nature of friendships and whether a person is rejected by peers. In particular, social avoidance in new situations and fear of negative evaluation were tempered by new friendships, including those that developed over the course of a new school year. However, general social avoidance and distress were more stable over time. Furthermore, peer exclusion and rejection over the course of the school year were significantly predictive of childrens' social anxiety and avoidance.

Others have reported as well that children with social anxiety and phobia tend to be lonelier and may have more difficulty forming friendships and joining peer groups compared to controls (Inderbitzen-Pisaruk, Clark, & Solano, 1992; La Greca, 2001; Strauss & Last, 1993). For example, Beidel and colleagues (1999) found that that 75% of youths with social phobia reportedly had no or few friends and that 50% did not like school and did not participate in extracurricular or peer activities. Albano and colleagues have noted further that children with social phobia often choose odd, solitary activities, have poor social networks, and are viewed by parents and teachers as shy, quiet people who tend to stay alone or in the company of just one friend (Albano et al., 2003; Albano, DiBartolo, Heimberg, & Barlow, 1995).

RIDICULE AND EXCLUSION FROM PEER GROUPS

Walters and Inderbitzen (1998) compared nonclinical youths described by peers as cooperative, friendly dominant, hostile dominant, or submissive. Submissive children reported significantly higher levels of social anxiety than children of the other groups, including greater fears of negative evaluation and new situations as well as social avoidance. Peer nominations also revealed submissive group members to be rarely viewed as "most liked" and often viewed as "least liked." These findings support others that submissive or anxious children, compared to controls, have more interpersonal concerns and are less well liked or less likely to receive positive responses by peers (Parkhurst & Asher, 1992; Spence et al., 1999; Strauss,

Frame, & Forehand, 1987). Walters and Inderbitzen (1998) concluded that "socially anxious adolescents are viewed by peers as likely targets of exclusion, ridicule, and aggression and as not being very dominant" (p. 194). Indeed, Ginsburg and colleagues (1998) found that high socially anxious children with anxiety disorders had more negative peer interactions compared to low socially anxious children, including having enemies at school and being ridiculed and teased.

Inderbitzen, Walters, and Bukowski (1997) also found that rejected and neglected children reported more social anxiety than youths classified as popular, average, or controversial. Within two rejected subgroups, aggressive and submissive, the latter reported substantially higher levels of social anxiety. In particular, fear of negative evaluation among submissive youths was related to rejection by peers. These data supported earlier findings that neglected children report more social anxiety than children of other status groups (La Greca, Dandes, Wick, Shaw, & Stone, 1988; La Greca & Stone, 1993). However, others have found neglected children to report *lower* levels of social anxiety than average children, indicating that some neglected children may not necessarily be distressed by a lack of peer relationships (Crick & Ladd, 1993).

Poor Perceptions of One's Social Qualities

La Greca and Lopez (1998) found that higher levels of social anxiety in adolescents correlated significantly with less support from classmates and poorer perceptions of one's social acceptance and romantic appeal to others. In addition, higher levels of social anxiety among adolescent girls correlated significantly with having fewer best friends, feeling less competent in friendships, and perceiving friendships as less intimate, less emotionally supportive, and lower in companionship. These associations were less strong for boys, although high social anxiety in boys was strongly related to less support from close friends and perceptions of themselves as less competent in friendships. Social anxiety was not closely linked to perceptions of parents and teachers.

Others have found as well that children with anxiety disorders in general, especially those with high social anxiety and compared to controls, tend to see themselves as less socially and otherwise competent and have significantly more expectancies of being disliked and rejected by peers (Chansky & Kendall, 1997; Ginsburg et al., 1998; Panella & Henggeler, 1986; Smari, Petursdottir, & Porsteindottir, 2001; Spence et al., 1999). This finding is not universal, however, as some children with social phobia rate themselves just as socially and physically competent as children with other anxiety disorders and controls (Beidel, 1991). In general, however, youths with emotional disorders and/or high social anxiety tend to have low global self-worth and do not feel well liked or accepted by their peers (La Greca & Stone, 1993; Leary, 1990; Mallet & Rodriguez-Tome, 1999; Riley, Ensminger, Green, & Kang, 1998).

POOR DEVELOPMENT OF SOCIAL SKILLS

Spence and colleagues (1999) found that youths with social phobia and their parents rated the youths as less socially skilled and assertive compared to controls. In addition, direct observations revealed that youths with social phobia initiated fewer school-based peer interactions, had less overall school-based peer interactions, and spoke fewer words following a prompt compared to controls. However, no differences were found with respect to eye contact or latency of response.

Other researchers have also reported that youths with shyness or social phobia, compared to controls, are generally less assertive, less socially skilled, and less confident about their social skill (Beidel et al., 1999; Francis & Radka, 1995; Henderson & Zimbardo, 2001b), or are rated by others as less assertive and socially skilled (Ginsburg et al., 1988). Indeed, several researchers believe that shyness and general and social anxiety help *prevent* the development of adequate social skills, general social competence, and friendships (Rubin, LeMare, & Lollis, 1990; Strauss, Lahey, Frick, Frame, & Hynd, 1988). One caveat, however, is that anxious children *in general* are often rated as socially incompetent and maladjusted (Strauss, Lease, Kazdin, Dulcan, & Last, 1989).

OTHER CHILD CHARACTERISTICS

BEHAVIORAL INHIBITION AND PERSONALITY

Behavioral inhibition seems closely related to social phobia because the construct pertains to withdrawal, avoidance, and fear regarding unfamiliar people (see Chapter 1). Researchers have found, for example, that children with behavioral inhibition are more likely than controls to show various fearful behaviors and anxiety and avoidant disorders (Biederman et al., 1990; 1993; Hirshfeld et al., 1992; Kagan, Snidman, McManis, & Woodward, 2001). In young adults as well, symptoms of social anxiety and phobia have been shown to be related to retrospective reports of childhood behavioral inhibition (Dell'Osso et al., 2002; Mick & Telch, 1998; Wittchen et al., 1999). Behavioral inhibition has also been linked to later diagnoses of social phobia in youths. A more detailed discussion of this linkage is presented in Chapter 3.

Less work has been done regarding other specific personality variables of children with social phobia. Beidel (1991) found no differences between children with social phobia or overanxious disorder and controls with respect to general and sleep activity, approach-withdrawal, flexibility-rigidity, mood, task orientation, distractibility, persistence, and rhythmicity in sleep, eating, and daily habits. However, Beidel and colleagues (1999) did find that youths with social phobia had less extraversion and more neuroticism compared to controls. This led the authors to conclude that the clinical group was often overresponsive to different events and situations and generally overaroused.

COGNITIVE AND AFFECTIVE CHARACTERISTICS

Children with high anxiety or anxiety disorders and social dysfunction often have cognitive and attributional biases, attend selectively to threatening stimuli in ambiguous situations, engage in self-denigration, and emphasize negative outcomes and poor coping even in nonthreatening situations (Barrett, Rapee, Dadds, & Ryan, 1996; Bell-Dolan, 1995; Chorpita, Albano, & Barlow, 1996; Crick & Ladd, 1993; Daleiden & Vasey, 1997; Ehrenreich & Gross, 2002; Muris, Rapee, Meesters, Schouten, & Geers, 2003; Vasey, Daleiden, Williams, & Brown, 1995; Vasey, El-Hag, & Daleiden, 1996). Adult studies indicate as well that people with social phobia tend to underestimate their level of social skill, interpret social events negatively, perceive their anxiety symptoms as highly visible, and overattend to real or perceived errors in their own social functioning (Clark & McManus, 2002; Hirsch, Clark, Mathews, & Williams, 2003; Hope, Rapee, Heimberg, & Dombeck, 1990; Rapee & Lim, 1992; Stopa & Clark, 1993, 2000).

Youths with social phobia are commonly described as excessively (1) self-conscious, (2) self-focused with respect to their arousal level, (3) sensitive to indicators of negative evaluation by others, (4) overestimating threat from others and underestimating personal social competence, and/or (5) having thoughts of negative outcomes, self-deprecation, embarrassment, and ridicule, rejection, and negative evaluation by others (Albano et al., 2003; Albano & Detweiler, 2001; Mallet & Rodriguez-Tome, 1999; Ollendick & Hirshfeld-Becker, 2002). Empirical work regarding cognitions among youths with social phobia is emerging, but data are somewhat mixed. A greater explication of these findings is presented in Chapter 3.

Less work has been conducted regarding the affective or emotional characteristics of youths with social phobia per se, which is unfortunate given that positive and negative affect are highly pertinent to youths with internalizing disorders (Chorpita, Plummer, & Moffitt, 2000) (see

Chapter 3). However, Melfsen and colleagues (2000) did examine facial expressiveness in children with and without social anxiety. Children with social anxiety showed less emotional expressiveness than controls with respect to happiness, surprise, and fear but not anger, disgust, or sadness. These children also showed more miscellaneous and incorrect facial expressions and less "affective blends," or "simultaneous expression of positive and negative facial elements" (p. 257). Interestingly, socially anxious youths did not generally rate their performance on various tasks lower than controls, although this may have been due to lack of insight on their part. The authors concluded that socially anxious children may fail to (1) provide adequate empathy or emotional feedback (e.g., happiness) to potential friends, (2) emphasize their own intentions via facial expressions, and (3) develop effective social interactions in general.

Simonian and colleagues (2001) similarly examined 15 youths with social phobia and controls along a facial recognition task for identifying emotional content. Children with social phobia were much more anxious about completing the task. In addition, the clinical group made significantly more errors with respect to emotions of happiness, sadness, and disgust, though no differences were found with respect to anger, surprise, or fear. The authors thus advocated the use of facial recognition training for treating youths with social phobia. A related study that included some youths with social phobia indicated that the clinical group had more difficulty understanding the concepts of hiding and changing emotions compared to controls, although no differences were found with respect to understanding emotional cues and the idea of multiple emotions (Southam-Gerow & Kendall, 2000). In general, data indicate that many youths with social phobia have at least some moderate impairment with respect to identifying and expressing emotional states (see also Battaglia et al., 2004).

SUBTYPES

As mentioned in Chapter 1, social phobia is currently differentiated into generalized and nongeneralized diagnostic subtypes. Adults with generalized social phobia, compared to those of the nongeneralized subtype, tend to display an earlier age of onset, less extraversion, and more psychopathology, symptom severity, and impairment (Mannuzza et al., 1995; Turner, Beidel, & Townsley, 1992). In addition, generalized social phobia may be related more to childhood shyness, whereas nongeneralized social phobia may be related more to specific traumatic experiences (Beidel, 1998; Stemberger, Turner, Beidel, & Calhoun, 1995). Indeed, this distinction may be related to Buss' (1986) fearful and self-conscious shyness subtypes (see Chapter 1). Other reports, however, contain mixed data and provide less clear differentiation of the nongeneralized and generalized subtypes (Boone et al., 1999; Bruch & Heimberg, 1994; Kessler, Stein, & Berglund, 1998; Weinshenker et al., 1996/1997).

With respect to youths, empirical data regarding social phobia subtypes are marked by contradictions. For example, Lieb and colleagues (2000) reported that generalized social phobia (1.1%) was much less frequent than nongeneralized social phobia (4.4%) among a large sample of 14–17-year-olds. However, Beidel and others (1999) found that nongeneralized social phobia comprised only 11% of their sample of youths with social phobia. In addition, seemingly nongeneralized problems such as test anxiety are often part of a highly complex clinical picture (Beidel & Turner, 1988).

In related fashion, Wittchen and colleagues (1999) examined 14–24 year olds with social phobia and found those of the nongeneralized subtype to be largely characterized by fears of performance and test situations (60.5%) and public speaking, especially at school (45.8%). Those with generalized social phobia, however, reported substantially greater fear of humiliation and many more social fears, especially public speaking (86.8%), performance and test situations (81.0%), talking to others (75.5%), participating in social activities (66.2%), and eating or drinking before others (46.9%). Those of the generalized subtype also had greater self-reported behavioral inhibition at ages 5–12 years, long-term separation from a parent, and parental psychopathology than those of the nongeneralized subtype.

On the other hand, Hofmann and colleagues (1999) found that adolescents with generalized and non-generalized social phobia were quite *similar* in terms of age, gender, and levels of comorbid psychopathology, fear, and depression. However, youths with generalized social phobia did report significantly more general anxiety than those with nongeneralized social phobia. Furthermore, the way the authors classified subtypes, using social situation domains and not diagnostic criteria, was unconventional (Velting & Albano, 2001).

COURSE AND OUTCOME

The manifestations of social anxiety and social phobia change as children age. As mentioned in Chapter 1, very young children often experience stranger distress and separation anxiety, which tend to wane over time. During preschool years, children will sometimes experience embarrassment and often react negatively to criticism and censure from others (Hudson & Rapee, 2000), and others will continue to display considerable behavioral inhibition or shyness. As children age during early elementary school grades, development normally accelerates with respect to self-consciousness, capability to experience embarrassment, sensitivity to rejection, taking another's perspective, anticipating and worrying about negative evaluations from others, and understanding subtle social cues and multilayered interactions (Albano & Detweiler, 2001; Velting & Albano, 2001). Coupled with the onset of new social, academic, and performance tasks (e.g., tests, sports, recitals), some children will naturally experience some level of social anxiety (Albano & Hayward, 2004).

For some of these young children, social anxiety can be problematic and often experienced in the form of somatic complaints such as stomachaches and headaches, clinging physically to familiar caregivers, crying, showing temper tantrums and oppositional behavior, and hiding from others (Albano & Hayward, 2004). As children enter middle school, personal, social, and evaluative demands on them become more frequent and intense, and normal anxiety can evolve into clinical forms of anxiety (Velting & Albano, 2001). Older children and adolescents with social anxiety often have severe cognitive distortions, withdraw from social contact and evaluative situations, and worry about their performance and appearance before others (Albano et al., 2003). As adolescents with severe social anxiety enter adulthood, many of their symptoms remain similar, though not identical (Beidel & Morris, 1993, 1995). As such, many of these adolescents are unprepared for college and general adult life and may become dependent on their families for a long time (Albano, 2003).

Detailed longitudinal data regarding childhood social phobia are lacking, though several related findings from various studies seem to indicate that at least some cases of social anxiety and social phobia have a moderately stable course over time. First, as mentioned earlier, adults with social phobia often report that their symptoms and related characteristics (e.g., behavioral inhibition) began in childhood or adolescence and persisted into adulthood (Davidson, Hughes, et al., 1993). In addition, people with social phobia often report very long durations of the disorder (DeWit et al., 1999; Turner, Beidel, Dancu, & Keys, 1986; Wittchen et al., 2000).

Second, the presence of childhood anxiety disorder in general seems predictive of risk for anxiety and other disorders in adults (Pollack, Otto, Rosenbaum, & Sachs, 1992; Woodward & Ferguson, 2001). Some have found this to be specifically true for social phobia in adolescence and adulthood (Pine, Cohen, Gurley, Brook, & Ma, 1998). In addition, Newman and colleagues (1996) found that 79.3% of diagnoses of social phobia made at age 21 years had also been present at ages 11, 13, 15, or 18 years.

Third, behavioral inhibition, a highly stable temperamental characteristic, has been charted from early ages and linked to some degree to the development of social phobia in young adolescents (Schwartz et al.,

1999). Other factors related to social phobia are quite stable across the lifespan as well, including shyness, self-consciousness, and worry about negative evaluations from others (Rubin, Nelson, Hastings, & Asendorpf, 1999; Velting & Albano, 2001). Fourth, the presence of childhood avoidant disorder has been shown to be somewhat stable and associated with various psychiatric disorders over a 4-year period (Cantwell & Baker, 1989). Finally, Essau and colleagues (1999, 2000) found that the frequency of social fears and types of feared social situations did not change much from 12–13 to 16–17 years of age, although the prevalence of social phobia did increase somewhat with age.

These findings generally reveal the possibility that some forms of social anxiety and social phobia have a fairly stable course over time. Several factors prevent a more definitive conclusion in this regard, however. First, little longitudinal data are available specifically for youths with social phobia. Second, the results of the above studies are not highly conclusive. Third, some have reported that childhood anxiety disorders in general, including social phobia, are *not* very stable over time (Costello & Angold, 1995; Essau, Conradt, & Petermann, 2002; Last, Perrin, Hersen, & Kazdin, 1996). In fact, some have found a *negative* correlation of age and symptoms of social phobia (Muris, Merckelbach, Mayer, & Meesters, 1998). Perhaps some youths with social anxiety and social phobia eventually improve as protective and ameliorative factors develop, perhaps some show fluctuating symptoms over time, and perhaps others continue to display severe impairment or worsen over time (see Figure 2.1) (Wittchen & Fehm, 2001).

Little work has been conducted as to what protective factors may help prevent a child from developing social phobia. DeWit and colleagues (1999) conducted a retrospective analysis of *adults* with social phobia and found

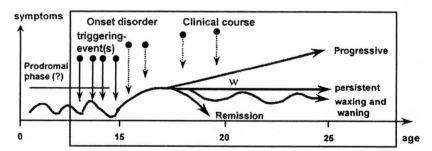

FIGURE 2.1. Developmental framework of onset and natural course. Vulnerability and risk factors for first onset include genetic/familial, temperament, and triggering events. Development of complications includes demoralization leading to depression or suicidal behavior, self-medication (i.e., substance use), and increased social dysfunction and disability. (Used with permission).

that recovery was related to having few siblings, living in a small town during childhood, onset after age 7 years, presence of less than three social fears, presence of health problems and depression before the onset of social phobia, and the absence of major health problems, physical abuse, and depression. Children may be protected from anxiety disorders in general by the presence of fewer risk factors (see Chapter 3), fewer primary and comorbid symptoms, fewer traumatic events, problem-focused coping strategies, appropriate parenting, social support, and early screening and detection (Essau et al., 2002; Kearney, Sims, Pursell, & Tillotson, 2003). However, much more research is needed regarding specific protective factors for youths with social phobia.

FINAL COMMENTS

Youths with social phobia clearly show many associated characteristics that help explain the pervasive and debilitating nature of the mental disorder. While perhaps not as heterogeneous as other childhood behavior problems, social phobia in youths is clearly as prevalent and potentially destructive as any child psychopathological condition. In addition, the breadth of symptoms and impairment in this population necessarily demands complex approaches to assessment and treatment.

CHAPTER 3

THE ETIOLOGY OF SOCIAL ANXIETY AND SOCIAL PHOBIA IN YOUTHS

The previous chapter covered the primary child-based characteristics of youths with social anxiety and social phobia. In this chapter, a discussion is held of the factors most pertinent to the etiology of social anxiety and social phobia in youths. Specifically, a presentation will be made of the major risk factors posited for this population, including genetics, temperament, other biological variables, cognitive characteristics, parental and familial influences, and learning experiences. These risk factors will serve as the essential building blocks for a later discussion of an integrated etiological model and a proposed developmental pathway for youths with social anxiety and social phobia.

RISK FACTORS FOR YOUTHS WITH SOCIAL ANXIETY AND SOCIAL PHOBIA

Many etiological conceptualizations of psychopathology are based to some degree on a *diathesis-stress model*, or the idea that risk factors for a mental disorder involve a biological predisposition in conjunction with environmental events or stressors that trigger or facilitate the expression of this predisposition. With respect to anxiety disorders in general, including social phobia, a common method for grouping risk factors follows Barlow's (2002) model of biological, generalized psychological, and specific psychological vulnerabilities. Biological vulnerabilities are those predispositions that occur very early in life, generalized psychological vulnerabilities are those factors that generally pervade a person's life as he or she develops, and specific psychological vulnerabilities refer to learning what is dangerous or threatening in one's environment. The synergistic combination of these sets of vulnerabilities is thought to be highly predictive of a specific anxiety disorder in a given person. This method of distinguishing risk factors is thus adopted for this chapter.

BIOLOGICAL VULNERABILITIES

Biological vulnerabilities for those with social phobia are often thought to include genetics, temperamental qualities, and other biological variables. These are described separately next.

GENETICS: SOCIAL PHOBIA

Various avenues of research indicate that anxiety disorders may have some moderate genetic predisposition because they seem quite familial in nature. Data to support this conclusion come largely from adult family studies indicating that family members of people with social phobia are more likely to have social phobia themselves compared to controls (Fyer, Mannuzza, Chapman, Liebowitz, & Klein, 1993; Reich & Yates, 1988; Tillfors, Furmark, Ekselius, & Fredrikson, 2001). This seems to be the case especially with respect to *generalized* social phobia (Mannuzza et al., 1995; Stein, Chartier, Hazen, et al., 1998).

Unfortunately, the presence of small sample sizes in these studies, in addition to the fact that *other* anxiety disorders and depression may also predispose some family members to social phobia, make definitive conclusions about genetic contributions difficult to make (Biederman et al., 2001; Horwath et al., 1995). In addition, adult twin studies often do not reveal large differences in concordance rates of social phobia between identical and fraternal twins (Andrews, Stewart, Allen, & Henderson, 1990; Skre, Onstad, Torgersen, Lygren, & Kringlen, 1993; Torgersen, 1983). Furthermore, linkage of social phobia to specific genes has not yet proved overly fruitful (e.g., Stein, Chartier, Kozak, King, & Kennedy, 1998).

An important exception was Kendler and colleagues (1992), who found social phobia concordance rates among identical and fraternal twins to be 24.4% and 15.3%, respectively. These authors initially determined the heritability of social phobia to be 30%, and later 51% (Kendler, Karkowski, & Prescott, 1999). Unfortunately, this particular study evaluated only females, used DSM-III criteria, and did not differentiate generalized from nongeneralized social phobia. As such, the study's utility is limited for understanding the genetic predisposition for social phobia.

With respect to children, parents with anxiety disorders often have children with anxiety, related disorders such as depression, and behavioral inhibition (Beidel & Turner, 1997; Biederman, Faraone, et al., 2001; Last, Hersen, Kazdin, Francis, & Grubb, 1987; Last, Hersen, Kazdin, Orvaschel, & Perrin, 1991; Rosenbaum et al., 1988, 1991; 2000; Turner, Beidel, & Costello, 1987). In addition, modest genetic heritability has been demonstrated with respect to several anxiety symptoms and disorders in children (Eley, 2001). The presence of anxious parents may also contribute to poorer treatment outcome in youths with anxiety disorders (Cobham, Dadds, & Spence, 1998), suggesting a possible anxiety link for some families.

With specific respect to childhood social phobia, however, available data do not clearly support or refute a proposed genetic predisposition. For example, Rowe and colleagues (1998) found that the dopamine transporter gene (DAT1) was associated with several anxiety-related disorders in youths, including social phobia. However, this gene has been associated with many *other* disorders as well, including depression and attention deficit hyperactivity disorder. Merikangas and colleagues (1999) found that the presence of two parents with an anxiety disorder was related to diagnoses of social phobia in 36.4% of their children, compared to 12.5% if one parent had an anxiety disorder and 0.0% if neither parent had an anxiety disorder. In addition, some youths of parents with social phobia, especially adolescents, often meet criteria for social phobia (23.4%) themselves in addition to other anxiety disorders (Mancini, Van Ameringen, Szatmari, Fugere, & Boyle, 1996).

Nelson and colleagues (2000), examining adolescent twins, found additive genetic factors for social phobia to be only 28%, compared to major depression (45%) and alcohol use disorder (63%). Lieb and colleagues (2000) found that offspring of parents with social phobia had social phobia themselves (9.6%) more so than offspring of controls (2.1%). However, parental depression and panic disorder and alcohol use disorder may increase rates of social phobia and social interaction problems in offspring as well (Biederman, Faraone, et al., 2001; Lieb et al., 2000; Rende, Warner, Wickramarante, & Weissman, 1999). Turner and colleagues (1987) also found that youths of parents with anxiety disorders had poorer social adjustment, spent more time in solitary activities, and had fewer friends compared to controls.

Albano and colleagues (2003), reviewing the extant data with respect to anxiety disorders in children, concluded that a genetic risk factor may generally predispose some youths toward various anxious or depressive disorders. However, environmental influences often help determine the direction of these psychopathologies. In addition, separating the different contributions of genetic predispositions and environmental influences is extremely difficult. Although a genetic predisposition to social phobia has not yet been clearly established, temperamental constructs *related* to social phobia do appear to have stronger heritability, and these are discussed next.

GENETICS: CONCEPTS RELATED TO SOCIAL PHOBIA

Warren and colleagues (1999) examined 7-year-old twins and found that genetic influences accounted for 34% of the variance in children's *social anxiety* scores, which were likened to shy behaviors or behavioral inhibition. Relatedly, Robinson and colleagues (1992) examined twin pairs and found heritability indices for *behavioral inhibition* to be .64, .56, and .51 at age 14, 20, and 24 months, respectively. DiLalla and colleagues (1994) similarly examined 2-year-olds for behavioral inhibition and found that concordance for identical twins (.70) was substantially higher than for fraternal twins (.38). *Changes* in shy, inhibited behavior in early developmental stages also appear to be more specific to identical than fraternal twins (Matheny, 1989; Plomin et al., 1993). Other characteristics similar to social phobia, such as childhood *shyness* or *anxiety-based school refusal behavior*, also appear to have a familial or heritable link (Cooper & Eke, 1999; Daniels & Plomin, 1985; Martin, Cabrol, Bouvard, Lepine, & Mouren-Simeoni, 1999).

The heritability of other social phobia-related constructs has also been examined, though more so in adults. For example, *harm avoidance* has been found to be highly representative of first-degree relatives of people with generalized social phobia (Stein, Chartier, Lizak, & Jang, 2001). Rose and Ditto (1983) found that fears of negative social interaction, social responsibility, and dangerous places had significant genetic modulation in 14–34-year-olds. In addition, Stein and colleagues (2002) examined hundreds of twins and found that genetic influences accounted for a moderate 42% of the variance with respect to fear of negative evaluation, a cognitive construct similar to social phobia. Fear of negative evaluation was also closely linked to submissiveness, anxiousness, and social avoidance.

Other social anxiety-related constructs seem to have some genetic basis as well, including introversion, neuroticism, and anxiety sensitivity (Arbelle et al., 2003; Eaves, Eysenck, & Martin, 1989; Stein, Jang, & Livesley, 1999). Others have argued as well that social anxiety has an evolutionary-genetic basis. In essence, social anxiety may help maintain social order by inducing some people to submit to more dominant ones, thus avoiding conflict and forming clear hierarchies (Gilbert, 2001; Ohman, 1986).

Temperament: Behavioral Inhibition

A temperamental quality most often linked to general and social anxiety in youths is behavioral inhibition, or a pattern of fearfulness, timidity, avoidance, and guardedness surrounding new stimuli such as strangers or novel objects or events (Kagan et al., 1988). This temperament is usually associated with *behavioral features* such as withdrawal, close proximity to caregivers, idleness, and frequent expressions of distress, as well as *physiological features* such as increased heart rate, blood pressure, and muscle tension, among others. Behavioral inhibition has been linked to highly reactive infants who often cry and show much motor activity in response to new stimuli (Kagan, 1994, 1997). These children as toddlers tend to be shy and subdued, and as young children tend to be anxious and fearful with a highly reactive sympathetic nervous system (Kagan, 2001).

Behavioral inhibition and the related construct of shyness have been shown to be enduring characteristics in developmental stages from toddlerhood to adulthood (e.g., Caspi & Silva, 1995; Fordham & Stevenson-Hinde, 1999; Goldsmith & Lemery, 2000; Scarpa, Raine, Venables, & Mednick, 1995). As mentioned in Chapter 2, children with behavioral inhibition are more likely than controls to eventually show various fearful behaviors and anxiety and avoidant disorders, and symptoms of social anxiety and phobia have been related to adult retrospective reports of childhood behavioral inhibition. Behavioral inhibition has been linked to social anxiety in youths at various developmental levels as well, and supporting data are discussed next.

With respect to young children, for example, Biederman, Faraone, and others (2001) examined 2–6-year olds of parents with or without panic disorder and/or depression. Children identified as behaviorally inhibited (i.e., fearful and with few vocalizations, spontaneous comments, or smiles) were much more likely to be diagnosed with social anxiety disorder (defined as social phobia or avoidant disorder) (17%) than those identified as not behaviorally inhibited (5%). However, this result was largely due to the difference in avoidant disorder per se (i.e., 9% versus 1%, respectively), which is an antiquated diagnosis (see Chapter 1).

With respect to young adolescents, Schwartz and colleagues (1999) examined 13-year-olds previously identified with or without behavioral inhibition at 21 or 31 months of age. A key difference was the presence of significant social anxiety, which was quite higher in the inhibited (61%) than the uninhibited group (27%). In fact, only 20% of those with behavioral inhibition never had generalized social anxiety. In addition, youths with generalized social anxiety commonly reported related problems such as other specific fears (71%), performance anxiety (65%), and separation fears (44%). Inhibited youths also produced less smiles and spontaneous comments than uninhibited youths. Muris, Merckelbach, Wessel, and van de Ven (1999) also found, among 12–14-year olds, that 4.8% of those self-rated as high in behavioral inhibition had social phobia. This compared to significantly lower 2.7% and 1.7% rates in youths self-rated as moderate and low behavioral inhibition, respectively.

With respect to older adolescents, Hayward and colleagues (1998) examined high schoolers over a 4-year period and eventually divided them into those with social phobia, depression, social phobia and depression, or no mental disorder. Various aspects of behavioral inhibition were also assessed, including social avoidance, fearfulness, and illness behavior. Social avoidance and fearfulness were found to predict the later development of social phobia in boys and girls. In fact, 22.3% of adolescents who were socially avoidant *and* fearful developed social phobia, compared to only 4.5% of those with neither predictor.

Although behavioral inhibition has been a very rich source of information about the development of anxiety and social anxiety in children, some important caveats must be considered. First, not all youths classified as highly reactive or behaviorally inhibited necessarily develop social anxiety disorder (Caspi, Moffitt, Newman, & Silva, 1996; Prior, Smart, Sanson, & Oberklaid, 2000). In fact, even a majority do not. Second, not all youths with anxiety disorder, including social phobia, display features of behavioral inhibition. In fact, a majority possibly do not. Third, youths with behavioral inhibition have been shown to develop depression as well as anxiety disorders other than social phobia.

Fourth, some studies of behavioral inhibition have relied heavily or exclusively on child self-report. Fifth, behavioral inhibition has been found to be a highly multifaceted, malleable, and inconsistent construct (Asendorpf, 1994; Rubin, Hastings, Stewart, Henderson, & Chen, 1997). Sixth, behavioral inhibition may operate in concert with other temperaments (e.g., neuroticism, harm avoidance, anxiety sensitivity) to help produce anxiety (Hirshfeld-Becker, Biederman, & Rosenbaum, 2004). Despite these caveats, however, some youths who are highly reactive or who show very strong features of behavioral inhibition do seem more likely to develop internalizing psychopathology compared to youths without such characteristics.

TEMPERAMENT: NEGATIVE AFFECT, POSITIVE AFFECT, PHYSIOLOGICAL HYPERAROUSAL, AND CONTROL

The investigation of personality or temperamental qualities related to childhood anxiety disorders has also focused on *negative affect* (sometimes linked to introversion/ neuroticism), *positive affect* (sometimes linked to extraversion), and *physiological hyperarousal* (Austin & Chorpita, 2004; Chorpita et al., 2000; Clark & Watson, 1991; Joiner, Catanzaro, & Laurent, 1996; Lonigan, Vasey, Phillips, & Hazen, 2004; Turner & Barrett, 2003). Negative affect has been linked with anxiety, low positive affect with depression, and physiological hyperarousal with fear (Chorpita, Albano, & Barlow, 1998). Examining a sample of clinically-referred youths with anxiety disorders and depression, Chorpita and colleagues (2000) found that social anxiety was significantly negatively related to positive affect but unrelated to negative affect or physiological hyperarousal. Among normal children, however, social anxiety *has* been found to be significantly related to negative affect (Chorpita, 2002).

Given that negative emotions seem intricately related to general and social anxiety in children, work has been conducted to identify which processes help produce these emotions. Several possibilities are mentioned in this chapter (e.g., family, cognitive, learning processes), but another that has received increased attention is the idea of *perceived control* over one's environment. In essence, some have proposed that one's historical sense of uncontrollability (i.e., inability to control outcomes) and unpredictability about life events represents a generalized psychological vulnerability that helps produce negative emotions and then perhaps anxiety disorders (Barlow, 2000, 2002; Chorpita & Barlow, 1998). As such, control may become a mediating factor between stressful life events and negative affect, as negative experiences of lack of control regarding these events accumulate over time and facilitate anxiety and depression. Life events most salient to this process may involve caregivers, oneself, and the world (Chorpita, 2001).

Others have contended that anxiety disorders are related to a combination of behavioral inhibition, high negative affect or neuroticism, and *poor effortful control*, the latter defined as difficulty in "self-regulation of affect through management of attention and other behaviors" (Lonigan & Phillips, 2001, p. 65). Some have argued as well that negative emotions in anxious children are largely marked by a "single temperamental risk factor" (Albano et al., 2003, p. 311) that may involve a confluence of the variables mentioned here. Unfortunately, however, work in this area remains beset by assessment differences and difficulties (Chorpita & Daleiden, 2002), and specific extensions to youths with social anxiety remain few. However, the constructs do seem to have great potential for applicability to this population. For example, children with social anxiety commonly report feelings of helplessness and futility as reasons for their negative emotions in social and evaluative situations.

OTHER BIOLOGICAL VARIABLES

Other biological variables have been associated with social phobia and may have some bearing on the development of the disorder. In adults, for example, those with social phobia and those with other anxiety disorders or controls have been differentiated along dopaminergic, serotonergic, noradrenergic, and GABAergic brain systems (Moutier & Stein, 2001). Structural brain changes or differential activation in the amygdala, hippocampus, and various cortical areas may distinguish people with social phobia from controls as well (Birbaumer et al., 1998; Davidson, Krishnan, et al., 1993; Pine, 2001; Schneider et al., 1999; Tupler et al., 1997). Adults with social phobia, more so than controls, also have significantly more neurological disorder and peptic ulcer disease (Davidson, Hughes, et al., 1993). Adults with social phobia have also been found to have differential patterns of heart rate and blood pressure next to some, though not all, comparative samples (Beidel, Turner, & Dancu, 1985; Davidson, Marshall, Tomarken, & Henriques, 2000; Heimberg, Hope, Dodge, & Becker, 1990; Hofmann, Newman, Ehlers, & Roth, 1995; Stein, Asmundson, & Chartier, 1994). Less strong results have been found with respect to chemical challenge and peripheral abnormality studies in adults with social phobia (Argyropoulos, Bell, & Nutt, 2001; Tancer & Uhde, 2002).

Significantly less work in this area has been conducted with respect to youths with social phobia or related constructs. Elevated heart rates following evaluative stressors have been found more so among high than low test-anxious children, but less conclusive results have been reported with specific respect to maintenance of these heart rates over time and youths with social phobia (Beidel, 1989). For example, Beidel (1991; Turner, Beidel, & Epstein, 1991) found no statistically significant differences in baseline heart rate or heart rate changes following stressful tasks in youths with social phobia compared to controls. Indeed, children exposed to various stressors do not always display increased heart rate (Beidel, 1989).

Growth hormone deficiency (GHD) has been linked to children who are socially constricted, withdrawn, and isolated (Money & Pollitt, 1966), and adolescents and adults who had GHD as children have a high incidence (60%) of social phobia (Stabler et al., 1996). This may be due to both neuroendocrine and psychosocial problems. In addition, children referred for GHD treatment tend to show decreased social competence and substantial anxiety, somatic complaints, and shy/withdrawn behavior (Stabler et al., 1994).

Finally, with respect to behavioral inhibition, Kagan (1997) hypothesized that hypersensitivity of the amygdala and related brain connections may be responsible for its presence. In addition, behavioral inhibition or high reactivity in children has been linked to increased 3-methoxy-4-hydroxy phenylglycol (MHPG), cortisol, heart rate and sympathetic nervous system activity, right frontal activation, and right frontal electroencephalograph asymmetry (Fox, Henderson, Rubin, Calkins, & Schmidt, 2001; Kagan et al., 1988; 2001; McManis, Kagan, Snidman, & Woodward, 2002). However, the physiological study of youths with social phobia remains in its infancy.

GENERALIZED PSYCHOLOGICAL VULNERABILITIES

Recall that generalized psychological vulnerabilities for mental disorder are those factors that generally pervade a person's life as he or she develops. With respect to childhood social phobia, these factors include cognitive characteristics, parental and familial influences, and learning experiences. These factors are discussed separately next.

COGNITIVE CHARACTERISTICS

As mentioned in Chapter 2, youths with social phobia are commonly described as excessively (1) self-conscious, (2) self-focused with respect to their arousal level, (3) sensitive to indicators of negative evaluation by others, (4) overestimating threat from others and underestimating personal social competence, and/or (5) contemplative of negative outcomes, self-deprecation, embarrassment, and ridicule, rejection, and negative evaluation by others. However, data from recent empirical studies indicates that definitive conclusions regarding these descriptions are not yet available.

Epkins (1996b), for example, found that children with social anxiety had many more cognitive distortions compared to controls but not more than youths with dysphoria. One important difference that did emerge, however, was that socially anxious and not dysphoric children had more cognitive distortions of overgeneralization and personalization compared to controls. Although the presence of dysphoria heavily confounded the cognitive biases in socially anxious children, the latter result led the author to conclude that socially anxious children's biases tend to be future-oriented and attentive toward "threat cues with an exaggerated estimate of vulnerability" (Epkins, 1996b, p. 96). Epkins (1996a), drawing from the same sample, also found that socially anxious children tended to perceive social rejection by others and that, when combined with dysphoria, experienced excessive social problems with actual peer rejection (p. 466).

Spence and colleagues (1999), using social-evaluative role-play and reading tasks, found that youths with social phobia expected to feel more anxious prior to these tasks, and expected to be less successful than peers on these tasks, than controls. Indeed, these youths were reportedly more anxious following the tasks although their actual performance was no different than controls. In addition, youths with social phobia were less likely to expect the presence of positive social events, but *no* significant difference was found with respect to expectations of negative social events. Furthermore, youths with social phobia did report the presence of more negative cognitions, but *no* significant difference was found with respect to positive cognitions. No differences were found as well with respect to self-performance ratings following the tasks. The authors concluded that youths with social phobia tend to have many negative expectancies and thoughts, but that these cognitions may be justified given their poor level of social skill (see Chapter 2).

Others have also found tepid or mixed results in this area. For example, Bogels and Zigterman (2000) examined 15 children with anxiety disorders, 6 of whom had social phobia as a primary or comorbid diagnosis, as well as clinical and nonclinical control groups. Nine stories were presented to the children that contained ambiguous themes of possible separation, social, or generalized anxiety. Childrens' responses to the stories were evaluated by examining positive, negative, and neutral cognitions as well as overestimations of danger and underestimations of competence and coping abilities. Results indicated that anxious children interpreted these stories in a negative manner significantly more so than the clinical control group but *not* the nonclinical control group, and did *not* differ from controls with respect to positive interpretations. In addition, anxious children had more dysfunctional cognitions and underestimations of competency.

Data regarding overestimations of danger were mixed, as anxious children did not differ from other groups with respect to number of such cognitions but did judge the stories as more dangerous when answering specific questions about them compared to controls. Anxious children also saw themselves as significantly less influential in these situations compared to nonclinical but *not* clinical controls. Although the authors concluded that anxious children do "have a cognitive bias for threat" (p. 210), the use of a small sample size, the mixed results, and the decision not to separately analyze youths of different diagnostic categories makes the study difficult to extrapolate to youths with social phobia.

Muris, Merckelbach, and Damsma (2000) examined a large sample of youths defined as socially anxious but not phobic, and controls. Youths listened to 5-sentence stories of common social situations that were either ambiguous (6) or threatening (1), and identified the point at which they found they story to be scary. Ratings of threat were also obtained. Results indicated that socially anxious youths, compared to controls, determined a story to be scary in less time, more often perceived threat during the stories, more often viewed the stories as threatening in general, and reported more negative emotions and cognitions. The authors concluded that the data provided strong support for a threat perception and interpretation bias in this population, but their heavy reliance on child self-report and examination of a nonclinical sample does not necessarily support such a conclusion for youths with social phobia.

Other, related studies have shown even more tepid results. For example, children with high test anxiety tend to have more negative self-evaluations and off-task thoughts compared to youths with low test anxiety but *also* high frequencies of on-task and coping thoughts (Prins, Groot, & Hanewald, 1994; Zatz & Chassin, 1985). In addition, Beidel (1991) found that youths with social anxiety tended to have more negative cognitions compared to controls, though this finding was not statistically significant. Youths with social anxiety did, however, rate themselves as less cognitively competent than controls. Chansky and Kendall (1997) found that social anxiety but not self-perceived social competence was predictive of negative social expectations among children with general anxiety disorders (see also Bogels, Snieder, & Kindt, 2003; Kindt, Bogels, & Morren, 2003; Rheingold, Herbert, & Franklin, 2003).

Furthermore, Perrin and Last (1997) found that anxious children, including some with social phobia, worried more about social evaluation than nonclinical but *not* clinical controls. Magnusdottir and Smari (1999) found that adolescent social anxiety correlated significantly with measures of perceived general and social threat to oneself, but only at .17 and .38, respectively. Finally, Field and colleagues (2003) found that positive or negative information given to normal youths about different social situations had *no* effect on social fear beliefs. In fact, negative information given about a public speaking situation actually *reduced* fear beliefs.

Alfano and colleagues (2002), in a thorough review of the literature, concluded that "research on the cognitive aspects of childhood anxiety has produced divergent and confusing findings" (p. 1230). This statement seems particularly relevant to findings regarding social phobia in youths. In particular, several caveats regarding the literature were discussed, including methodological and definitional differences across studies, incomplete assessments, failure to examine processes behind cognitive content findings, and failure to attend more closely to developmental differences. The authors even suggested that assuming that cognitive therapy is a necessary component of treating anxious children is not yet fully warranted.

Daleiden and Vasey (1997), in a widely cited paper, provided a sample framework to understand the cognitive processes that may underlie findings relevant to anxious children. In their *information-processing perspective*, the authors proposed that anxious children selectively attend to, focus on, and become distracted by threatening stimuli in their environment. As such, anxious children may tend to view even ambiguous stimuli as threatening, assume negative attributions and outcomes, and see themselves as unable to cope with threats and accompanying anxiety. As these children process information in such a negative way over time, they may overpractice strategies of escape and avoidance to enhance personal safety and thus fail to accurately evaluate their thoughts in anxiety-provoking situations. Although not tied directly to youths with social anxiety, such a model does help explain the common descriptions made of this population in the literature (see above and Chapter 2). In addition, such a model provides an excellent starting point for understanding the automatic processes that underlie cognitive content as well as why such content is maintained over time. Such a model, which is also sensitive to developmental differences (Vasey & McLeod, 2001), may also help provide a framework for organizing disparate information in this area.

PARENTAL AND FAMILIAL CHARACTERISTICS

Specific parental or familial characteristics might also be related to the familial aggregation of social phobia. These characteristics include parenting style and family environment, attachment, and modeling of social anxiety and avoidance. These are discussed separately next.

Parenting Style and Family Environment

Parents of anxious children are often described as controlling, partial, meddling, affectionless, overprotective, demanding, encouraging of avoidant behaviors, discouraging of proactive or prosocial behaviors, and/or anxious, withdrawn, avoidant, and socially isolated themselves (Barrett, Rapee, et al., 1996; Dadds, Barrett, Rapee, & Ryan, 1996; Dumas, LaFreniere, & Serketich, 1995; Krohne & Hock, 1991; Lindhout et al., 2003; Rapee, 1997; Woodruff-Borden, Morrow, Bourland, & Cambron, 2002). With respect to *social anxiety-related constructs*, maternal expressed emotion seems related to behavioral inhibition in youths (Hirshfeld, Biederman, Brody, Faraone, & Rosenbaum, 1997), shyness is evident in adoptive parents and their adoptive children (Daniels & Plomin, 1985), and lack of authoritative (e.g., authoritarian) parenting has been linked to peer rejection and lower levels of social competence in children (Dekovic & Janssens, 1992).

With respect to social phobia *per se*, adult retrospective studies implicate several parental or familial practices that may have facilitated the development of social anxiety:

- isolating a child from social activities (Bruch, Heimberg, Berger, & Collins, 1989)
- overemphasizing the opinions and negative evaluations of others (Bruch & Heimberg, 1994; Bruch et al., 1989)
- poor family sociability and avoidance of social situations (Bruch & Heimberg, 1994; Bruch et al., 1989)
- less warmth and caring and greater overprotectiveness of the child (Arrindell, Emmelkamp, Monsma, & Brilman, 1983; Arrindell et al., 1989; Parker, 1979)
- rejection of the child (Arrindell et al., 1983, 1989)
- general instability, characterized by separation from or lack of close relationships with adults, marital conflict in parents, parental history of mental disorder, moving frequently, involvement with the legal system, running away from home, physical and sexual maltreatment, school failure and dropout, and need for special education (Chartier, Walker, & Stein, 2001; Wittchen et al., 1999)

A serious problem with these retrospective studies is bias, of course, as accurate recall can be affected by many factors such as depression (Parker et al., 1997). However, some have evaluated youths with social or test anxiety and their *current* family environment. For example, Caster and colleagues (1999) found that adolescents with high levels of social anxiety, compared to controls, viewed their parents as overconcerned about the opinions of others, ashamed of the youths' shyness and poor performance, and focused on isolating the youths. In addition, high socially anxious adolescents perceived themselves and their parents as less socially active than controls. However, parental perceptions of the families did not differ between the two groups.

Other findings with specific respect to socially anxious children have been more tepid. In particular, Bogels and colleagues (2001) examined how socially anxious children aged 8–18 years perceived their current family environment. Although maternal social anxiety did predict child social anxiety, parental warmth and rejection were *not* closely related to child social anxiety unless the child's level of social anxiety was extreme. In addition, maternal overprotectiveness was found only somewhat related to child social anxiety, and family sociability among socially anxious children was less than normal children but no different from a clinical control group. The tepid findings were further underscored by the fact that parents of socially anxious children emphasized the opinions of others less than parents of normal controls. The authors also found that first or only children tended to have less social anxiety, a finding opposite others (Bruch, 1989).

Melfsen and colleagues (2000) also found that mothers of socially anxious children differed little with respect to facial expressions compared to mothers of non-socially anxious children. One key exception, however, was that mothers of socially anxious children generally showed less intense facial expressions of emotions, leading the authors to conclude that the children of these parents could have great difficulty modeling facial expressions in key social situations and thus fail to interact appropriately with others.

Lieb and colleagues (2000) also found that higher parental overprotectiveness and rejection were associated with increased rates of social phobia in children, though other mental disorders (e.g., depression, alcohol use disorder) were *also* found to be related to these parenting variables. In addition, Peleg-Popko and Dar (2001) found that increased social anxiety was positively correlated with family cohesion or overprotectiveness. With respect to children with test anxiety, Peleg-Popko (2002) found these youths to generally have families with reduced communication, encouragement of personal growth, and system maintenance (i.e., highly inconsistent parental behavior). Fathers of youths with test anxiety also tend to have more obsessive-compulsive symptoms than controls (Messer & Beidel, 1994).

Attachment

Parent-child attachment problems, such as an insecure or disorganized or anxious ambivalent attachment style, may also be related to childhood anxiety and related problems (Cowan, Cohn, Pape-Cowan, & Pearson, 1996; Manassis, 2001; Radke-Yarrow et al., 1995; Rosenstein & Horowitz, 1996; Van IJzendoorn & Bakermans-Kranenburg, 1996). In addition, attachment problems may be related to later social anxiety. Warren and colleagues (1997), for example, identified infants with anxious/resistant, avoidant, and secure attachments and reexamined 172 at age 17.5 years. Of 26 adolescents who later had developed an anxiety disorder, 28.1% were of the anxious/resistant attachment type, 16.2% were of the avoidant attachment type, and 11.6% were of the secure attachment type. The most frequent anxiety disorder was social phobia (38.5%). Attachment type was also found to be a better predictor of anxiety disorder than temperament or maternal anxiety. Conversely, securely attached infants, or those with warm, responsive caregivers, tend later to be more popular, socially effective, interactive with peers, and viewed by others as socially positive compared to insecurely attached infants (Masia & Morris, 1998).

Parental Modeling of Social Anxiety and Avoidance and Other
Parental Practices

Parents of anxious children do appear to model and reinforce anxious, avoidant behaviors in their children (Chorpita et al., 1996; Dadds et al., 1996; Kashdan & Herbert, 2001). Little work has been done in this regard with specific respect to youths with social phobia, but older children and adolescents would seem likely to model behaviors consistent with this disorder (Dadds, Davey, & Field, 2001). Modeled behaviors most likely include avoidance and statements of fear, dangerousness, threat, difficulty coping, and uncontrollability regarding social and evaluative situations (Barrett et al., 1996; Ollendick, Vasey, & King, 2001). With respect to social competence and status in children, these are greatly affected by positive (e.g., less controlling) parent-child play experiences, appropriate (e.g., inductive) disciplinary practices, opportunities for early socialization, parental social support, and useful social information conveyed to a child (e.g., about entering a play group) (Masia & Morris, 1998).

These variables may thus be instructive for understanding the development of social anxiety in some youngsters. For example, youths with social anxiety may be likely to have parents who are socially anxious themselves, who are more controlling, who are harsh or critical in their discipline, who shelter youths from socialization experiences, and who consistently warn their children of danger even in ambiguous play and other social and evaluative situations. Some have theorized that a combination of (1) parental modeling of anxiety and avoidance, overcontrol and overprotection, and reduction of socialization experiences, (2) child inhibition and shyness, distress, and demands for close proximity to and comfort from caregivers, and (3) insecure attachment lead to an anxious-coercive parent-child relationship that spurs the development of anxiety disorders, perhaps including social phobia, in youths (Dadds & Roth, 2001).

LEARNING EXPERIENCES

Common pathways for learning fear in childhood involve modeling, information transfer, and direct conditioning (Rachman, 1977). When fears develop in older childhood and adolescence, as is the case for many social and evaluative fears, the mechanism of learning is often modeling and information transfer (Dadds et al., 2001). As mentioned above, parents may be excellent models of socially phobic behavior, and information from parents is often integral to shaping play and other social behaviors in children. In addition, adults with social phobia do report that modeling and information transfer were directly responsible for the onset of their disorder

(Ost & Hughdahl, 1981). Of course, memory bias in this regard must be considered as well.

Direct conditioning may also help spur the acquisition and maintenance of social and evaluative fears in children. With respect to acquisition, traumatic or stressful events may facilitate the disorder via classical conditioning, and many adults with shyness or social phobia indeed link their condition to specific negative social events (Ishiyama, 1984; Ost & Hughdahl, 1981). This may be particularly true for people with specific social phobia, although 20% of people *without* social phobia also report traumatic social experiences (Stemberger et al., 1995).

As mentioned in Chapter 2, children with social phobia often experience negative and possibly traumatic peer interactions as well (Beidel & Turner, 1998), although the direction of causality among these factors remains unclear. For example, children with social phobia may have certain temperaments (e.g., shyness, behavioral inhibition) or cognitive biases that lead them to withdraw from many socialization opportunities and thus *later* experience peer rejection, neglect, or humiliation as well as underdeveloped social skills. Indeed, childhood learning experiences are typically linked in the literature to temperamental and other vulnerabilities when describing the onset of social phobia in youths (e.g., Dadds et al., 2001). In essence, some children may be more particularly predisposed to learn to fear social and evaluative situations than others.

With respect to maintenance of social and evaluative fears in children, several learning possibilities are evident. First, parents may inadvertently or deliberately reinforce socially anxious behavior in their children via ongoing praise, sympathy, or acquiescence to child requests to avoid key socialization experiences (Eisen & Kearney, 1995). Second, a child may continually avoid or escape social and evaluative situations, and subsequent fear reduction may thus serve to negatively reinforce the withdrawn behavior. Subsequent approach toward a nonthreatening place (e.g., home, caregiver position) may serve to positively reinforce withdrawn behavior as well (Delprato & McGlynn, 1984; Mowrer, 1960). Third, punishment of approach responses toward social and evaluative opportunities, especially incompetent approaches that involve deficient social skills, may suppress such responses in the future (Vasey & Dadds, 2001).

Fourth, rule-governed behavior and extensive stimulus generalization could extend fearful behavior to other social contexts (McNeil, Lejuez, & Sorrell, 2001). Fifth, ongoing learning experiences with stressors could help prevent a child from overcoming developmentally appropriate fears that should normally fade over time, prevent him or her from exposure to fearful socialization experiences and thus habituation to them, and/or prevent satisfactory development of social skills (Vasey & Dadds, 2001).

Learning experiences may also lead a youth to view internal sensations or social/evaluative situations as dangerous, thus creating a *specific psychological vulnerability*. These maintaining processes likely intersect with other vulnerabilities mentioned in this chapter. However, learning processes with respect to socially anxious children remain highly speculative and require more empirical work.

AN INTEGRATIVE MODEL AND DEVELOPMENTAL PATHWAY OF SOCIAL ANXIETY DISORDER

Having described the major biological and psychological vulnerabilities posited for social anxiety disorder, attention is turned next to an etiological model and a developmental pathway that integrates these vulnerabilities. This is done at the adult level to illustrate a global etiological picture, and then at the youth level to illustrate more detailed pathways.

ADULTS

One widely cited and highly comprehensive etiological model for adult social phobia is that espoused by Hofmann and Barlow (2002) (see Figure 3.1). In this model, generalized biological and psychological

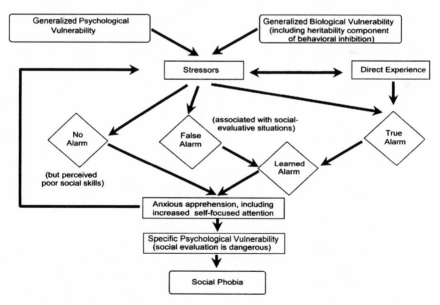

FIGURE 3.1. A model of the etiology of social phobia. (Used with permission).

vulnerabilities for anxious apprehension intersect with negative life events and direct social/evaluative experiences. For some people, particularly those with specialized social phobias (e.g., of public speaking or other circumscribed situations), a fear reaction or panic attack(s) may develop following particularly stressful, traumatic, or highly embarrassing social/evaluative situations (i.e., *true alarm*). An example might be a person who develops intense fear during or shortly after a disastrous public speaking engagement.

For other people, particularly those with generalized social phobia, a more diffuse anxiety response with feelings of embarrassment and shame may develop. This anxiety response may lack a specific alarm reaction, but could still be associated with intense anxious apprehension about perceived deficits in one's social skills. The development of social phobia is less likely in this pathway unless the previously mentioned vulnerabilities are strongly present (Barlow, 2000). In addition, the anxiety response could be associated with Barlow's notion of *false alarms*, which involve fear or panic largely in the absence of a specific, provoking stimulus but which, in this case, follow generally stressful social/evaluative situations. This pathway likely becomes ingrained over time as feelings develop of lack of control in social/evaluative situations and as one comes to believe that such situations are potentially dangerous and threatening.

Each of these pathways can be maintained by several variables such as self-focused attention and cognitive processing errors. This may help explain why many cases of social phobia in adults strongly persist over time. One should note, however, that other etiological models of adult social phobia have been proposed and are based more heavily on biological (Pine, 2001), representational or cognitive (Roth & Heimberg, 2001), or behavioral/learning variables (Beidel & Turner, 1998).

YOUTHS

With respect to youths, the development of integrated etiological models of social phobia has been largely eschewed in favor of exploring potential developmental pathways to the disorder. This is not to say that overall models have been neglected altogether, and those that have been proposed are generally more inclusive of family and peer relationships than adult models. Morris (2001), for example, noted that social phobia likely reflects a combination of temperamental qualities, family processes, peer relationships, performance inhibition, and social skills deficits. Albano and Hayward (2004) added that any model of social phobia in youths must include the intermingling of biological vulnerabilities with contextual variables such as parenting style, peer interactions, academic settings, and culture. Specific developmental pathways to childhood social phobia would involve variations of these risk factors.

Many developmental pathways can, of course, lead to social phobia and related outcomes and psychopathologies in youths. Indeed, several authors have proposed developmental pathways or links that apply to the development of childhood social phobia (Albano et al., 2003; Beidel et al., 1999; La Greca & Lopez, 1998; Morris, 2001; Neal & Edelmann, 2003; Ollendick & Hirshfeld-Becker, 2002; Rubin et al., 1990; Stemberger et al., 1995; Vasey & Dadds, 2001). Rather than separately explicating each of these pathways, an amalgam is presented here that involves one general pathway with many distinct parts and subpaths. Protective and ameliorating factors are presented subsequently as well.

Most proposed developmental pathways for childhood social phobia begin with biological vulnerabilities such as predispositions toward autonomic overarousal, behavioral inhibition, high negative affect, and/or low positive affect. In essence, some children do seem innately geared toward excitability, fear, and withdrawal from different situations, especially novel or interactive situations. As these infants develop, they may be exposed to parents who are temperamentally anxious, inhibited, or unresponsive themselves. This scenario could lead to:

- poor child-parent attachment
- parental confusion or ineptitude about how to care for a child who is fussy, clingy, fearful, and demanding
- an underdeveloped child-parent social relationship

In essence, the stage may be set quite early for some children to falter in social situations. As these children enter toddlerhood and the early preschool period, for example, they may engage in excessive self-reliance or self-isolation (e.g., playing in a corner by themselves) that is encouraged or not discouraged by others. In addition, these children may be isolated *by parents* from social situations that are potentially embarrassing for the parents (e.g., "What if he throws a fit at the birthday party? I'd rather not have to deal with it"), or that the parent worries may be too stressful for the child ("She can't handle this right now"). The results of this process may involve:

- initial modeling of poor strategies for addressing social situations (e.g., avoidance, withdrawal, verbal complaints, conflict, feigned illness as an excuse for escape)
- reduced opportunities to build and practice effective social skills and to receive and appropriately process feedback from others

- increased anxiety and inhibition in social situations and less desire to be in these situations
- poor mastery of social fears and loss of opportunities for habituation or beneficial emotional processing
- coping strategies marked more by avoidance than by seeking support from others

These outcomes may be especially pertinent to children not enrolled in preschool or in other social activities where adults other than the child's parents can supervise and help develop his or her social skills and mastery of social situations.

As these children enter and proceed through elementary school, various social, academic, athletic, and other demands are made of them. For children with biological and psychological predispositions toward social withdrawal in infancy and toddlerhood, these increased demands may serve as highly aversive experiences that interact with their vulnerabilities. Although direct conditioning experiences may occur (e.g., direct peer rejection), vicarious experiences or episodes of negative information transfer may occur as well. For example, a child could see another child rejected or assaulted or be told by parents or peers that interacting with certain (or many) children is dangerous and should be avoided. As such, the following may occur:

- anxiety may increase as a child begins to perceive social and evaluative situations, particularly those involving unfamiliar peers, to be dangerous, threatening, unpredictable, and uncontrollable; such perceptions may be reinforced by family members as well
- even in the absence of a specific anxiety-provoking event, anxiety symptoms themselves could become viewed as highly uncomfortable, uncontrollable, dangerous, and expected
- even in the presence of mildly stressful social or evaluative events, intense anxiety and avoidance/escape may occur, leading to failures to habituate, engage in beneficial emotional processing, master anxiety, and/or modify relevant erroneous beliefs and cognitive distortions
- as avoidance/escape becomes a more frequently used strategy, social skill development may remain arrested due to limited opportunities for practice
- a cycle may become well-ingrained over time of anxiety and inhibition in social/evaluative situations that leads to avoidance and subsequent worry about future social/evaluative situations

One should note as well that many children who are *strongly* predisposed to social retraction (e.g., via genetics, temperament, attachment) may *not* experience highly stressful social/evaluative events but may *still* develop social phobia or go on to have problems in peer relationships or social withdrawal (see Chapter 1). Other psychopathologies may develop as well, most notably depression and/or generalized anxiety, separation anxiety, or panic disorders. Conversely, some children may be *weakly* predisposed toward social retraction but still experience highly negative episodes of social interaction and evaluation and, via learning mechanisms, later develop social anxiety or related disorders.

As these children enter middle and high school, ongoing practices of self-isolation and avoidance/escape/withdrawal from social/evaluative situations may facilitate more ingrained problems with peers. As noted in Chapter 2, for example, peer exclusion, ridicule, and rejection are intimately tied to a child's social anxiety and avoidance. For example, both the child and his or her peers may perceive the other party as unfriendly, mean-spirited, or snobbish. As such, the child may engage in even more solitary activities, spend more time with family members, eschew development of close friendships, and view himself or herself as socially incompetent. Perhaps these behaviors, which may be continually reinforced by family members, serve to foster social worry and distress, increase negative self-evaluation, further impair development of social skills and friendships, produce fewer opportunities for socialization, and extend an anxious, depressive, fearful, and avoidant cycle in social and evaluative situations.

In such a complicated pathway, biological factors intersect with family factors, and this combination later intersects with negative peer experiences. Along the way, several practices serve to cement the pathway and increase the likelihood of social phobia or other psychopathology. These practices most likely involve cognitive and behavioral avoidance, poor skill development, erroneous beliefs and cognitive distortions, destructive parent/family responses (e.g., overprotectiveness, reinforcement of anxiety and avoidance), and peer rejection and hostility. As children in this pathway age, risk factors compound and deviation from the pathway likely becomes more difficult. However, particular patterns of risk factors and when they occur along the pathway would certainly lead to very different effects for individual children. For example, youths with multiple, early risk factors and negative family and peer experiences in early childhood would seem to be more likely to develop social anxiety-related problems compared to youths with fewer risk factors and whose problems with family members and peers do not present until adolescence.

Several general factors may also protect certain children from fully progressing along this hypothetical pathway. Examples include less intense biological predispositions, supportive parenting, ongoing and positive exposures to socialization experiences, parental initiation of these experiences ("Yes, you are going to the soccer game"), good development of social and coping skills and friendships, realistic thinking patterns, and early intervention. More specific protective factors were described in Chapter 2 as well.

As mentioned earlier, this hypothesized pathway represents an amalgam of what has been proposed in the literature. Although perhaps a bit unwieldy, the pathway covers different risk factors that children typically face and how such risk factors may produce social phobia. However, extensive empirical support remains necessary, and may be derived from longitudinal prospective, twin, adoption, and intervention studies (Ollendick & Hirshfeld-Becker, 2002). In addition, investigations are sorely needed with respect to alternative pathways, how children are derailed from these pathways, how one might prevent such pathways from occurring, how cultural variables influence these pathways, and why some youths experience many risk factors but do *not* develop psychopathology or social problems. Regarding the latter, protective factors identified via developmental research (e.g., resilience) may be instructive.

FINAL COMMENTS

The pathways to childhood social phobia are likely as diverse and numerous as the characteristics of these children. Not to be lost in all of this information, however, is the fact that childhood social phobia is a potentially crippling form of mental disorder that can lead to devastating consequences. This fact necessitates the development of effective assessment and treatment strategies for this population, and the remainder of the book is thus devoted to these strategies.

CHAPTER 4

RESEARCH-BASED ASSESSMENT OF SOCIAL ANXIETY AND SOCIAL PHOBIA IN YOUTHS

Previous chapters have covered the primary characteristics of youths with social anxiety and social phobia. In this chapter, the major research-based assessment techniques that have been designed for this population are discussed. These techniques include interviews, child self-report question-naires, parent and teacher scales, family assessment measures, behavioral assessment tests, self-monitoring procedures, cognitive and physiological assessment measures, functional assessment strategies, and other meth-ods. Chapter 5 will concentrate on suggestions for tailoring these tech-niques to general *clinical* settings during screening, formal evaluation, and consultation phases. For the purposes of this chapter, one should note that many assessment techniques have been devised for constructs *related* to social anxiety and phobia, such as introversion/shyness, self-esteem, de-pression, and social skills, withdrawal, and competence. However, a full description of these related measures is outside the scope of this book.

INTERVIEWS

Interviews for assessing anxious youths may be structured or more general in nature. Suggested topics for more general interviews are dis-cussed in Chapter 5. With respect to *structured* interviews, several have been designed for children and some have been used to help study anxious youths. Although psychometrically strong, these interviews tend to devote less attention to anxiety than to other mental disorders (Silverman, 1994). Common examples include the:

- *Child and Adolescent Psychiatric Assessment* (Angold & Costello, 2000)
- *Child Assessment Schedule* (Hodges, McKnew, Cytryn, Stern, & Kline, 1982)
- *Diagnostic Interview for Children and Adolescents* (Welner, Reich, Herjanic, Jung, & Amado, 1987)
- *Interview Schedule for Children* (Kovacs, 1985)
- *National Institute of Mental Health Diagnostic Interview Schedule for Children* (Shaffer et al., 1996)
- *Pediatric Anxiety Rating Scale* (Research Units on Pediatric Psychopharmacology Anxiety Study Group, 2002)
- *Schedule for Affective Disorders and Schizophrenia for School-Age Children-Present and Lifetime Version* (Kaufman et al., 1997)

For assessing anxiety disorders in youths, including social phobia, the primary interview that has been used is the *Anxiety Disorders Interview Schedule for Children* (ADIS-C) (Silverman & Albano, 1996; Silverman & Nelles, 1988), a downward extension of the ADIS adult version (Brown, DiNardo, & Barlow, 1994; DiNardo, O'Brien, Barlow, Waddell, & Blanchard, 1983). The ADIS-C has both child and parent versions and concentrates heavily on anxiety and anxiety-related disorders along a largely structured, DSM-based format. Although anxiety disorders are the main focus of the ADIS-C, other internalizing and externalizing childhood disorders are included as well. The social phobia section in the most current ADIS-C child version (see below) (Silverman & Albano, 1996) is in Figure 4.1. Questions generally surround DSM criteria, specific targets of social anxiety, and ratings of fear, avoidance, and interference.

The original version of the ADIS-C was based on DSM-III-R criteria. Several studies examined the psychometric strength of this version and generally found strong reliability and validity (Silverman & Eisen, 1992; Silverman & Nelles, 1988; Silverman & Rabian, 1995). Regarding social phobia in particular, however, only moderate Kappa coefficients were reported (i.e., .46 and .54 for child and parent interview, respectively) (Silverman & Eisen, 1992). Rapee and colleagues (1994), examining a large sample of children with anxiety disorders, found higher interrater reliability for social phobia diagnoses based on combined child and parent report (i.e., Kappa coefficients = .82 and .77 for principal and any diagnosis of social phobia, respectively). In addition, Kappa coefficients were generally strong

Social Phobia (Social Anxiety Disorder)

Initial Inquiry

Some kids (teenagers) feel *really* scared and uncomfortable in situations with other people—so scared and uncomfortable that they might want to *stay away* from these places. Some kids (teenagers) might also cry, or even have a temper tantrum, or get angry when they have to be in situations with other people. What happens is that they might be told to go to these places, but they would rather not. They are much more afraid of these situations than other kids their age are.

1a. **When you are in certain places with other people like school, restaurants, or parties, do you feel that people might think that something you do is stupid or dumb?**   ☐ Yes ☐ No ☐ Other

If "Yes," place a check mark in the circle.   SYMPTOM

1b. **When you are in certain places with other people, like school, restaurants, or parties, do you think that people might laugh at you?**   ☐ Yes ☐ No ☐ Other

If "Yes," place a check mark in the circle.   SYMPTOM

1c. **When you are in these situations with other people, do you worry that you might do something that will make you feel ashamed or embarrassed?**   ☐ Yes ☐ No ☐ Other

If "Yes," place a check mark in the circle.   SYMPTOM

 If one or more "Yes" responses to Questions 1a–1c, place a check mark in the diamond.   CRITERION

For any of Questions 1a–1c that the child endorsed, the interviewer might wish to obtain further elaborations to determine if that area is clinically significant. Also, if the child responded

FIGURE 4.1. ADIS child version. (Used with permission).

regardless of child gender and age and format for rating the interview (i.e., live versus videotaped). Lower agreement was found between child and parent reports (i.e., Kappa coefficients = .44 and .25 for principal and any diagnoses of social phobia, respectively).

The ADIS-C was subsequently and extensively revised to reflect DSM-IV criteria, incorporate more extensive rating scales, and improve its utility,

"No" to Questions 1a–1c, the interviewer may use discretion in inquiring about the situations listed in Question 2c.

Fear (Yes or No)

2a. **Now I am going to give you a list of some situations** (see list following Question 2c). **I want to know if you think you get more nervous or scared in these situations than other kids your age do. Answer "Yes" only if these situations almost always make you scared or nervous, not if it has just happened once or twice. First, just tell me "Yes" or "No."**

Note. The interviewer may use discretion inquiring about age-relevant situations. Those situations more common to older children and adolescents are grouped at the end of the list. Also, if the child responded "No" to Questions 1a–1c, the interviewer may use discretion in inquiring about all the situations listed.

Fear Ratings (0–8)

2b. For each situation to which the child responded "Yes," obtain fear ratings using the Feelings Thermometer (found on the back cover of the Clinician Manual). Ask, **When you say that you're afraid or nervous** (e.g., giving an oral report), **how afraid do you feel when you're** (e.g., giving an oral report)? **Use the thermometer to show me how afraid or nervous you get.**

Avoidance/Distress (Yes or No)

2c. For each situation in Question 2b with a fear rating of 4 *(Some)* or greater, inquire about avoidance behavior and endurance with distress. Ask, **For those things you rated some or more fear (4 or higher), I now want to know if you ever try to avoid or stay away from these situations** (e.g., working in groups)?

If one or more situations in the list are endorsed as either avoided or endured, place a check mark in the diamond.

FIGURE 4.1. (*Continued*)

clarity, and psychometric strength. The result was the *Anxiety Disorders Interview Schedule for DSM-IV: Child and Parent Versions* (ADIS for DSM-IV: C/P) (Silverman & Albano, 1996). The reliability of this measure was examined by Silverman and colleagues (2001) among children referred for anxiety treatment. Kappa coefficients for social phobia diagnoses based on child, parent, and combined (child + parent) reports were .71, .86, and

	Fear		Fear Rating (0–8)	Avoidance/ Distress	
	Yes	No		Yes	No
Answering questions in class	☐	☐	☐	☐	☐
Giving a report or reading aloud in front of the class	☐	☐	☐	☐	☐
Asking the teacher a question or for help	☐	☐	☐	☐	☐
Taking tests	☐	☐	☐	☐	☐
Writing on the chalkboard	☐	☐	☐	☐	☐
Working or playing with a group of kids	☐	☐	☐	☐	☐
Gym class	☐	☐	☐	☐	☐
Walking in the hallways or hanging out by your locker	☐	☐	☐	☐	☐
Starting or joining in on a conversation	☐	☐	☐	☐	☐
Using school or public bathrooms	☐	☐	☐	☐	☐
Eating in front of others (e.g., home, school cafeteria, restaurants)	☐	☐	☐	☐	☐
Meetings such as girl or boy scouts or team meetings	☐	☐	☐	☐	☐
Answering or talking on the telephone	☐	☐	☐	☐	☐
Musical or athletic performances	☐	☐	☐	☐	☐
Inviting a friend to get together	☐	☐	☐	☐	☐
Speaking to adults (e.g., store clerk, waiters, principal)	☐	☐	☐	☐	☐
Talking to persons you don't know well (e.g., strangers, new or unfamiliar people)	☐	☐	☐	☐	☐
Attending parties, dances, or school activity nights	☐	☐	☐	☐	☐
Having your picture taken (e.g., for the yearbook)	☐	☐	☐	☐	☐
Dating	☐	☐	☐	☐	☐
Being asked to do something that you really don't want to do, but you can't say no. For example, if someone wants to borrow your homework or favorite toy, is it hard to say no?	☐	☐	☐	☐	☐
Having someone do something to you that you don't like, but you can't tell them to stop. For example, if someone is teasing you, is it hard for you to tell them to leave you alone?	☐	☐	☐	☐	☐

FIGURE 4.1. (*Continued*)

.92, respectively. Reliability was also good regardless of child age and for social phobia symptom scales (.81–.87) and parent and clinician ratings of impairment (.81 and .84, respectively). Poor reliability was found for social phobia child ratings of impairment (.10).

Are there any other times that being around people makes you   ☐ Yes ☐ No ☐ Other
nervous or scared?

If "Yes," **Could you tell me about that?** _____

_____

_____

✋ If the child responded "No" to any of Questions 1a–1c and reports
no fear or avoidance in any situation in Questions 2a–2c, skip to
Specific Phobia (p. 23).

To meet diagnostic criteria for Social Phobia, the child must
respond "Yes" to at least one question from Questions 1a–1c,
respond "Yes" to at least one situation listed in Question 2a, and
either avoid or endure social situations with intense anxiety or
distress. In addition, there must be evidence of significant interference in the child's normal routine as indicated by the response
in the Interference section.

Now I want to find out more details about some of those things that
bother you. When you tell me that (insert specifics of the child's fear,
e.g., "you don't like to start a conversation"):

3. **Does it make a difference if the people are friends or strangers?**   ☐ Yes ☐ No ☐ Other

   If "Yes," **Which is easier?**
   ☐ Friends ☐ Strangers

4. **Does it make a difference if the group is boys, girls, or boys and**   ☐ Yes ☐ No ☐ Other
   girls?

   If "Yes," **Which is easier?**
   ☐ Boys ☐ Girls ☐ Boys and Girls Together

5. **Does the age of the people matter?**   ☐ Yes ☐ No ☐ Other

   If "Yes," **Which is easier—older than you, younger than you, or the**
   same age as you?
   ☐ Older than you ☐ Younger than you ☐ Your age

6. **Does the size of the group make a difference?**   ☐ Yes ☐ No ☐ Other

   If "Yes," **Which is easier—big groups, small groups, or medium size**
   groups?
   ☐ Big ☐ Small ☐ Medium

FIGURE 4.1. (*Continued*)

Wood and colleagues (2002) also found good concurrent validity for
the ADIS for DSM-IV: C/P among youths with anxiety disorders. For example, the authors found that youths with social phobia, compared to
youths with other anxiety disorders, scored significantly higher on the social anxiety subscale of the Multidimensional Anxiety Scale for Children

7. **What do you think will happen when you are in** (give specifics of feared social situation)? _____

_____

_____

Interference

Okay, I want to know how much you feel this problem has messed things up in your life. That is, how much has it messed things up for you with friends, in school, or at home? How much does it stop you from doing things you would like to do? Tell me how much by using the Feelings Thermometer we discussed earlier, okay? If necessary, review the scale with the child. Show the child the Feelings Thermometer (found on the back cover of the Clinicial Manual) and obtain an overall rating of interference. Record the number corresponding to the child's anchor response, 0–8.

If clinical interference is indicated (a rating of 4 or greater), place a check mark in the diamond.

If all three diamonds are checked, consider Social Phobia (Social Anxiety Disorder) diagnosis and place a check mark in the star.

FIGURE 4.1. (*Continued*)

(MASC) (March, 1997). This was true for both child (MASC-C) and parent (MASC-P) reports of child social anxiety, and for younger and older children. Furthermore, good agreement between clinicians and a consensus team was found for social phobia diagnoses (Kappa = .94) and severity ratings (r = .75).

The ADIS for DSM-IV: C/P is currently the gold standard for assessing anxious youths, including those with social phobia, via structured interview. The measure is psychometrically strong and has been used widely in empirical studies of anxious children both as a means of assessing their characteristics and as an outcome measure. Concerns regarding the interview include sensitivity to developmental differences, tight linkage to DSM criteria, and varying reports across interviewees.

Regarding the latter, for example, DiBartolo and colleagues (1998) examined youths with social phobia using the ADIS-C and found that child and parent reports were similar for child social fear but *not* social avoidance. In particular, children reported less social avoidance on their part than parents. Child reports of less social avoidance may have been influenced by social desirability concerns, meaning that clinicians should take care when interpreting such reports and may wish to include a measure of social desirability during assessment (e.g., Revised Children's Manifest Anxiety Scale lie subscale) (see below) (DiBartolo, Albano, Barlow, & Heimberg, 1998). Research is needed, however, to assess whether such concerns apply to the revised version of the ADIS-C.

CHILD SELF-REPORT QUESTIONNAIRES

In addition to clinical interview, a common method for assessing child-hood social anxiety is a self-report questionnaire. This method is especially important given the subjective and internalized nature of social anxiety, and is now an essential component of empirical research in this area. Special attention is given in this section to the two scales that have been most commonly used and researched.

SOCIAL ANXIETY SCALE FOR CHILDREN

One of the first and most venerable child self-report measures of social anxiety is the *Social Anxiety Scale for Children* (SASC) and its subsequent revision, developed by La Greca and her colleagues (La Greca et al., 1988). Items for this scale were originally crafted by examining existing anxiety measures and rewording items that were relevant to peer relations and three hypothetical aspects of social anxiety: *fear of negative evaluation, social avoidance*, and *social distress*. Items were evaluated by experts and ten items were retained. Children responded to items on a 0–2 scale of never true (0), sometimes true (1), or always true (2). The scale was administered to second- to sixth-graders along with sociometric ratings and child self-reports of anxiety via the Revised Children's Manifest Anxiety Scale (RCMAS) (Reynolds & Richmond, 1985).

Factor analysis indicated the presence of two main factors: *fear of negative evaluation* (FNE; 6 items; 64.4% of variance) and *social avoidance and distress* (SAD; 4 items; 23.5% of variance). The first factor refers to worry or nervousness in peer-related social/evaluative situations. Results further indicated that total SASC scores had good internal consistency (r = .76) and test-retest reliability (r = .67), as did the two factor scores. In addition, total, FNE, and SAD scores were significantly related to total and subscale RCMAS scores (i.e., physiological anxiety, worry/oversensitivity, and social concerns/concentration). Children identified as neglected also showed significantly higher total SASC scores than popular or controversial children and were no different than rejected children. This was particularly so for FNE scores, and the authors concluded that this subscale may be psychometrically stronger than SAD.

La Greca and Stone (1993) revised the SASC by expanding the number of items to 26 (9 FNE, 13 SAD, 4 filler) and evaluating them as before. Fourth- to sixth-graders responded to the items on a 1–3 or 1–5 scale (not at all to all the time), the latter of which was found to have better psychometric strength (range of total scores thus 18–90). Three primary factors were identified: *fear of negative evaluation from peers* (FNE; 8 items; 68.9% of variance), *social avoidance and distress specific to new situations* (SAD-N; 6 items; 13.1% of variance), and *generalized social avoidance and distress* (SAD-G; 4 items; 7.8% of variance). Four items loaded improperly on these factors and were deleted, and four filler items loaded on separate factors as expected. Results further indicated that each revised (i.e., SASC-R) subscale had good internal consistency (r = .69–.86) and that neglected and rejected youths had significantly higher SASC-R scores than popular or average children. The authors concluded that the SASC-R is a more precise instrument than the SASC, especially with respect to social avoidance and inhibition. Other studies have shown similar results to support the psychometric strength of the SASC-R (Ginsburg et al., 1998; Peleg-Popko & Dar, 2001; Vernberg et al., 1992).

La Greca and Lopez (1998) modified the SASC-R for use with adolescents and examined the psychometric properties of the new *Social Anxiety Scale for Adolescents* (SAS-A). The SAS-A is largely similar to the SASC-R but items were reworded to reflect the greater sophistication of adolescents (e.g., use of the word "peers"). High school students completed the scale and other measures, and factor analytic results were identical to the SASC-R. The subscales also displayed good internal consistency (r = .76–.91).

Inderbitzen-Nolan and Walters (2000) replicated the 3-factor structure of the SAS-A. In addition, they found that SAS-A total and subscale scores correlated significantly with subscales of the Revised Children's Manifest Anxiety Scale and with negative mood, anhedonia, and negative self-esteem subscales of the Children's Depression Inventory (CDI) (Kovacs, 1992). Interestingly, no significant correlation was found between SAS-A and CDI interpersonal problems and ineffectiveness subscale scores. However, an important result of these studies was that social anxiety could now be measured reliably across youths of various developmental levels.

Myers and colleagues (2002) further examined the SAS-A in a large sample of high school students. The factorial model identified by La Greca and Lopez (1998) was not fully supported, as several items loaded on more than one factor or failed to load properly onto one factor. Instead, exploratory factor analysis revealed three new factors: fear of negative evaluation, novel social situation fears, and general social situation fears. Retaining only items that had a factor loading of .40+ whittled the items in each factor to 6, 4, and 3, respectively (i.e., a 13-item SAS-A short form). Concurrent validity of this short form was supported by significant correlations of the subscales with a measure of negative affectivity. Although the SAS-A structure was altered in this study, evidence still supported the scale's general utility for measuring social anxiety in adolescents.

La Greca (1998, 1999) summarized the major research conducted with respect to her social anxiety scales as well as various normative data and cutoff scores. In doing so, the recommendation was made to use subscale rather than total scores in clinical and research practice given the distinct differences among the subscales. The scales were also recommended for purposes of screening community samples, identifying youths with impaired social functioning and social anxiety disorder, measuring social distress, and serving as dependent measures in treatment outcome and longitudinal studies. Indeed, the SASC-R and SAS-A are now considered staples for assessing social anxiety in youths.

SOCIAL PHOBIA AND ANXIETY INVENTORY FOR CHILDREN

Another common and psychometrically strong child self-report measure of social anxiety is the *Social Phobia and Anxiety Inventory for Children* (SPAI-C), developed by Beidel and her colleagues (Beidel, Turner, & Morris, 1995). The SPAI-C was derived from an adult self-report measure for social phobia and agoraphobia: the 32-item *Social Phobia and Anxiety Inventory* (SPAI) (Turner, Beidel, Dancu, & Stanley, 1989). Items on this scale surround social anxiety-related thoughts and somatic concerns about situations involving strangers, authority figures, and people of the opposite gender and in general.

Clark and colleagues (1994) provided psychometric information regarding the SPAI for 12–18-year olds. Two expected scale factors, social phobia and agoraphobia, were found. In addition, the scale demonstrated excellent internal consistency (Cronbach's alpha = .91–.97), differentiated youths who did or did not meet DSM-III-R criterion A for social phobia (see Chapter 1), and correlated significantly with measures of fear, trait anxiety, willingness and ability for dating, and assertiveness (inversely with the latter two constructs). In addition, SPAI social phobia and total scores differentiated youths with social phobia from youths with other anxiety, other mental, or no other mental disorders. The authors concluded that the SPAI could be used as a valid measure of social anxiety in adolescents. Other researchers also found the SPAI to be a reliable and valid measure for assessing Spanish adolescents (Olivares, Garcia-Lopez, Hidalgo, Turner, & Beidel, 1999).

Beidel and her colleagues revamped the SPAI for use with younger children (aged 8–14 years) (SPAI-C) and to measure social *phobia* in youths as well as social anxiety. The scale measures social distress across various situations in general and those involving adults and familiar and unfamiliar peers. Items are scored on a 0–2 scale of never or hardly ever (0), sometimes (1), and most of the time or always (2). In the final version, 16 of 26 items require multiple responses, mean ratings are summed across various items, and the range of scores is 0–52.

Beidel, Turner, and Morris (1995) examined youths with social phobia, other anxiety disorders, and controls in the initial development of the SPAI-C. Items were derived from childrens' responses to interviews, daily diary information, and the adult-based SPAI. The number of items was trimmed to 26 by deleting those that failed to significantly differentiate anxious and nonanxious youths. The final version of the SPAI-C clearly differentiated socially anxious and non-socially anxious children. In addition, a suggested cutoff score (18), internal consistency (Cronbach's alpha = .95), and short-term ($r = .86$) and long-term ($r = .63$) test-retest reliabilities were established. With respect to concurrent validity, the SPAI-C was significantly related to (1) the trait ($r = .50$) but not the state subscales of the State-Trait Anxiety Inventory for Children (Spielberger, 1973), (2) factors of the Fear Survey Schedule for Children-Revised (Ollendick, 1983), including failure and criticism ($r = .53$), and (3) parent ratings of internalizing ($r = .45$) but not externalizing behavior on the Child Behavior Checklist (Achenbach & Edelbrock, 1983).

Factor analysis of the SPAI-C also revealed three main factors: *assertiveness/general conversation* (13 items; 48% of variance), *traditional social encounters* (9 items; 6% of variance), and *public performance* (7 items; 5% of variance). Some items loaded strongly on more than one factor. Each factor significantly differentiated children with and without social anxiety, and the authors noted that the factors may correspond, respectively, with generalized social phobia, social anxiety in limited encounters with others, and specific social phobia.

Beidel, Turner, and Fink (1996) further examined the convergent, discriminant, and construct validity of the SPAI-C via interview and daily diary information in children with or without social phobia. Regarding convergent validity, SPAI-C scores were somewhat related to number of distressing social events per day ($r = .50$) and ratings of distress regarding those events ($r = .41$). Regarding discriminant validity, SPAI-C scores differentiated youths with social phobia from those with no mental disorder as well as those with externalizing behavior problems. Regarding construct validity, factor analysis yielded five factors: *assertiveness* (7 items; 35.0% of variance), *general conversation* (6 items; 7.5% of variance), *physical and cognitive symptoms* (4 items; 5.8% of variance), *avoidance* (4 items; 5.3% of variance), and *public performance* (4 items; 4.7% of variance).

Beidel and colleagues further examined the discriminative and external validity of the SPAI-C (Beidel, Turner, Hamlin, & Morris, 2000). SPAI-C scores from anxious and nonanxious children were compared to parent reports of social anxiety in their children and independent observer ratings of social skill and anxiety in interaction role-play and performance-based reading tasks. Regarding discriminative validity, SPAI-C scores differentiated youths with social phobia from those with other anxiety disorders. Regarding external validity, SPAI-C scores were only somewhat related to parental ratings of social anxiety ($r = .31$) and independent observer ratings of role-play effectiveness or skill ($r = -.29$) and speech latency ($r = .37$). No substantial relationship was found between SPAI-C scores and role-play and reading anxiety or reading effectiveness. The SPAI-C, like the SASC-R, is now a widely used child self-report measure for youths with social anxiety and social phobia.

COMPARISONS OF THE SASC-R AND SPAI-C

Several researchers have compared the SASC-R and SPAI-C. For example, Morris and Masia (1998) examined elementary school children and presented normative data for total and subscale SASC-R and SPAI-C scores. Total scores correlated modestly (.63) and all subscale scores from both measures correlated significantly with one another (range, .34–.65). In addition, ranges of scores from one measure corresponded with ranges of scores for the other measure 63% of the time. The authors endorsed the concurrent validity of the scales but warned that they likely assess somewhat different constructs *and* that a substantial number of children exceed the recommended cutoff scores on each measure.

Extending these findings, Epkins (2002) examined SPAI-C and SASC-R scores and parent ratings of behavior in youths referred or not referred for outpatient therapy. The SPAI-C and two SASC-R subscales (FNE, SAD-New) differentiated the two groups but many non-referred children did exceed clinical cutoff scores on each measure (37% and 20%, respectively). In addition, higher SPAI-C and SASC-R scores were related to more parent-reported internalizing problems and lower social competence in children. Total SPAI-C and SASC-R scores significantly correlated in the non-referred and referred groups ($r = .75$ and .81, respectively) and ranges of scores from one measure generally (82–91%) corresponded with ranges of scores for the other measure. The authors concluded that the instruments appear to measure somewhat different constructs and that greater research attention is needed with respect to cutoff scores and normative data for subgroups.

Garcia-Lopez and colleagues (2001) also examined the SAS-A, SPAI, Fear of Negative Evaluation Scale, and Social Avoidance and Distress Scale (Watson & Friend, 1969) in a large sample of Spanish adolescents. An adult-based structured diagnostic interview (social phobia section) was also used (ADIS-IV-L) (DiNardo, Brown, & Barlow, 1994). Numbers of feared social situations derived from the interview correlated well with total and subscale scores of each dependent measure (range, .57–.78) and total and subscale scores from the dependent measures largely correlated significantly with one another.

Factor analysis of the measures yielded one social anxiety factor, and the measures were found to significantly differentiate adolescents with or without social phobia and adolescents with specific or generalized social phobia. In addition, test-retest reliability was good for all SAS-A and SPAI subscale scores (range, .75–.86). The authors concluded that the measures in general were psychometrically strong and that they appear to largely tap one general construct of social anxiety. Another, similar study conducted by the authors revealed two factors ("cognitive symptoms" and "behavioral and somatic symptoms") that were highly intercorrelated and that represented a "unidimensional structure" of social anxiety (Olivares, Garcia-Lopez, Hidalgo, & Caballo, 2004) (see also Garcia-Lopez, Olivares, & Vera-Villarroel, 2003).

Storch and colleagues (2004) similarly compared the SAS-A and SPAI-C in a large sample of adolescents. In addition to providing normative data, the authors found the SAS-A and SPAI-C to identify 18.1% and 19.9% of youths, respectively, as socially anxious. Factor analysis also supported La Greca and Lopez's (1998) 3-factor SAS-A model and Beidel and colleagues' (1996) 5-factor SPAI-C model. All subscales of each measure showed good internal consistency (Cronbach alpha range = .65–.93) and modest test-retest reliability over a one-year period. Scores significantly declined at time two administration. All subscales of each measure also correlated significantly with all other subscales, and total scores from each measure correlated at .76. In particular, the SAD-New and SAD-General subscales of the SAS-A correlated most strongly with the SPAI-C Avoidance subscale. The authors concluded that the two instruments do appear to be measuring somewhat different aspects of social anxiety.

Inderbitzen-Nolan, Davies, and McKeon (2004) also compared the SAS-A and SPAI-C in a large sample of adolescents. The ADIS for DSM-IV: C/P was also used to identify youths with diagnoses of social phobia ($n = 78$), and youths were classified with high or low social anxiety based on SAS-A and SPAI-C cutoff scores. Interestingly, like earlier findings, SAS-A and SPAI-C total scores correlated at .79. Furthermore, social anxiety classification (high and low) by one measure was largely confirmed by the other measure (high: 63–77%; low: 84–91%). Using interview information, sensitivity to diagnoses of social phobia was only 43.6% for the SAS-A, but 61.5% for the SPAI-C. Using both measures' cutoff scores reduced sensitivity to 39.7%, but using one cutoff score from either measure increased sensitivity to 65.4%. The scales were much more sensitive to *no* diagnosis of social phobia (82.7% for each). The authors concluded that the SPAI-C is perhaps a better instrument for identifying youths with clinically significant symptoms of social phobia. However, many youths (38.5%) with social phobia did not exceed the SPAI-C cutoff score, meaning that a combination of interview and child self-report measures is likely a good option when assessing this population.

Overall, adolescent measures of youth social anxiety seem to overlap more so than child measures. Regarding the latter, some contend that the SPAI-C is somewhat more salient when assessing *clinical* populations and may be more sensitive to specific aspects of social anxiety such as assertiveness, avoidance, and concerns about conversations and public performance. However, the SASC-R does contain many items for cognitive symptomatology, so a good strategy might be to use both measures for a particular child.

Other Child Self-Report Questionnaires

Other anxiety self-report questionnaires also contain *subscales* or *subsections* that are relevant to social anxiety and social phobia in youths. Common examples include the:

- *Multidimensional Anxiety Scale for Children*, a measure of childhood anxiety with subscales for harm avoidance and physical, separation, and social anxiety (i.e., humiliation and performance fears) (March, 1997; March, Sullivan, & Parker, 1999)
- *Screen for Child Anxiety-Related Disorders*, a measure of childhood anxiety with five main factors: somatic/panic, general anxiety, separation anxiety, school phobia, and social phobia (Birmaher et al., 1997, 1999). A revision of this scale has also been reported (Muris, Merckelbach, Schmidt, & Mayer, 1999)
- *Spence Children's Anxiety Scale*, a measure of childhood anxiety with subscales for social phobia, separation anxiety, panic attacks/agoraphobia, obsessive-compulsive disorder, generalized anxiety, and fears of physical injury (Spence, Barrett, & Turner, 2003)
- *Fear Survey Schedule for Children-Revised*, a measure of general fearfulness with a factor related to fear of failure and criticism (Ollendick, 1983)
- *School Refusal Assessment Scale-Revised*, a measure of the relative strength of different functions of school refusal behavior with a subscale for escaping aversive social and/or evaluative situations at school (Kearney, 2002)

Other anxiety self-report questionnaires also contain *items* that are relevant to social anxiety and social phobia in youths. Common examples include the:

- *Childhood Anxiety Sensitivity Index*, a measure of fear of dangerousness of internal physical symptoms with items surrounding worry about others' knowledge of these symptoms (Silverman, Ginsburg, & Goedhart, 1999)
- *Revised Children's Manifest Anxiety Scale* and *State-Trait Anxiety Inventory for Children*, measures of general anxiety and negative affectivity with items relevant to worries about making mistakes and others' perceptions and reactions (Reynolds & Richmond, 1985; Spielberger, 1973)
- *Daily Life Stressors Scale* and other hassles scales, measures of difficulties that youths encounter daily with items surrounding conversations with, and performances before, others (Kearney, Drabman, & Beasley, 1993)
- *Test Anxiety Scale for Children*, a measure of test anxiety with items surrounding worry about performance in this area (Sarason, Davidson, Lighthall, Waite, & Ruebush, 1960)
- *Youth Self-Report*, a measure of internalizing and externalizing behavior problems with items relevant to social anxiety and withdrawal (Achenbach & Rescorla, 2001).

Other measures pertinent to the assessment of childhood social phobia have also been reported, but require more empirical attention. Examples include the *Dating Anxiety Scale for Adolescents* (Glickman & La Greca, 2004), *Liebowitz Social Anxiety Scale for Children and Adolescents* (Masia, Klein, Storch, & Corda, 2001), *Social Fears Belief Questionnaire* (Field et al., 2003), *Social Worries Questionnaire* (and its parent version) (Spence et al., 1999), and *Worry Scale* (Perrin & Last, 1997).

PARENT AND TEACHER QUESTIONNAIRES

Parent-based interviews are commonly used to assess social anxiety and social phobia in youths, but parent and teacher questionnaires regarding these constructs have not received as much empirical attention. Exceptions include parent versions of the *Social Anxiety Scale for Children-Revised* and *Social Anxiety Scale for Adolescents* (SAS-A) (La Greca, 1998). These versions are nearly identical except that "My child" in the parent versions replaces the "I" in the child versions. Data regarding the SAS-A were reported by La Greca (1998), who stated that the parent version had a very similar factor structure to the adolescent version as well as good internal consistency. In addition, parent and adolescent SAS-A scores correlated modestly but more so for girls, two-parent households, adolescents with higher levels of social anxiety, and items about observable events. The author encouraged users of the SAS-A parent version to exercise caution, especially regarding boys, and that adolescents are likely the best source for assessing their social anxiety. Other measures containing subscales for social anxiety have also been modified for parent-based ratings (e.g., Birmaher et al., 1999).

General parent and teacher measures of child behavior also include subscales related to social anxiety and social phobia. These most commonly include the *Child Behavior Checklist* and *Teacher's Report Form* (Achenbach & Rescorla, 2001) *Conners Rating Scales* (Parent and Teacher Versions-Revised) (Conners, 1997), and *Child Symptom Inventory-4* (Sprafkin, Gadow, Salisbury, Schneider, & Loney, 2002). In general, however, teachers may not be accurate reporters of youth social anxiety given the subjective and often covert nature of the problem. Indeed, peer ratings are often better predictors of a child's social anxiety than teacher ratings, although teachers are good at identifying youths with test anxiety (La Greca, 2001).

FAMILY ASSESSMENT MEASURES

Investigations of family dynamics with respect to childhood anxiety disorders are burgeoning (see Chapters 2 and 3). As such, assessment technology in this area is also burgeoning, and consists primarily of questionnaires and behavioral observation. Questionnaires typically focus on key family dynamics such as cohesion, flexibility, conflict, control, independence, expressiveness, and affective involvement. Common examples include the *Family Environment Scale, Family Adaptability and Cohesion Evaluation Scale*, and *Family Assessment Measure* (Moos & Moos, 1986; Olson, Portner, & Lavee, 1987; Skinner, Steinhauer, & Santa-Barbara, 1995, respectively). Measures of parental expectancies and practices regarding a child's social performance, such as the *Parental Expectancies Scale* and *Alabama Parenting Questionnaire*, are also relevant to socially anxious children (Eisen, Spasaro, Brien, Kearney, & Albano, 2004; Shelton, Frick, & Wootten, 1996, respectively).

A more intensive and specific form of family assessment regarding anxious children, including those with social phobia, was conducted by Barrett and colleagues (1996). The authors presented 12 ambiguous scenarios that could be construed as physically or socially threatening or nonthreatening (e.g., having a strange feeling in stomach, seeing other children laugh upon approach to them). Children and parents answered questions about what they believed was happening in each situation, their explanations for each situation (chosen from two threat-based and two neutral choices), and what the child would do in the situations. Videotaped responses were later coded along avoidant, aggressive, and proactive categories. After answering the questions, families engaged in 5-minute discussions regarding one physical and one social threat scenario. Following parental help, children were instructed to give a final answer about what they would do in the given situation. Results indicated that parents enhanced avoidant responses in anxious children. Woodruff-Borden and colleagues (2002) similarly videotaped parents and their anxious children, some with social phobia, during speech preparation and problem-solving tasks. Parental behaviors were coded as engaging, withdrawn, overcontrolling, and negative. Compared to controls during the tasks, parents of anxious children were more withdrawn and less productively engaged.

Although these *formal* observations were nicely designed and conducted, their practicality for many clinical settings may be limited. Still, results of these and related studies do indicate the importance of evaluating family processes among anxious children, including those with social phobia. Questionnaire information is likely helpful in this regard, though some *general* in-session observation of family dynamics can be quite instructive as well. Suggestions for doing so are presented in Chapter 5.

BEHAVIORAL ASSESSMENT TESTS

Another common form of evaluating children with social phobia is a *behavioral assessment test*, or BAT, which usually involves having a child role play a given situation or perform in some way before others. As the child does so, various measures can be employed, such as ratings of distress (e.g., 0–100 Subjective Units of Distress Scale), independent observer ratings of child behavior, and even psychophysiological recordings. Among adults with social phobia, common BATs include conversations with others, writing or solving problems before others, and public speaking, the latter of which may have the best external validity (Hofmann, 2000; McNeil, Ries, & Turk, 1995). These scenarios may apply to youths as well.

Among children with social phobia, common BATs in research settings involve taking tests (e.g., subsections of a standardized achievement test) (Beidel, 1991), reading a story aloud, and engaging in social interactions. Beidel and colleagues (1999), for example, asked children to read aloud the story of Jack and the Beanstalk for 10 minutes before a small audience. In addition, children interacted with a trained, same-age/gender peer in different role play scenarios. These scenarios included having a conversation, giving and receiving a compliment, asking someone to change a negative behavior, and receiving an offer of help. The scenarios were then videotaped and rated for skill and perceived anxiety by independent but blind observers. In addition, child ratings of distress were obtained and speech latency was measured. In this study, interrater reliability regarding the BAT variables was very good ($r = .80-.94$).

Behavioral assessment tests for this population are often standardized in research settings, but should probably be tailored more to a client's particular concerns in clinical settings. Among my cases of youths with social phobia, common observations involve those mentioned above in addition to approaching others for help (e.g., asking for the time, directions, or additional information), ordering food, interacting with others in a naturalistic setting (e.g., church, school, birthday party), and using appropriate social mannerisms for a given situation. Particular attention is also paid to a child's skill and effectiveness in these situations. The observations may be conducted in-session but in community-based settings as well. Before, during, and after the observations, the child usually rates his or her anxiety and/or desire to escape the situation. In addition, the therapist may rate the child's level of skill, effectiveness, anxiety, or other relevant behaviors. In urgent cases, these observations may be linked quickly to exposure-based treatment practices (see Chapter 9).

SELF-MONITORING PROCEDURES

Behavioral assessment of youths with social phobia may also be done via *self-monitoring*, or child-based daily logs of anxiety-related behaviors. Self-monitoring may be particularly useful for measuring subjective anxiety states that are best reported by a child, but may also be used to gather information about anxiety-provoking events, degree and strategies of avoidance and escape, efforts to cope with a given situation, and anxiety-based thoughts, emotions, and physical symptoms. In many cases, separate but parallel parent or teacher monitoring forms may be given as well. However, compliance regarding this form of assessment is often problematic among youths and the psychometric strength of self-monitoring remains in need of further study.

The utility and validity of self-monitoring for anxious children has been supported on a preliminary basis (Beidel, Neal, & Lederer, 1991). In this particular study, children were asked to complete a daily diary for 14 days regarding type of anxious situations, time and setting of the situations, the child's response to the situations, and endorsement of an illustration that represented how the child felt in the situations. Incentives were offered for compliance, but only 31–39% of the youths completed the measure for all 14 days. Among children with social phobia, Beidel and colleagues (1999) used daily diary ratings over a 14-day period to assess avoidance, physical symptoms, and coping skills. Despite the use of incentives, children engaged in self-monitoring for an average of only 12.1 days.

In clinical settings, self-monitoring should be tailored to the concerns of a particular client, tied to detailed instructions about their completion, linked to incentives and consequences for compliance and noncompliance, and supervised by significant others. In addition, compliance to self-monitoring forms may be enhanced by regular contact with a child (e.g., between-session calls) and simplification (e.g., checklist, single rating). Obstacles to compliance should be addressed as well, and the importance of the measure for treatment purposes should be made repeatedly clear. If a child continues to fail to comply with self-monitoring, then other methods may be emphasized.

COGNITIVE ASSESSMENT MEASURES

As mentioned in Chapters 2 and 3, anxious children may have biased thought processes and self-focused attention that contribute to, and/or help maintain, their high levels of general and social anxiety. Assessing relevant types of cognitions may be done in various ways, including self-report questionnaires, thought listing and think-aloud procedures, and stories. Laboratory-based measures such as Stroop color-naming and probe detection tasks have also been used to assess biased attention in youths with anxiety disorders (Martin, Horder, & Jones, 1992; Vasey et al., 1995). These often computer-based measures focus on response latency to emotionally threatening words, which is sometimes longer for anxious children than controls. These measures are not generally applicable to clinical settings, however, and have methodological and theoretical limitations (Vasey, Dalgleish, & Silverman, 2003). Therefore, they are not emphasized here.

Common examples of questionnaires to measure self-statements in anxious children include the *Cognition Checklist* (for children), *Cognitive Triad Inventory for Children, Automatic Thoughts Questionnaire, Thought Checklist for Children, Children's Negative Cognitive Error Questionnaire, Negative Affect Self-Statement Questionnaire,* and *Children's Cognitive Assessment Questionnaire* (CCAQ) (Ambrose & Rholes, 1993; Kaslow, Stark, Printz, Livingston, & Tsai, 1992; Kazdin, 1990; Laurent & Stark, 1993; Leitenberg, Yost, & Carroll-Wilson, 1986; Ronan, Kendall, & Rowe, 1994; Zatz & Chassin, 1983, respectively). However, no specific self-statement-based questionnaires have been designed for youths with social anxiety or social phobia. In addition, such questionnaires are problematic anyway given children's sometimes limited cognitive development, and even adult measures in this area have been criticized with respect to clinical utility (Woody, Chambless, & Glass, 1997).

As an alternative, *thought listing* requires a child keep a written log of thoughts before, during, and after various social and/or evaluative situations (Kendall & Chansky, 1991). The child may be asked to log thoughts in such situations as they are encountered on a daily basis or do so in a clinical setting during a behavioral assessment test. Spence and colleagues (1999), for example, assigned social-evaluative tasks to children with or without social phobia and videotaped their behaviors. Following the tasks, videotapes were reviewed with each child, who then gave ratings of their performance and recalled their cognitions during different segments. Cognitions were then coded into categories and interrater reliability was excellent (kappa = .88). *Think-aloud procedures* are similar to thought listing but require a child to *verbalize* thoughts and feelings before, during, and after a behavioral assessment test (Houston, Fox, & Forbes, 1984). Cognitions derived from these procedures may then be coded along different categories of content and valence (e.g., negative, positive, neutral) (Chansky & Kendall, 1997).

Although thought listing and think-aloud procedures are potentially useful, compliance is often problematic because of high anxiety or forgetfulness, the procedures are subject to reactivity, administration and scoring vary widely across settings, and the obtained information is sometimes limited and not clinically useful (Eisen & Kearney, 1995). For example, many children give incomplete, solitary, or only positive or only negative responses (Kendall & Chansky, 1991). Furthermore, in a comparison of questionnaire (CCAQ) and thought listing procedures among children with test anxiety, Prins and Hanewald (1997) found that the latter produced fewer positive and coping cognitions and predicted task performance less well. However, thought listing and think-aloud procedures would seem useful for assessing certain cases, particularly those involving older youths, youths whose social anxiety is clearly associated with cognitive biases, and youths for whom cognitive therapy will be used in treatment.

Another cognitive assessment method is to read very short *stories* or scenarios to children and obtain questionnaire information or ratings of threat and emotion (Field et al., 2003). Muris, Merckelbach, and Dansma (2000), for example, read seven, 5-sentence stories to children and periodically assessed their ratings of threat perception and their emotions. Childrens' thoughts were also obtained about whether they believed the stories would be threatening or nontheatening. Raters of the childrens' answers largely agreed (Kappa = .85). Bogels and Zigterman (2000) also read nine stories to children surrounding separation, social, and generalized anxiety situations. Following each story, children were asked open- and closed-ended questions about threat, emotions, and coping strategies. Cognitions were coded as positive, negative, and neutral. Interrater reliability was generally good regarding cognition valence (kappa = .78) and categorization of negative cognitions (kappa = .63). Although the importance of cognitive content in anxious children remains controversial, the use of cognitive assessment measures is likely key to certain cases of social phobia that are clearly maintained by cognitive biases and distortions.

PHYSIOLOGICAL ASSESSMENT MEASURES

Physiological assessment of anxious children most commonly includes measures of heart rate and blood pressure, skin conductance and resistance, perspiration, adrenergic activity, and muscle tension (King, 1994). Cardiac measures have been most frequently used for youths with social phobia (Beidel, 1989). Several limitations are associated with physiological assessment of anxiety in children, however. These include unstable responses, lack of psychometric and normative data, poor clinical relevance, expense, and demands for technical sophistication and training (Schniering, Hudson, & Rapee, 2000). In addition, very little data are available with respect to the physiological status of youths with social anxiety and social phobia, and assessment in this area remains in its infancy. However, future research into how children with social phobia react in various situations may be instructive with respect to choice and priority of treatment options (e.g., somatic management exercises).

FUNCTIONAL ASSESSMENT

The measures described so far concentrate heavily on the *form* of behavior, or symptomatology. Of equal concern, however, is the *function* of behavior, or why socially anxious behaviors such as avoidance are maintained over time. In many cases, of course, social avoidance is maintained by *negative reinforcement,* or relief from anxiety as a child withdraws from a given situation. In some cases, however, social avoidance can also be maintained by factors such as *attention* and *tangible reinforcement.* For example, an anxious child may leave a birthday party early and receive extensive comfort from his parents, who have now inadvertently but positively rewarded the escape behavior. During treatment for this child, a therapist may have to address escape that is motivated as much by attention or tangible rewards as by negative reinforcement. Functional assessment of

anxiety-related behaviors has been developed for youths with school refusal behavior (Kearney, 2001), but has yet to be fully extended to youths
with social phobia. Suggestions regarding the latter are presented in Chapter 5.

OTHER ASSESSMENT METHODS

Although not commonly used, other methods may also be relevant for
assessing children with social anxiety. *Formal testing*, for example, including achievement or intellectual or personality instruments, can be used to
assess a child's academic standing, cognitive developmental status, temperament, or other variables that could influence treatment. In addition,
projective testing may be useful for youths with difficulty expressing specific
anxiety-related thoughts or emotions or for youths who require extensive
rapport-building. Finally, *sociometric measures* in the form of peer-based
questions (e.g., who do you most/least like to play with?) can be useful
for identifying a child's social status and degree of social isolation.

FINAL COMMENTS

The development of assessment methods for anxious children in general and youths with social anxiety and social phobia in particular has
proceeded with increased pace in recent years. As such, clinicians have a
wider array of tools to discover the exact nature of a child's form and function of behavior. In related fashion, the development of this wide array
of measures now allows clinicians to adopt a multisource, multimethod
assessment approach for this population. In addition, greater sensitivity to
developmental differences may now be incorporated into an assessment
approach. These themes are expanded in the next chapter, which covers
recommendations for assessment in general clinical settings.

CHAPTER 5

CLINICAL ASSESSMENT OF SOCIAL ANXIETY AND SOCIAL PHOBIA IN YOUTHS

The previous chapter covered the major research-based assessment techniques that have been used to evaluate youths with social anxiety and social phobia. In this chapter, general clinical assessment procedures for this population are discussed. The chapter is organized according to screening, formal evaluation, and consultation phases, and includes recommendations pertinent to each phase as well as important pre-treatment considerations. Ideas and a sample case are also presented for synthesizing assessment material to help determine treatment direction and techniques.

SCREENING

When initially screening a referral for potential social phobia, certain sets of questions may be considered to see whether a true problem exists and to help structure a possible formal evaluation. For example, *demographic information*, in particular the child's age, should be requested. Knowledge of age will help determine (1) whether the child's behavior problem is developmentally appropriate (e.g., a young preschooler versus an adolescent), (2) the child's general cognitive status and potential fit for cognitive therapy (e.g., limited versus advanced), and (3) function of the child's social anxiety. Regarding the latter, for example, many younger children display anxious behavior for negative reinforcement and attention, whereas many older children and adolescents display anxious behavior for negative reinforcement and tangible rewards (e.g., being allowed to stay home and watch television). Information about gender may also be somewhat instructive, as girls tend to have more social anxiety than boys (see Chapter 2).

A second set of screening questions should obviously surround the *nature and form* of the anxiety-based behavior problem. In particular, brief questions may be asked about the problem's history, symptoms and associated problems, severity, and functional impairment. Knowing the history and duration of the problem may provide an early glimpse into how comprehensive treatment will need to be. For example, if the problem is very new, such as at the beginning of the school year, then treatment may not yet be necessary or may be brief as many initial social worries fade with habituation to new surroundings and peers. However, if the problem has persisted or lasted many weeks or longer, then more rigorous treatment is much more likely to be needed.

Knowing the breadth and severity of symptoms and associated problems may provide further information about the scope and urgency of treatment, particularly if a child's social anxiety is associated with severe depression, suicidal behavior, drug use, or school refusal behavior. Symptom-related questions may surround the physiological, cognitive, and behavioral response sets of social anxiety. In addition, asking these questions may help a clinician derive an early picture of whether social anxiety is the primary problem or one that is symptomatic of something larger such as depression or another disorder. For example, a child's anxiety about performing academically before others may be closely related to his or her learning disorder, such that alleviation of the learning disorder might naturally decrease the child's performance anxiety. Knowing whether social anxiety is the primary or a secondary problem will help a clinician better tailor his or her main assessment choices (e.g., measures of depression, achievement, drug use) during formal evaluation.

In related fashion, information should be obtained about what areas of the child's functioning are currently impaired. In many cases of childhood social phobia, school refusal behavior is a prominent issue that should be investigated at length. However, severe avoidance of different social and/or evaluative situations should certainly be probed as well. In essence, questions should be raised as to whether a child's social anxiety significantly interferes with his or her, or the family's, daily life functioning. Treatment is more warranted in cases where social or performance anxiety has led to extensive absenteeism or avoidance of key situations. However, therapy may be necessary as well for children who *do* attend social events or perform before others, but who do so with great dread and reduced quality of life.

In some screenings for social anxiety symptomatology, parents will focus more on a child's externalizing and disruptive behavior problems (e.g., noncompliance about school attendance, tests, and recitals) than on equally relevant internalizing behaviors. Clinicians should take care to cover *all* relevant behaviors and, if possible, contact others (e.g., teachers) who may have additional information. Furthermore, parents often seek treatment for their child's social anxiety following some crisis or otherwise difficult event, and may frantically portray the problem in the worst possible light. Clinicians in this situation may wish to model a calm approach, adopt a methodical questioning process, and convey that excessive social anxiety is a common difficulty that many children face and overcome.

A third important set of screening questions surrounds any *medical or familial variables* that may be affecting a child's social anxiety. For example, many youths with social anxiety have somatic complaints, and social anxiety with school refusal behavior is often associated with headaches, stomachaches, asthma, and gastrointestinal problems (see Chapter 2). In such cases, referral to a physician for medical assessment is recommended prior to formal evaluation. Neuropsychological testing may also be appropriate in some cases. In essence, clinicians should know whether a true organic basis exists for somatic complaints or whether significant attention-seeking and exaggeration may be occurring. In other cases, consultations with psychiatrists will be necessary to address possible pharmacotherapy and/or comorbid conditions such as severe depression or other anxiety disorders. Knowledge about recent family stressors and transitions (e.g., move to a new location) may also be instructive, as a child's social anxiety may spike during these times.

Formally evaluating a child's social anxiety is generally more warranted if the problem is developmentally inappropriate *and* has lasted at least several weeks, proliferated to many symptoms and associated problems, reached at least a moderate level of severity, or caused significant interference in a child's and/or family's daily life functioning. Scheduling the first session for formal evaluation will be more urgent for cases of social anxiety that also include pervasive avoidance, destructive behavior, or school absenteeism. In addition, formal evaluation of this population should focus on multiple methods, informants, and domains (March & Albano, 2002). Suggestions regarding the formal evaluation process for general clinical settings are discussed next.

FORMAL EVALUATION

Formally evaluating a youth with social anxiety/phobia would ideally include as many of the procedures discussed in Chapter 4 as possible.

Outside of research-based environments, however, this is often difficult to do. As such, suggestions are made here for tailoring research-based assessment procedures to general clinical settings. Of course, variations must be made depending on the dynamics and characteristics of a particular case.

INTERVIEW

A preferred method for assessing youths with social anxiety and social phobia is a structured interview with good psychometric strength, such as the Anxiety Disorders Interview Schedule for Children: DSM-IV: Child and Parent Versions (ADIS-C: DSM-IV: C/P) (Silverman & Albano, 1996) (see Chapter 4). Although highly comprehensive and useful, the ADIS-C: DSM-IV: C/P can take several hours to administer for complex cases. Even for less complex cases, administering just one interview version (child or parent) will usually take longer than a typical clinical session (March & Albano, 2002).

If time is limited and a particular case clearly involves social or performance anxiety, then a clinician may opt to administer only the ADIS-C: DSM-IV: C/P social phobia and other relevant sections. The social phobia sections have good reliability, though authors of psychometric studies of the ADIS-C: DSM-IV: C/P generally administered the entire measure. Still, using particular sections can provide important and quick information about child and parent perspectives of the problem, symptoms, ratings of fear, types of avoided situations, mediating factors, and degree of interference.

Although a structured interview is preferred, a general interview can still cover topics most pertinent to a case of childhood social phobia. In doing so, particular attention should be paid to developmental variables (Albano & Hayward, 2004; Morris, Hirshfeld-Becker, Henin, & Storch, 2004). Important interview topics thus include the following:

- relevant demographic characteristics and contact information
- symptomatology, including physiological, cognitive, and behavioral aspects of social and performance anxiety; this includes information for assigning a diagnosis of social phobia and ruling in or out closely associated problems such as generalized anxiety disorder and depression
- current effects of symptomatology on the child's and family's daily life functioning
- child's current life stressors and his or her ability and techniques for coping with these stressors in particular and with social and performance anxiety in general

- child's current status in various areas, including academic, social, intellectual, and mental functioning; this includes the child's level of performance and satisfaction in each area as well as detail about the child's interpersonal relationships, friendships, and social skills
- etiological factors such as family dynamics and applicable cognitive, social, traumatic, temperamental, and biological variables
- maintaining factors (e.g., negative reinforcement, attention-seeking, pursuit of tangible rewards) and antecedents and consequences pertinent to episodes of intense social and performance anxiety
- potential crisis issues such as extensive depression, destructive behavior, and school absenteeism
- history regarding the child's and/or family member's psychiatric/mental health diagnoses/treatment, development and delay of key milestones, transitions, academic performance, personality/temperament, and medical conditions
- child's current health status and medication usage
- family member perspectives of the child's social and performance anxiety
- family contextual issues such as marital status, finances, social support, and living situation, among others
- other contextual issues such as maltreatment, school violence/bullying, divorce, homelessness, unemployment, and distance from social events, among others
- relevant cultural variables, including differences in language, norms, problem-solving methods, and perspectives on social and performance anxiety
- reasons for seeking treatment at this time, informant variance, anticipated resistance or obstacles to treatment, and other important sources of information (e.g., peers, siblings, teachers, dating partners, grandparents and other relatives)
- relevant information for treatment, including practical issues (e.g., frequency of sessions) and family motivation, optimism, and expectations regarding treatment

CHILD SELF-REPORT QUESTIONNAIRES

As with interviews, information regarding child self-report measures has burgeoned tremendously in recent years (see Chapter 4). Given that many child anxiety researchers believe that youths are the best descriptors of their internal anxiety states, using self-report questionnaires for youths with social phobia seems indispensable. These measures are inexpensive and can be given quickly and without extensive technical expertise. The self-report measures most pertinent to social anxiety/phobia and most empirically supported are the *Social Anxiety Scale for Children-Revised*, *Social Anxiety Scale for Adolescents*, and the *Social Phobia and Anxiety Inventory for Children* (SPAI-C). The use of at least one of these measures is strongly suggested during screening or formal evaluation, though each contains unique characteristics that may fit better with a particular case (see Chapter 4).

Other child self-report measures may also pertain to children with social anxiety or phobia, particularly those children with concurrent fear, depression, general anxiety, worry, or even externalizing behavior problems (see Chapter 4). Furthermore, cognitive assessment via questionnaires can be done to identify relevant self-statements, biases, self-consciousness, and self-focused attention that may be relevant to treatment.

PARENT AND TEACHER QUESTIONNAIRES

Parent-based questionnaires regarding a child's social and performance anxiety remain largely under development (see Chapter 4). However, using parent versions of the main child self-report measures for this population may be instructive and will, at a minimum, reveal any informant variance that may be important. Using measures to explore more general childhood behavior problems, such as the *Child Behavior Checklist* and *Teacher's Report Form* (Achenbach & Rescorla, 2001), are highly recommended as well. In addition, parent-based questionnaires that explore family functioning, such as the *Family Environment Scale* (Moos & Moos, 1986), are easy to administer and can provide important information about contributing family dynamics.

BEHAVIORAL OBSERVATIONS

Methods of observing youths with social and performance anxiety have been nicely designed in the literature, and include various role-play and problem-solving tasks as well as scenario and story presentations (see Chapter 4). Observed child behaviors are then usually coded along predetermined categories. Although useful, these procedures are not always amenable to general clinical settings because of their time requirements and complexity. Still, certain behaviors can be closely observed in-session to identify baseline patterns of responding as well as possible treatment targets.

Behavioral observations of youths with social and performance anxiety can pragmatically consist of simple in-session role play and annotations about parent-child interactions and avoidance. Feasible in-session role plays, for example, include reading aloud or giving oral presentations before a small audience, test-taking (e.g., from sample tests sent from a teacher), initiating and maintaining conversations with others, greeting and requesting help from others, and excusing oneself from a room. Of course, other social- and performance-based tasks may also apply to a particular case.

Brief naturalistic observations in community-based settings can also involve these tasks as well as others such as ordering food in a restaurant, interacting with peers at a large social gathering, and responding to spontaneous attention from others. In addition, a child may be asked to attend certain settings (e.g., classroom, cafeteria) when no one else is there. This helps confirm that the presence of others is indeed the main variable causing his or her avoidance (e.g., as opposed to noncompliance or specific phobia). Although formal coding of behavioral categories from all of these observations may not be feasible, obtaining regular anxiety ratings from a child before, during, and after each observation is highly recommended. In addition, thought-listing or think aloud procedures may be employed to assess a child's thoughts during the observations (see Chapter 4).

In-session parent-child interactions and child avoidance can also be observed. In particular, therapists should watch for instances of conflict, overprotectiveness, parental reinforcement of anxious or attention-seeking behavior, and other inappropriate parental responses (e.g., offering excessive tangible rewards for compliance). A common scenario, for example, is for a socially anxious child to refuse to speak with the therapist to try to force parental acquiescence (e.g., to leave the office) or some incentive for participation. Parental responses to child reluctance are quite instructive, and range the gamut from appropriate encouragement to hostility or vigorous defense of the child.

Other means of child avoidance should be monitored closely as well, including lack of eye contact, adherence to simple (e.g., yes/no) answers, pleas to end the interview prematurely, crying, defensiveness, and forms of resistance. Discrepancies between the child's verbal statements and his or her actions can be instructive as well, especially in cases where the child denies any social or performance anxiety. Observations of the child's general appearance, level of social skill, odd motor mannerisms, fidgeting or other overt signs of nervousness, posture, and physical proximity to parents may also be informative. If a child's social and performance anxiety is linked to school refusal behavior, then observations relevant to different functions are advised (see Kearney & Albano, 2000).

DAILY ASSESSMENT METHODS

Excellent ways of assessing anxiety and related variables that are highly amenable to most clinical settings are child and parent diaries or logbooks. Although compliance can be problematic (see Chapter 4), recordings from daily logbooks often improve an understanding of a child's episodes of social and performance anxiety, child and parent motivation in treatment, and informant variance among family members. A logbook could allow a child and parents to list episodes of the child's social and performance anxiety, antecedents and consequences to these episodes, coping strategies and cognitions pertinent to these episodes, anxiety and depression ratings (e.g., 0–10), and other behaviors or situations deemed important for treatment (e.g., child compliance to commands, progress on therapeutic homework assignments). Of course, simplified or more tailored logbooks can be administered as well depending on a child's cognitive status and particular needs.

In many cases, logbook compliance will have to be monitored regularly, and any problems addressed immediately. Educating family members about the importance of the logbooks, providing a rationale for their use, and training members to complete them are highly recommended. In cases where logbooks are not feasible, or where compliance remains highly problematic, then retrospective ratings and behavior descriptions for the past 2–3 days can be solicited during each treatment session or via telephone.

CONTACTING SCHOOL OFFICIALS

When assessing youths with social anxiety and social phobia, contact with various school officials is strongly suggested. School officials such as general and special education teachers, specialized (e.g., physical education) teachers, guidance counselors, deans and principals, school psychologists, nurses, librarians, and even bus drivers and other staff members are often rich sources of information about a child's avoidance, symptomatology, social status, and academic functioning. In addition, school records and other documentation, including daily report cards and weekly progress reports of behavior, can be quite valuable.

If a child with social phobia has even modest in-school avoidance and/or school refusal behavior, then information from school officials and records should be obtained about several pertinent variables. From school officials, important information may concern the child's social and performance and classroom behaviors/skills, peer status, others' attitudes toward the child, and previous school-based attempts to remediate the child's behavior (e.g., incentives, punishments). From school officials or records and documentation, important information may also concern attendance, school policy regarding absenteeism, course schedules, layout of the school, alternative school programs, missed assignments and tests, required make-up work, performance expectations and assigned homework/external projects, past behavior problems, standardized test scores, and rating scale information.

The willingness of school officials to participate in various school-based adjustments and treatment plans (e.g., 504 plan, class schedule changes, gradual re-exposure to social/performance situations and classes) should be gauged and developed as well. Ongoing conflict between parents and school officials, or potential school-based obstacles to treatment, should also be explored and addressed as necessary. In many cases of childhood social phobia, a close working relationship between the therapist, parents, and school officials is crucial for successful treatment. As therapy progresses, consultation with school officials should continue in order to sustain rapport, eliminate new obstacles to treatment, obtain feedback about the effectiveness of the treatment plan, and ensure that parents are notified quickly of any problems. A rapprochement of parents and school officials should also be pursued as necessary to help prevent future relapse.

SYNTHESIZING ASSESSMENT INFORMATION

In cases of childhood social anxiety/phobia, clinicians should solicit information from various methods and informants about as many child and family behaviors as possible. In doing so, care should be taken with respect to issues of social desirability, informant variance, gender, and important developmental factors (see previous chapters) (Sweeney & Rapee, 2001). Synthesizing assessment information can be challenging, but a good strategy is to begin with interview and questionnaire information to develop initial hypotheses about the scope and nature of a child's presenting problems. Some of the most crucial hypotheses or questions that the clinician should bear in mind during this process include the following:

- Is the child's social phobia specific to certain situations or stimuli or more generalized in nature?
- What response sets, physiological, cognitive, and/or behavioral, are most problematic in this particular case?
- Does the child have primary social phobia or is the condition secondary to other mental disorders or behavior problems? If the child's social phobia is primary, does he or she have comorbid conditions that need to be addressed?
- Is the child's social phobia primarily anxiety-based or do concurrent social skills deficits also need to be addressed?
- Is the child's social phobia also associated with specific functions of behavior such as excessive attention-seeking or pursuit of tangible rewards from others?

• What external factors may be influencing the child's social phobia and are they relatively circumscribed or broad in scope?

As answers to these questions become clearer following interviews and questionnaires, behavioral observations may be done to confirm one's initial hypotheses. In cases involving significant informant variance, however, behavioral observations will be needed to help develop these hypotheses in the first place. Daily logbook information will also be helpful in this regard. A good conceptualization of the child's social phobia must precede treatment so that an appropriate strategy may be chosen. For example, a child with specific social phobia and substantial social skills deficits may require a more child-based behavioral approach, whereas another child with generalized social phobia, school refusal behavior, and associated functional elements may require an intense cognitive-behavioral approach that involves the child, parents, and school officials.

A clinician's hypotheses about a child's social anxiety may change during the course of treatment as new data become available and as the child's behavior is modified. Therefore, aspects of the formal evaluation process should never completely end, even during treatment. Furthermore, initial and ongoing consultation with family members about the clinician's hypotheses is critical, and this process is described next.

CONSULTATION

The consultation session generally involves summarizing extant assessment findings, providing treatment rationales, addressing pretreatment considerations, and covering procedures regarding sessions and treatments. These areas are discussed next.

SUMMARIZING EXTANT ASSESSMENT FINDINGS

Summarizing extant assessment findings may be done by evaluating patterns of responses across individuals and across measures. A clinician may wish to concentrate on recurring themes that most people agreed on during formal assessment, such as pervasive avoidance, anxiety, physiological symptoms, and reduced quality of life. However, discrepancies across information sources are instructive as well and could be used as fodder for further investigation and education. For example, a child may report excessive anxiety and little avoidance, whereas a mother may complain of her child's excessive avoidance but not anxiety. A discussion of such discrepancies may help inform certain family members about the true nature of the child's problem, especially if such a discussion can be facilitated by third-party input (e.g., teachers, clinician).

Assessment findings regarding diagnoses, severe symptoms and behavior problems, function of social anxiety, and interference in daily life functioning should be emphasized. In addition, priorities should be assigned to the problems at hand, with higher priority given to severe anxiety and avoidance, depression, destructive behavior, and school absenteeism. During the summary process, which may be done separately with children and parents, feedback and questions should be solicited in case someone wishes to dispute the findings. In some cases, further assessment or a better synthesis of information is needed. In other cases, a family member will need evidence that their viewpoint is less than accurate.

During the consultation process, care should be taken not to assign blame to any one individual for the child's social anxiety problem, especially the child per se. In related fashion, because etiology in these cases is usually unclear, an extended discussion of causal factors with family members is rarely helpful. Instead, clinicians may wish to focus on the multifaceted nature of the child's symptoms and the various factors that can impinge upon them. For example, one could generally cover issues of temperament, cognitive bias, reinforced avoidance, family dynamics, problematic peer interactions, and other variables within the context of a manifold explanation of the child's social phobia. Of course, conspicuous etiological variables (e.g., traumatic events, excessive shyness) in a particular case should be discussed, especially if they are clearly and highly relevant to treatment. In general, though, emphasizing a collective responsibility for a child's social phobia will be consistent with the cooperative parent-child-school approach necessary for treatment.

PROVIDING A TREATMENT RATIONALE

Following a summary and discussion of assessment results, a treatment rationale may be given and tailored to the cognitive developmental status of the child. A treatment rationale may be given first in a general way and then more specifically. More generally, children and parents can be reminded of the difficulties they presently face and the child's current preferred method of coping with severe social anxiety (i.e., avoidance). One should point out that avoidance is a passable way of reducing anxiety in the short run but, in the long run, only leads to more problems (e.g., distress when around peers, loss of friends, panic when asked to perform, school absenteeism). Particular examples of the child's physiological and cognitive symptoms may be provided in this regard.

Following this preamble, the clinician may convey that he or she wishes to help the child learn a different way of coping with social and performance anxiety. In essence, new skills will be taught to help the child control negative feelings, change upsetting thoughts, and cope with difficult situations in ways he or she has not done before. An important idea that should be stated at this point is that the child and parents must be prepared to work hard and give substantial effort for treatment to succeed. In essence, the therapist must convey that he or she will be a guide or teacher but that the "heavy lifting" aspects of therapy will have to be done by the child and parents.

A more specific treatment rationale may then be given. This surrounds the idea that treatment will generally involve remediation of the major physiological, cognitive, and behavioral aspects of social phobia via different techniques. For example, the child and parents can be informed that unpleasant physical symptoms will be addressed via somatic control exercises, self-reinforcement, and practice. In addition, aversive thoughts may be addressed via cognitive restructuring and other exercises as well as development of effective social skills and self-confidence. Furthermore, behavioral avoidance may be addressed by gradual exposure to anxiety-provoking social and performance situations and practice in real-life situations. Other, more overarching treatment procedures can be discussed as well, including psychoeducation, contingency management, reduction of family conflict and other obstacles, and treatment of comorbid conditions, among relevant others. During this process, clinicians should solicit questions from family members about suggested treatment procedures and obtain information about potential problems.

PRETREATMENT CONSIDERATIONS

Various factors can derail even the best laid plans for treating youths with social phobia. Significant impediments include extremely high levels of anxiety and avoidance, poor child or parent motivation, treatment non-compliance and willingness to sabotage treatment, refusal to speak to the therapist, inflexible personality traits, intense comorbid conditions such as depression, severe health or academic problems, rigid parenting strategies, lack of financial and other familial resources, highly dysfunctional family dynamics and communication/problem-solving skills, excessive parental psychopathology, marital conflict, poor cognitive developmental status, highly discrepant therapist-client cultural variables, poor cooperation from school officials, legal obligations (e.g., family court dates, school expulsions), and events that naturally exacerbate a child's social or performance concerns (e.g., bullying or other forms of true victimization).

If any of these factors exist to a substantial degree, then treatment will have to be adjusted or the impediments will have to be addressed almost immediately. In many cases, these impediments will slow or stop treatment progress, mandate a broader treatment strategy, alter treatment goals (e.g., part-time, not full-time school attendance), or require a referral to another mental health professional. In addition, these cases will usually require extensive consultation with other professionals such as school officials, psychiatrists and pediatricians, social workers, legal case workers, and other mental health specialists.

GENERAL TREATMENT CONSIDERATIONS

The consultation session can also be used to lay the ground rules for future therapy. This includes scheduling future sessions, placing limits on a therapist's time, and reiterating the amount of work that will be needed between sessions. The average length of treatment from research-based protocols is often 8–16 sessions or weeks, and this can be given to family members as a general timeline. However, many cases take more time to resolve, and this should be conveyed as well. In addition, sessions may be held twice per week but should be held at least once per week to assess progress and maintain an even course of therapy. If substantial school refusal behavior is evident, then sessions should be held in late afternoon or evening so the child does not miss school for therapy appointments. Contingency plans for missed sessions should also be developed.

Many cases of childhood social phobia, especially those involving a mixture of behavior problems, can be quite intense in nature. Therefore, clinicians should advise clients of any limits on their time with respect to answering telephone calls, attending school-based or other meetings, extending specific session lengths, and conducting treatment procedures (e.g., exposures) outside of the office. These limitations will not preclude a clinician from conducting therapy with this population, but may slow treatment progress if all relevant techniques cannot be covered or if all exigencies cannot be addressed immediately. Finally, the consultation session should end with a reminder that a significant amount of work will be required of parents and children for treatment to be successful. This includes maintaining daily logbooks, practicing treatment techniques and new skills between sessions, and contacting school officials and other relevant persons as necessary. Reconveying this point throughout treatment is also recommended.

SAMPLE CASE: SCREENING, FORMAL EVALUATION, AND CONSULTATION

Alisha was a 12-year-old multiracial female referred for treatment by her parents and school guidance counselor. During the screening phase,

Alisha's mother (Mrs. A.) told the therapist that her daughter was struggling to maintain attendance at her new middle school. Although she did go to school, each day was marked by dawdling and reluctance, crying, shaking, and statements from Alisha that she did not like school and felt lonely there. Mrs. A. reported that Alisha did not appear to have other behavior problems except occasional bouts of sadness and lack of motivation to be with peers. Furthermore, Alisha was described as a typically shy child who always stayed close to two friends during elementary school. Upon entry to middle school, however, Alisha's contact with these friends had diminished greatly as she had a different class schedule and isolated herself more from social activities.

When asked about Alisha's current level of functioning, Mrs. A. said that her daughter rarely wished to attend social gatherings and usually stayed close to family members. She said further that Alisha's grades were very good and that her daughter enjoyed solitary activities like doing homework and watching television. Mrs. A. also reported the recent onset of physical symptoms in Alisha, including headaches and stomachaches, although no medical cause had been found. Both Mrs. A. and the school guidance counselor were concerned about Alisha's mood and the fact that she was becoming increasingly isolated from peers.

During formal evaluation, the therapist utilized sections of the ADIS-C: DSM-IV: C/P pertinent to social anxiety, social interaction, and depression. In addition, Alisha completed questionnaires regarding social anxiety (Social Anxiety Scale for Children-Revised), depression (Children's Depression Inventory), and general behavior problems (Youth Self-Report). Mr. and Mrs. A. completed the Child Behavior Checklist, and all parties completed relevant versions of the School Refusal Assessment Scale-Revised.

Information from these measures revealed that Alisha had a high level of social anxiety, particularly with respect to new social situations at school. In essence, she had great trepidation about new experiences with peers, although she tended to be less anxious once she knew a person better. Unfortunately, her avoidance of most social situations maintained her anxiety and precluded the development of more friendships. In addition, she had subclinical depression that was determined to be secondary to her social anxiety. Brief behavioral observations with different clinic personnel confirmed Alisha's anxiety and difficulty when meeting new people and her gradual ease once more social interactions were completed (e.g., with the therapist). Logbook information also revealed that Alisha's social anxiety was intense during school mornings but less so in the afternoons as she habituated to her surroundings.

Consultation with Alisha and her parents was designed to summarize assessment results, outline a potential treatment plan and its rationale, and assess potential obstacles. The therapist recommended an intense behavioral treatment program of role play and practice in new social situations, gradual enrollment in more extracurricular activities, class schedule adjustments so Alisha could spend lunch with her two close friends, and somatic control exercises to help Alisha manage her physical anxiety symptoms. All parties agreed that the treatment plan would be implemented by attending one formal treatment session per week, receiving one call from the therapist between sessions per week, and daily practice of skills learned in therapy. Logbook information during treatment revealed that Alisha's level of social anxiety in new situations and depression eased considerably over the next several weeks, and that her willingness to attend school and more diverse social activities did improve.

CHAPTER 6

THE TREATMENT OF SOCIAL ANXIETY AND SOCIAL PHOBIA IN YOUTHS

Previous chapters have covered the major characteristics and assessment strategies for youths with social anxiety and social phobia. In this chapter, a *brief* introduction is made regarding the major psychosocial and pharmacological treatments that have been designed to ameliorate these problems. In addition, empirical evidence is discussed for these treatments. A greater explication of these procedures for clinical settings is made in the remaining chapters of this book. Many of the procedures described here can also apply to youths who are shy, inhibited, or otherwise socially withdrawn. However, the focus of this and remaining chapters will be on youths with social anxiety and social phobia.

PSYCHOSOCIAL TREATMENT PROCEDURES FOR YOUTHS WITH SOCIAL ANXIETY AND SOCIAL PHOBIA

Psychosocial treatments for youths with social anxiety and social phobia involve child-, parent-, and family-based and other procedures. Each of these is discussed in turn.

CHILD-BASED TREATMENT PROCEDURES

Child-based psychosocial techniques for this population are generally cognitive-behavioral in nature, and include psychoeducation, self-monitoring, somatic control exercises, cognitive therapy, social skills and assertiveness training, and exposure-based practices. Each of these is briefly discussed in turn.

Psychoeducation

A common treatment technique for youths with social phobia is *psychoeducation*. Psychoeducation in this context partially refers to informing a child and often his or her family members about the nature of anxiety and its main response components: physiological, cognitive, and behavioral. Furthermore, children and family members are educated about how anxiety is triggered and maintained (Birmaher & Ollendick, 2004). In doing so, specific examples from a child's own experience can be used. In addition, the sequence of anxiety-based response components particular to that child can be illustrated to show how anxiety builds over time.

Psychoeducation is often helpful when conveying treatment rationales to family members, and so is usually conducted early in treatment (March & Ollendick, 2004). Specifically, different treatment techniques can be discussed that are most pertinent to the primary anxiety-based response components for a particular child. Supportive psychotherapy is also intertwined with psychoeducation in many treatment approaches for anxious children (Last, Hansen, & Franco, 1998; Silverman et al., 1999b).

Self-Monitoring

In conjunction with psychoeducation, *self-monitoring* is often used to further identify and understand aversive physiological symptoms, irrational thoughts, and avoidant behaviors associated with social phobia (Ginsburg & Walkup, 2004). Self-monitoring may take the form of diaries or logbooks (see Chapters 4 and 5), and can focus on specific episodes of fear or anxiety that a child experiences during a certain time. Self-monitoring helps a clinician and child recognize important antecedents and consequences to these episodes as well as anxiety sequences that are specific to different situations. In addition, self-monitoring is an excellent and sensitive method for gauging treatment progress.

Somatic Control Exercises

To help control aversive physiological symptoms of anxiety, *somatic control exercises* may be used. Two common forms of such exercises are relaxation training and breathing retraining. *Relaxation training* can involve many methods, including meditation, guided imagery, distraction, hypnosis, biofeedback, and even pharmacological intervention. One popular and portable relaxation training procedure, though, involves tensing and releasing different muscle groups. Examples include the hands, shoulders, face, jaw, stomach, and leg areas (Ollendick & Cerny, 1981). In this procedure, a child works with a therapist to practice tensing and releasing these areas and to comprehend the difference between a tense muscle and a relaxed one. Home-based practice of such relaxation is encouraged in addition to its regular use in anxiety-provoking situations.

In addition, *breathing retraining* is useful when a child is not inhaling appropriately during anxiety-provoking situations or is hyperventilating. The technique may require a child to practice inhaling slowly through his or her nose and exhaling slowly through his or her mouth. In younger children, counting or imagery may be used to enhance the technique (Eisen & Kearney, 1995). As with relaxation training, breathing retraining is simple, portable, and popular among children with anxiety disorders. Somatic control exercises are almost always integrated with other treatment techniques and are predominantly useful when a child's anxiety involves a strong physiological component.

Cognitive Therapy

To control irrational thoughts that help maintain anxiety, *cognitive therapy* or restructuring may be used. This process often involves key steps such as educating a youth about various types of cognitive distortions, identifying and classifying irrational thoughts during anxiety-provoking situations, evaluating these thoughts via reflection and questioning, appraising events more realistically, and modifying irrational thoughts in an adaptive fashion. Specific techniques to do so include psychoeducation, examining evidence for and against specific thoughts, decatastrophizing, cognitive self-control, decentering, reattribution training, reframing/relabeling, behavioral experiments, self-instructional training, and cognitive rehearsal (Bond & Dryden, 2002; Friedberg & McClure, 2002; Reinecke, Dattilio, & Freeman, 2003).

Cognitive therapy is often embedded with other techniques such as social skills training and exposure-based practices. The therapy is indicated most when a youth has adequate verbal/intellectual abilities to absorb pertinent information, where cognitions are especially problematic in anxiety-provoking situations, and where compliance is good with respect to self-monitoring of thoughts and practice during exposures. However, the utility of cognitive therapy for youths with social phobia has been questioned by some researchers (see Chapter 3), and the general technique is not a central element of *all* treatment protocols for this population (see below). In general, cognitive techniques should be used cautiously, with care, and perhaps more so with adolescents than children.

Social Skills and Assertiveness Training

Another commonly used treatment technique for youths with social anxiety and social phobia is *social skills training*. This involves instructing youths about their skill deficiencies in various social and/or evaluative situations and training them to perform more adaptive behaviors (Blonk, Prins, Sergeant, Ringrose, & Brinkman, 1996; LaGreca & Santogrossi, 1980). Many social skills can be targeted in this regard, but key ones include making introductions, initiating and maintaining conversations, practicing appropriate social problem-solving methods, coping adaptively with anxiety-provoking events, engaging in oral/written presentations and other performances before others, expressing affection appropriately, and cooperating effectively with others. In addition, assertiveness to acquire information (e.g., directions, homework assignments) or stop unwanted behaviors from others (e.g., excessive requests, inappropriate touching) is a key social behavior and often enhanced via *assertiveness training* (Emmelkamp & Scholing, 1997).

Social skills and assertiveness training methods typically include modeling and role play procedures involving presentation of or interaction with a peer model, rehearsal of key social behaviors, feedback to enhance social and performance skills, and practice in real-life situations (Cartledge & Milburn, 1995). Other methods include developing and implementing alternative solutions to social problems (Christoff et al., 1985). Social skills training methods are often incorporated into exposure-based practices (King, Murphy, & Heyne, 1997). Social skills training may be less necessary in cases where a child has excellent social skills but simply fails to perform these skills at acceptable levels (Gresham & Evans, 1987). In many cases of childhood social phobia, however, social skills and assertiveness training are essential treatment components because the child's anxiety has impeded the development of these skills (see Chapter 2).

Exposure-Based Practices

To help control avoidant and other problematic behaviors related to anxiety, *exposure-based practices* may, and in most cases should, be used. Indeed, exposure is often considered to be the key ingredient of treatment for social anxiety and phobia (Albano, Detweiler, & Logsdon-Conradsen, 1999). Successful exposure treatment is likely based on habituation, beneficial emotional processing of anxious events, and a heightened sense of perceived self-efficacy in anxiety-provoking situations (see Chapter 9).

As mentioned earlier, exposure-based practices are often used in conjunction with somatic control exercises, cognitive therapy, and social skills training. The general goal of this treatment approach is to have a child practice somatic/cognitive anxiety management and social skills and experience lessened anxiety in different social and evaluative situations. In essence, the child should come to understand that avoidance, a maladaptive response, can be replaced with anxiety management/social skills and expositions that are more adaptive and more socially acceptable responses to anxiety.

Exposure-based practices typically begin with psychoeducation and the development of an *anxiety/avoidance hierarchy*, or a list of situations that range from least to most anxiety-provoking (Silverman & Kurtines, 1996). In cases of social phobia, these situations would naturally involve those that are social and/or evaluative in nature. Hierarchy items may be derived by examining stimuli that are most upsetting to youths with social phobia (see Chapter 2). Specific examples of hierarchy items for a particular child may be derived from formal assessment information. Each stimulus hierarchy item is rated (e.g., on a 0-10 scale) for level of fear or anxiety as well as degree of avoidance.

Exposure may begin on an *imaginal basis*, in which children are exposed to different scenes that may be verbally described by a therapist. These scenes may involve outcomes that a child fears most in social and evaluative situations, and should serve as a precursor to later in vivo exposures (Kearney & Albano, 2000). *In vivo exposures*, or real-life exposures, are also based on a child's stimulus hierarchy and involve practicing adaptive behaviors in actual, feared social and evaluative situations (e.g., Beidel, Turner, & Morris, 2000b). Initially this process may be more controlled and assisted by others in-session, but can later involve more independent practice in a child's natural environment. Finally, *interoceptive exposure* involves exposure to internal physical sensations that one may fear in social and evaluative situations (Craske, Barlow, & Meadows, 2000). This may be particularly useful for youths with clear panic attacks in these situations.

Exposures may be *contrived* in nature, meaning that contact with a feared stimulus is actively sought, or *non-contrived* in nature, meaning that contact with a feared stimulus is unavoidable (March & Albano, 2002). In addition, Albano and Barlow (1996) discussed the concept of *double exposures* in which youths with social phobia participate in exposures designed for other youths with social phobia. In fact, exposure-based practices are often conducted in a group format to do so, and even individual therapy for a youth with social phobia will likely require interaction with peers.

Exposure-based practices also involve extensive *generalization training* in which a child practices newly learned skills in situations that are ancillary to the primary targets of treatment (e.g., Beidel, Turner, & Morris, 2000b). For example, a child could apply skills learned in therapy to subclinical or even developmentally appropriate fears or apply them to upcoming stressful situations. Generalization training may be used in conjunction with *relapse prevention*, which involves identifying future stressors or challenges that may trigger anxiety and developing specific interventions to address them (see Chapter 10). Imaginal exposure to these future-based situations with somatic control exercises and cognitive therapy is often useful in this regard. Generalization training may also be used in conjunction with *response prevention*, or ongoing practice of nonavoidant strategies and/or control of compulsive rituals when encountering stressful stimuli (March & Albano, 2002).

PARENT-BASED CONTINGENCY MANAGEMENT PROCEDURES

Parent-based treatment regarding youths with social anxiety and social phobia generally involves contingency management procedures, or structuring consistent parental consequences for appropriate and inappropriate child behavior (Briesmeister & Schaefer, 1998). For youths with social anxiety or social phobia, contingency management and child-based treatment procedures are often integrated. Therefore, parental consequences may apply most to child behaviors such as compliance to therapeutic homework assignments (including exposures), attendance at school and social events, and daily social interactions and performances before others, among others (Kearney & Albano, 2000).

Contingency management may also involve other parent-based procedures such as providing disincentives or extinguishing inappropriate behavior, improving commands, and establishing daily routines to foster appropriate skills. In addition, the use of token economies with response cost as well as shaping and guiding appropriate behavior is common. Parental consistency in using these procedures is also emphasized.

FAMILY-BASED AND OTHER TREATMENT PROCEDURES

Family-based procedures are also relevant for treating youths with social anxiety and social phobia. *Contingency contracting*, for example, involves the development of written agreements between youths and parents to provide incentives for appropriate behavior and disincentives for inappropriate behavior (e.g., Cretekos, 1977; Vaal, 1973). In addition, the technique is very useful for developing negotiation and problem-solving strategies among family members (Kearney, 2001). Contracts may pertain to concurrent problems to social phobia such as school refusal behavior, but typically surround compliance to exposure-based and other therapeutic procedures (Silverman et al., 1999b). Contingency contracting may also conjoin other family therapy techniques such as reframing or communication and formal problem-solving skills training.

Other treatment procedures for socially anxious youth may focus on school-based techniques. Teachers and other school officials, for example, can help implement many of the procedures described here, including self-monitoring, reinforcement of proactive social behavior, token economies, and exposures. In addition, classroom environments can be altered to reduce peer-based threats or teasing, unnecessary stressors, excessive teacher-based reprimands, and child-based behavior problems such as absenteeism (Albano & Hayward, 2004). At a minimum, school officials should be consulted to derive information pertinent for treatment (see Chapter 5) and to help remove any obstacles to treatment success. The development of strong parent-school official relationships and the provision of booster sessions within school settings may also be crucial for relapse prevention.

GENERAL ANXIETY TREATMENT OUTCOME STUDIES

Several researchers have treated youths with various anxiety disorders, including youths with social phobia, using the procedures described here. Three excellent sets of examples are briefly presented next. First, Kendall (1994) utilized psychosocial treatment for 47 youths aged 9–13 years with various anxiety disorders. The treatment protocol (Coping Cat Workbook) involved helping youths recognize physical and cognitive anxiety symptoms, modify irrational cognitions and develop coping plans during anxiety-provoking situations, engage in self-evaluation of performance and self-reinforcement, complete therapeutic homework assignments, and undergo behavioral techniques such as modeling, role play, relaxation training, in vivo exposure, and contingent reinforcement.

Results from 16-session treatment indicated significant improvement on various dependent measures of anxiety and related constructs. In addition, 64% of treated youths no longer met criteria for an anxiety disorder at posttreatment. Subsequent studies have also supported the strength of this approach and its modifications (Flannery-Schroeder & Kendall, 2000; Kendall et al., 1997; Kendall & Southam-Gerow, 1996; Mendlowitz et al., 1999). Poorer treatment outcome seems best predicted by higher pre-treatment levels of child internalizing symptoms, maternal depression, and older child age (Southam-Gerow, Kendall, & Weersing, 2001).

Second, Barrett, Dadds, and Rapee (1996) compared cognitive-behavioral treatment (CBT), CBT with family-based treatment, and no treatment for youths aged 7–14 years with various anxiety disorders, including social phobia. Child-based treatment was similar to Kendall's approach (Coping Koala Workbook). Family-based treatment consisted of parent training to reinforce approach behaviors and extinguish anxiety-based behaviors, to address parent-based anxiety responses and model appropriate responses to anxiety, and to improve family communication and problem-solving skills. Results from 12-sesssion treatment indicated that both groups improved significantly on various dependent measures compared to controls. In addition, family-based treatment substantially enhanced the effects of CBT alone. For example, elimination of anxiety diagnoses at posttreatment was 57% for the CBT group and 84% for the CBT plus family treatment approach. Subsequent studies have generally supported these treatment approaches as well (Barrett, Duffy, Dadds, & Rapee, 2001; Cobham et al., 1998; Dadds et al., 1999; Dadds, Spence, Holland, Barrett, & Laurens, 1997).

Finally, Silverman and colleagues (1999a, 1999b) conducted two treatment outcome studies of youths aged 6-16 years with various anxiety disorders, including social phobia. The first study consisted of group CBT with parent-based contingency management procedures (GCBT), and the second study consisted of 10-session exposure-based cognitive self-control (SC) procedures versus exposure-based contingency management (CM). All treatments except CM were substantially more effective than control conditions. Elimination of anxiety diagnoses at posttreatment was 64% for GCBT, 88% for SC, and 56% for CM. Poorer treatment outcome seems best predicted by levels of child depression and trait anxiety and by parental depression, hostility, and paranoia (Berman, Weems, Silverman, & Kurtines, 2000).

A consensus has thus formed that child-based and parent/family-based cognitive-behavioral procedures are effective for treating youths with anxiety disorders, and may even inform prevention efforts (e.g., Albano & Kendall, 2002; Barrett, 2000; Essau & Petermann, 2001; Hudson, Kendall, Coles, Robin, & Webb, 2002; Nauta, Scholing, Emmelkamp, & Minderaa, 2003; Ollendick & March, 2004; Silverman & Treffers, 2001; Toren et al., 2000). Practice parameters for treating this population also concentrate heavily on education, exposure-based procedures, family interventions, and pharmacotherapy (American Academy of Child and Adolescent Psychiatry, 1997). Applying these procedures to youths with specific anxiety disorders such as social phobia has thus begun in earnest.

TREATMENT OUTCOME STUDIES FOR YOUTHS WITH SOCIAL PHOBIA

Several treatment outcome studies have been conducted specifically for youths with social phobia. Albano and colleagues (1995), for example, evaluated a 16-session group treatment protocol for five adolescents with social phobia. Uncontrolled treatment consisted of psychoeducation about the nature of social anxiety, rationale for treatment, skills building with modeling, role play, and shaping (i.e., social and problem-solving skills, assertiveness training, and cognitive therapy), and in-session and external in vivo exposures to feared social situations. Parents also received psychoeducation and treatment rationales and were prepared for exposure-based sessions. At three-month follow-up, 4 of 5 participants no longer met formal diagnostic criteria for social phobia.

This cognitive-behavioral group treatment approach has been expanded and refined with time (Albano, 1995; Albano & Barlow, 1996; Albano et al., 1999). The primary structure of this treatment consists of two, 8-session phases, the first of which includes psychoeducation, skills building, and snack time practice. The latter component involves eating-based exposures with therapist self-disclosure of socially embarrassing moments, guided imagery, relaxation training, modeling appropriate coping and problem-solving skills, social interactions, and shaping and feedback. The second treatment phase concentrates heavily on within-session contrived and more community-based exposures to feared social and performance situations as well as relapse prevention strategies. Parents are also involved intermittently to understand treatment and to prepare for exposure-based practices. An outline of this protocol is presented in Table 6.1.

Hayward and colleagues (2000) examined this protocol versus no treatment in female youths (mean age, 15.8 years) with social phobia. At posttreatment, treated youths showed statistically significant though moderate improvement in social phobia symptoms compared to controls. In addition, 55% of the treatment group still met criteria for social phobia at posttreatment compared to 96% of the control group. These figures improved to 40% and 56%, respectively, at one-year follow-up. Differences between the two groups were even more exaggerated when comorbid depression was considered.

Albano and Hayward (2004) issued several treatment recommendations for youths with social phobia with varying symptom severity levels. For youths with mild symptoms of social anxiety that cause little functional disturbance, psychoeducation and 6-month follow-up may be most appropriate. For youths with moderate symptoms of social anxiety that

TABLE 6.1. Session Content for CBGT-A

Session 1	(Parents attend)
	Ground rules for group
	Situations causing social anxiety
	Cognitive-behavioral model of social anxiety
	Snack time: Therapists share information
	Overview of treatment program and rationale
	Monitoring
	Homework: Monitoring and setting treatment goals
Session 2	(Parents attend)
	Review self-monitoring
	Three-component model of anxiety
	Dissecting social anxiety into three components: Use a common situation
	Snack time: Therapist's embarrassing moment
	Expectations for treatment
	Becoming detectives: Studying the three components
	Homework: Monitoring and life goals
Session 3	Review of self-monitoring, goals, and model of anxiety
	Labeling distortions: Introduction to automatic thoughts (ATs)
	Therapists' role play of ATs
	Snack time: Guided imagery to the moon
	Rational responses: Countering ATs
	Review of session
	Homework
Session 4	Review of homework
	Four steps to cognitive restructuring
	Therapists' role play of cognitive restructuring
	Snack time: Therapist deals with a problem
	Steps to problem solving
	Review
	Homework
Session 5	Review of homework
	Therapists model social skills versus "unskilled"
	Social skills training I: Identifying and improving upon weaknesses
	Snack time practice: Shaping oral reading skills
	Social skills training II: Assertiveness
	Review of session and homework assignment: Preparing a paragraph for next week's snack time
Session 6	Review of homework
	Social skills training III: Review of skill building steps and focus on perspective taking
	Group role play: Conversing in the cafeteria
	Snack time: Reading aloud prepared paragraphs
	Social skills training IV: More assertiveness
	Review and homework

(Continued)

TABLE 6.1. (*Continued*)

Session 7	Overview and review of skills covered to date: cognitive restructuring, problem solving, social skills Treatment rationale: Simulated exposures Evaluating expectations: "How much better should I be now?" Snack time: Group interaction exercise What to do with your parents: How to access support and be understood Homework
Session 8	(Parents attend) Review of homework Review of expectations: "What should have changed by now?" Treatment rationale: Simulated and between-session exposures Snack time: Informal socializing Role play: Perspective taking—parents and teens switch roles Enlisting support: The coaching team Homework
Sessions 9–14	Review of homework Simulated exposure #1 Snack time: Mini exposures to situations such as taking compliments, giving critical feedback to a friend, etc. Simulated exposure #2 Homework: individual hierarchy items are assigned for between-session exposure
Session 15 or 19	(Parents attend: Next to last session) Review of monitoring and exposure homework Exposures: Each group member is targeted in an exposure that all parents observe Snack time: Informal socializing Expectations and future plans: Relapse prevention; homework
Sessions 16–20	Review of self-monitoring and exposure homework Final exposures and relapse prevention Snack time: Pizza party Processing of termination and relapse prevention

Note. CBGT-A, Cognitive Behavioral Group Treatment for Adolescent Social Phobia.
(Used with permission).

do cause some functional disturbance, child-based cognitive-behavioral treatment methods may be most appropriate. For youths with severe symptoms of social anxiety and substantial functional disturbance, child-based cognitive-behavioral therapy, medication, and possible adjunctive treatments (e.g., parent-based procedures) may be most appropriate. Finally, for youths with extreme symptoms of social anxiety and highly severe functional disturbance, child-based cognitive-behavioral therapy, medication, and adjunctive treatments for sessions over a lengthy time period may be most appropriate.

Others have also investigated variations of CBT for socially anxious youths. For example, Spence and colleagues (2000) examined youths aged 7–14 years with social phobia and assigned them to 12-session (and two booster session) child-based cognitive-behavioral treatment (CBT), CBT with parental involvement, or wait-list control. CBT consisted primarily of relaxation training, social skills training, social problem solving skills training, cognitive therapy (i.e., positive self-instruction and cognitive challenging), gradual exposure to various social situations, and therapeutic homework assignments. Treatment was modified for younger children by deemphasizing cognitive components.

Parental involvement included modeling, prompting, and reinforcing child skills practice and homework assignments, modeling appropriate social behaviors for children, and not reinforcing anxiety-related behaviors in children. At posttreatment, 87.5% of the CBT group no longer met criteria for a clinical diagnosis, compared to 58.0% and 7.0% for the parental involvement and control groups, respectively. At 12-month follow-up, these figures were 81.0% and 53.0% for the two treatment groups, respectively. The authors concluded that both treatments were effective, particularly the use of social skills training. However, including parents may have diluted or impeded treatment outcome in some cases.

Another variation of CBT was investigated by Gallagher and colleagues (2004), who evaluated a brief, controlled, 3-week cognitive-behavioral group intervention in 12 youths aged 8–11 years with social phobia. Three, 3-hour treatment sessions consisted of psychoeducation, cognitive therapy, and in-session and external exposure-based practices. Furthermore, parents were informed of their children's homework assignments but no formal parent-based treatment was used. At posttreatment, 41.7% of children and 58.3% of parents in the treatment group still endorsed social phobia diagnoses, compared to 81.8% and 100.0%, respectively, for controls. Further improvement in the treatment group was noted at 3-week follow-up (16.7% and 50.0%, respectively). Findings regarding other dependent measures were more mixed. The authors concluded that short-term CBT group treatment for this population is effective but also that longer-term treatment may be necessary for more complete benefits.

Others have modified CBT procedures for school-based settings. Masia and colleagues (2001), for example, tested the Skills for Academic and Social Success, a 14-session, group-oriented treatment that focuses on education, realistic thinking, social skills training, exposure-based practices, and relapse prevention. Six adolescents received treatment at their school. At posttreatment, three participants no longer met criteria for social phobia and, overall, social phobia symptoms were significantly reduced. An advantage of this approach is that treatment was applied at school where impairment is often greatest, though several obstacles from school officials were also noted.

Finally, others have evaluated a more behavioral approach to treating youths with social phobia. Beidel, Turner, and Morris (2000) treated youths (mean age, 10.5 years) with social phobia via their Social Effectiveness Therapy for Children (SET-C). SET-C components include child and parent education, social skills training via modeling and role play, peer generalization experiences, in vivo behavioral exposures, and therapeutic homework assignments. Treatment was provided twice per week, once per week in group format and once per week individually. Control participants received study and test-taking skills training for the same length of time.

At posttreatment, the SET-C group showed more significant improvement than controls with respect to general and social anxiety, social skill and performance, and daily functioning in social encounters. In addition, two-thirds of the SET-C group no longer met criteria for social phobia compared to only 5% of the control group, and improvement largely continued to 6-month and 3-year follow-up (D.C. Beidel, personal communication, March 18, 2004). This study was one of the first to show that the use of strictly behavioral (and not cognitive) procedures was effective for treating youths with social phobia.

COMPARISON OF PSYCHOSOCIAL TREATMENTS

Three major psychosocial treatments for childhood social phobia were compared by the main authors of these protocols (Garcia-Lopez, Olivares, Turner, et al., 2002; Olivares, Garcia-Lopez et al., 2002) (see also Olivares & Garcia-Lopez, 2002; Olivares-Rodriguez et al., 2003; Rodriguez & Garcia-Lopez, 2001; Rodriguez et al., 2003). Spanish adolescents with generalized social phobia were assigned to either Social Effectiveness Therapy for Adolescents-Spanish version (SET-A$_{SV}$) (n = 14), Cognitive-Behavioral Group Therapy (for Adolescents) (CBGT-A) (n = 15), Intervencion en Adolescentes con Fobia Social Generalizada (IAFSG) (Therapy for Adolescents with Generalized Social Phobia) (n = 15), or a control group (n = 15). The treatment groups consisted of 29, 16, and 12 sessions, respectively. Measures were taken at pre- and post-treatment and one-year follow-up.

From pre- to post-treatment, active treatment participants were superior to controls with respect to measures of social and public speaking anxiety, lack of impairment, self-esteem, and number of feared social situations. In addition, from pre-treatment to follow-up, active treatment participants were superior to controls with respect to measures of social anxiety, lack of impairment, and social skills. From post-treatment to follow-up, active treatment participants were superior to controls with respect to measures of social anxiety (fear of negative evaluation), social skills, and number of feared social situations. At follow-up, participants in the SET-A$_{SV}$ and IAFSG groups tended to maintain gains or show improvement, whereas improvement for the CBGT-A group was less well maintained with respect to social and public speaking anxiety and number of feared social situations.

The researchers also examined effect sizes for the active treatments. Effect sizes per dependent measure were generally quite strong for each treatment condition (range = 0.95–2.72). The researchers also found the SET-A$_{SV}$, CBGT-A, and IAFSG groups, utilizing a 100% criterion, to have effectiveness rates of 35.7%, 53.3%, and 33.3%, respectively, at post-treatment and 57.1%, 26.7%, and 46.7%, respectively, at follow-up. This indicates that CBGT-A is somewhat better in the short-term than the long-term compared to other treatment methods. Using a 75% criterion, effectiveness rates for the SET-A$_{SV}$, CBGT-A, and IAFSG groups were 71.4%, 53.3%, and 66.7%, respectively, at post-treatment and 78.6%, 46.7%, and 73.3%, respectively, at follow-up.

The authors concluded that a cognitive component to treatment does not necessarily produce significant behavioral change over and above exposure-based practices. However, changes in anxious cognitions were noted. In addition, social skills training per se seemed less useful than integrating the technique with exposure-based sessions where participants must actively practice these skills and where a therapist can tailor an exposure to a child's unique social skill needs (Garcia-Lopez, Olivares, Turner, et al., 2002). The small sample size of the study and its heavy basis on adolescent self-report are significant limitations, however. Therefore, these conclusions are muted to some extent.

PHARMACOTHERAPY

Pharmacological treatments for youths with anxiety disorders have also been studied. However, these treatments are controversial because their efficacy is not strong and because many child-based pharmacological outcome studies are confounded by use of concurrent behavioral therapies, varying dependent measures, methodological drawbacks, and lack of control groups (Kearney & Silverman, 1998). In general, the use of selective serotonergic reuptake inhibitors (SSRIs) and the treatment of obsessive-compulsive disorder seem to show the strongest outcome effects (Albano & Hayward, 2004).

For youths with social phobia, SSRI treatment has been evaluated in conjunction with youths with other anxiety disorders, and moderate outcomes have been reported (Birmaher et al., 1994, 2003; Research Unit on Pediatric Psychopharmacology Anxiety Study Group, 2001; Van Ameringen, Mancini, Farvolden, & Oakman, 1999). More specific to social phobia, however, Compton and colleagues (2001) evaluated 14 youths (mean age, 13.6 years) with the disorder in an 8-week open trial of the SSRI sertraline (Zoloft) (mean 123.2 mg/day by end of study). Participants also received brief sessions of cognitive-behavioral treatment prior to drug treatment. At posttreatment, youths were classified as responders (5), partial responders (4), or nonresponders (5). In addition, substantial reductions were evident for social and general anxiety, depression, avoidance, and parent ratings of behavior problems. The authors concluded that the drug may be an effective short-term treatment for social phobia in youths, although the study was uncontrolled and perhaps confounded by the use of cognitive-behavioral treatment. Others have also reported some success using sertraline, paroxetine, or nefazodone for individual cases of youths with social phobia (Mancini, Van Ameringen, Oakman, & Farvolden, 1999).

As mentioned earlier, practice parameters for youths with social phobia have included both psychosocial and pharmacological treatment components. However, psychosocial treatments for this population have been subjected to substantially more frequent and stringent empirical analysis than pharmacological treatments. Therefore, the use of pharmacological agents should be used with substantial caution, perhaps only as an adjunctive or short-term treatment, and/or in cases with extreme social anxiety symptoms.

FINAL COMMENTS

The treatment of social anxiety and social phobia in youths has undergone substantial analysis in recent years, though certainly much more work remains. In particular, greater attention is needed with respect to dismantling studies that examine the efficacy of individual treatment components, prescriptive treatment studies that tailor different therapies to children of different ages and with other characteristics, and outcome studies that utilize a wide range of standardized and comparable dependent measures (Beidel, Ferrell, Alfano, & Yeganeh, 2001). In addition, outcome studies that better integrate the treatment of social phobia with related therapies for shyness, inhibition, and social withdrawal would be beneficial.

CHAPTER 7

TREATING YOUTHS WITH SOCIAL ANXIETY AND SOCIAL PHOBIA

LAYING THE GROUNDWORK

The previous chapter contained a brief overview of treatment components that are commonly used to address youths with social anxiety and social phobia. In this chapter as well as in Chapters 8 and 9, treatment procedures for use in general clinical settings are described in more depth. This chapter will concentrate on initial procedures designed to lay the groundwork for the more intense procedures discussed in Chapters 8 and 9. These initial procedures include psychoeducation, somatic control exercises, contingency management, and contingency contracting. Obstacles to treatment as well as homework assignments will also be discussed throughout. A sample case of a youth with social phobia and concurrent depression and school refusal behavior is provided as well.

Some caveats before proceeding. First, the procedures discussed in this book are covered in a way that implies their use more so for individuals than groups. However, many advantages exist for conducting group therapy for youths with social phobia, including increased social interaction, double exposures, and cost-effectiveness (see Chapter 6). Therefore, suggestions will be made intermittently for using these procedures in group settings. Second, the procedures do not necessarily apply to any particular case. Indeed, good clinical judgment is needed when selecting the course, pace, and techniques of therapy for a given child. In related fashion, treatment techniques must be modified and applied with sensitivity to a child's mental condition, developmental status, unique characteristics such as culture, and family and other variables (see Chapter 5). Finally, the procedures are not described like a treatment manual, and descriptions are made with the assumption that the reader has a good background with respect to general psychotherapy practice with youths.

PSYCHOEDUCATION

Psychoeducation for this population generally refers to informing a child and his or her family members about the nature of social anxiety and its response components: physiological, cognitive, and behavioral. In addition, children and family members are educated about how anxiety is triggered and maintained. In doing so, a rationale may be conveyed for the treatment techniques that are to be used. Impairment from social anxiety in the form of skills deficits, peer rejection, or other problems, as well as inappropriate coping strategies such as avoidance, can also be illustrated to punctuate the need for treatment and how quality of life can be improved. Psychoeducation may be tailored to the specific characteristics of a child by relying on past and present self-monitoring and other assessment information.

Psychoeducation is often described in the literature as a child-based technique, though I find it helpful to include parents in the process. The technique begins by describing separately the components of social anxiety and providing examples from a child's own experiences. In many cases, children can provide their own examples but, in other cases, the therapist must provide considerable help. On a large sheet of paper or a writing board, the therapist may draw three circles that contain one heading each: "What I feel," "What I think," and "What I do." The circles do not overlap.

The first circle contains physical feelings that the child experiences in anxious social and/or performance-based situations. The child may reiterate his or her own physical feelings from formal assessment, the therapist may prompt these responses from the child and parents, or the therapist may provide a list of physical feelings commonly experienced by youths with social anxiety (see Chapter 2) and ask the child to endorse those that he or she usually experiences. The therapist then writes the responses in the "What I feel" circle.

The second circle contains the child's thoughts during anxious social and/or performance-based situations. The child may reiterate these thoughts from assessment or the therapist may prompt the thoughts in some way. The thoughts are then written in the "What I think" circle. The third circle contains the child's actual physical behaviors during anxious social and/or performance-based situations. These behaviors most often include forms of avoidance as well as others such as excessive reassurance-seeking, oppositional, or noncompliant behaviors. Each circle can then be reviewed for completeness.

The therapist then explores with the child the specific *sequence* of anxiety that occurs in different anxiety-provoking situations. For example, a child may say that she experiences substantial stomach cramps at school immediately before going to the cafeteria for lunch. These cramps may then be followed by worries or thoughts about vomiting in the cafeteria and resultant embarrassment. Subsequent behaviors might then include obvious ones such as hiding in the bathroom during lunch or more subtle ones such as eating near the exit in case nausea becomes severe. Although an anxiety sequence is often similar across situations for a given child, this is not always so. Therefore, all major anxiety-provoking situations should be probed to identify the various sequences of physical feelings, thoughts, and behaviors that are evident.

As a child's anxiety sequences are identified, the therapist can outline how the child's anxiety is typically triggered and maintained. For many children, aversive physical feelings or troublesome thoughts are key triggers, but other children may avoid first and worry later. These sequences may change over time, however, which makes the use of self-monitoring quite important. Children and parents (if applicable) can monitor and rate a child's physical feelings, thoughts, and behaviors in anxiety-provoking situations to further illustrate these patterns, identify changes over time, and chart treatment progress.

Psychoeducation may also be done when providing rationales and goals for treatment. Because treatment procedures will target the major response components to anxiety, treatment rationales may be structured similarly. For example, physical feelings of anxiety could be managed via somatic control exercises, anxious thoughts could be modified via cognitive therapy, and avoidant behaviors could be eliminated via exposure-based practices. Each set of treatment techniques, and relevant others, can be explored in depth and divided into phases. For example, initial phases of treatment will likely concentrate on anxiety management techniques for aversive feelings and thoughts. Later phases of treatment will likely concentrate on using these anxiety management techniques to successfully engage in exposure-based practices to reduce avoidance.

Furthermore, specific goals for the child can be identified at this point. Examples include a substantial reduction in physical feelings and problematic thoughts (i.e., successful anxiety management), elimination of avoidant behaviors, development of social skills, and ancillary goals such as reduced family conflict or child noncompliance. Questions regarding proposed techniques should be answered fully to help prevent misconceptions, skepticism, and noncompliance regarding treatment. Family members should also be warned that the general therapy plan may change over time to adapt to new information, problematic behaviors, and obstacles.

One key obstacle that may arise during this process is a lack of problematic thoughts during anxiety-provoking situations. This may be due to a child's limited cognitive developmental status, but other reasons include a diffuse anxiety response (e.g., "I just feel bad"), true lack of problematic thoughts, or noncompliance. In this case, extensive self-monitoring with help from others may be necessary but, in other cases, problematic thoughts simply do not apply. If thoughts do not seem overly relevant to treatment, then an emphasis can be placed on addressing aversive physical feelings and avoidant and other misbehaviors.

Psychoeducation can be easily adapted for use in individual and group therapy. In group situations, however, extra care should be taken to ensure that all members fully understand the anxiety and treatment components. Pulling children aside during breaks to ensure this may be desirable. In addition, psychoeducation may be conducted in conjunction with "ground rules" to be set for a group, including attendance, homework assignments, group participation, and confidentiality (Albano, Marten, & Holt, 1991).

Finally, psychoeducation should not be viewed as a one-time procedure, but one to be reintroduced throughout treatment to remind individuals of the "big picture" and goals of therapy. In related fashion, I have found psychoeducation to be useful for building and maintaining rapport, offering encouragement, enhancing motivation, and easing tension. As a therapist calmly conveys the structure of anxiety and its treatment, clients are often eased by the knowledge that this is a common and fixable problem. Psychoeducation usually takes one session to complete, but can be condensed or extended as necessary.

SOMATIC CONTROL EXERCISES

Somatic control exercises are typically employed to help a child manage aversive physical feelings associated with his or her social and/or performance anxiety. Although different forms of somatic control exercises exist, the most common for anxious children include relaxation training and breathing retraining. *Relaxation training* comes in several forms as well, and a child and his or her family members should provide input about which methods have been tried in the past. A popular form of relaxation training is a *tension-release method* involving different muscle groups. In this method, a child sits in a comfortable chair before a therapist who slowly

TABLE 7.1. Relaxation Training Script (from Ollendick & Cerny, 1981)

Hands and arms

Make a fist with your left hand. Squeeze it hard. Feel the tightness in your hand and arm as you squeeze. Now let your hand go and relax. See how much better your hand and arm feel when they are relaxed. Once again, make a fist with your left hand and squeeze hard. Good. Now relax and let your hand go. (Repeat the process for the right hand and arm).

Arms and shoulders

Stretch your arms out in front of you. Raise them up high over your head. Way back. Feel the pull in your shoulders. Stretch higher. Now just let your arms drop back to your side. Okay, let's stretch again. Stretch your arms out in front of you. Raise them over your head. Pull them back, way back. Pull hard. Now let them drop quickly. Good. Notice how your shoulders feel more relaxed. This time let's have a great big stretch. Try to touch the ceiling. Stretch your arms out in front of you. Raise them way up over your head. Push them way, way back. Notice the tension and pull in your arms and shoulders. Hold tight, now. Great. Let them drop very quickly and feel how good it is to be relaxed. It feels good and warm and lazy.

Shoulders and neck

Try to pull your shoulders up to your ears and push your head down into your shoulders. Hold in tight. Okay, now relax and feel the warmth. Again, pull your shoulders up to your ears and push your head down into your shoulders. Do it tightly. Okay, you can relax now. Bring your head out and let your shoulders relax. Notice how much better it feels to be relaxed than to be all tight. One more time now. Push your head down and your shoulders way up to your ears. Hold it. Feel the tenseness in your neck and shoulders. Okay. You can relax now and feel comfortable. You feel good.

Jaw

Put your teeth together real hard. Let your neck muscles help you. Now relax. Just let your jaw hang loose. Notice how good it feels just to let your jaw drop. Okay, bite down hard. That's good. Now relax again. Just let your jaw drop. It feels so good just to let go. Okay, one more time. Bite down. Hard as you can. Harder. Oh, you really are working hard. Good. Now relax. Try to relax your whole body. Let yourself get as loose as you can.

Face and nose

Wrinkle up your nose. Make as many wrinkles in your nose as you can. Scrunch up your nose real hard. Good. Now relax your nose. Now wrinkle up your nose again. Wrinkle it up hard. Hold it just as tight as you can. Okay. You can relax your face. Notice that when you scrunch up your nose your cheeks and your mouth and your forehead all help you and they get tight, too. So when you relax your nose, your whole face relaxes too, and that feels good. Now make lots of wrinkles on your forehead. Hold it tight, now. Okay, you can let go. Now you can just relax. Let your face go smooth. No wrinkles anywhere. Your face feels nice and smooth and relaxed.

Stomach

Now tighten up your stomach muscles real tight. Make your stomach real hard. Don't move. Hold it. You can relax now. Let your stomach go soft. Let it be as relaxed as you can. That feels so much better. Okay, again. Tighten your stomach real hard. Good. You can relax now. Settle down, get comfortable and relax. Notice the difference between a tight stomach and a relaxed one. That's how we want to feel. Nice and loose and relaxed. Okay. Once more. Tighten up. Tighten hard. Good. Now you can relax completely. You feel nice and relaxed.

(Continued)

TABLE 7.1. (*Continued*)

This time, try to pull your stomach in. Try to squeeze it against your backbone. Try to be
as skinny as you can. Now relax. You don't have to be skinny now. Just relax and feel
your stomach being warm and loose. Okay, squeeze in your stomach again. Make it
touch your backbone. Get it real small and tight. Get as skinny as you can. Hold tight
now. You can relax now. Settle back and let your stomach come back out where it
belongs. You can feel really good now. You've done fine.

Legs and feet
Push your toes down on the floor real hard. You'll probably need your legs to help you
push. Push down, spread your toes apart. Now relax your feet. Let your toes go loose
and feel how nice that is. It feels good to be relaxed. Okay. Now push your toes down.
Let your leg muscles help you put your feet down. Push your feet. Hard. Okay. Relax
your feet, relax your legs, relax your toes. It feels so good to be relaxed. No tenseness
anywhere. You kind of feel warm and tingly.

Conclusion
Stay as relaxed as you can. Let your whole body go limp and feel all your muscles
relaxed. In a few minutes it will be the end of the relaxation exercise. Today is a good
day. You've worked hard in here and it feels good to work hard. Okay, shake your
arms. Now shake your legs. Move your head around. Open your eyes slowly (if they
were closed). Very good. You've done a good job. You're going to be a super relaxer.

(Used with permission).

reads a relaxation training script. The session may be audiotaped so the
child can practice the technique at home. A popular relaxation script from
Ollendick and Cerny (1981) is in Table 7.1.

The tension-release method requires a child to tense a specific muscle group, maintain the tension for 5–10 seconds, and release quickly. As
the therapist proceeds through different muscle groups, the child is encouraged to note the difference between a tense muscle and a relaxed one.
Important muscle groups are covered, but special attention should be paid
to groups (e.g., face, stomach) identified as most problematic for that child
in anxiety-provoking social and/or performance situations. The child may
then be asked to practice the relaxation technique at least twice per day
and in situations of intense anxiety.

Breathing retraining may also be used to enhance relaxation, and is particularly useful for youths who hyperventilate during anxiety-provoking
situations. A sample breathing retraining script from Kearney and Albano
(2000) is in Table 7.2. The child is asked to inhale slowly through his or her
nose and exhale slowly through his or her mouth. Having a child push a
finger into his or her diaphragm is recommended to ensure the accuracy
of the technique. Counting and imagery may also be used to enhance the
technique or make it more palatable for younger children.

TABLE 7.2. *Breathing Retraining Script* (from Kearney & Albano, 2000)

Ask the child to imagine going on a hot air balloon ride. As long as the hot air balloon has fuel supplied by the child's breathing, destinations are unlimited. Ask the child to breathe in through his or her nose and out through his or her mouth with a SSSSSSSSS . . . . sound. You may encourage this process through imagery (e.g., having a picture of a hot air balloon nearby). If necessary, have the child count to himself or herself slowly when breathing out.

Example:

Imagine going on a ride in a hot air balloon. Your breathing will give the balloon its power. As long as you breathe deeply, the balloon can go anywhere. Breathe in through your nose like this (demonstrate). Breathe slowly and deeply. Try to breathe in a lot of air. Now breathe out slowly through your mouth, making a hissing sound like this (demonstrate). If you want, you can count to yourself when you breathe in and out.

(Used with permission).

Somatic control exercises are particularly useful if a child experiences severe physical symptoms when anxious. However, these exercises per se may not provide much benefit. Indeed, in my experience, many children with social phobia discount the procedures or fail to use them because the procedures are less than helpful. However, other children do find the procedures quite useful, especially in conjunction with cognitive or other treatment procedures. If a child is noncompliant about using somatic control exercises, then a therapist should consider the possibility that the procedures are irrelevant.

CONTINGENCY MANAGEMENT

The procedures discussed so far are largely child-based in nature, but parents can be involved in treatment as well. *Contingency management* procedures, for example, are especially useful for treating children with social anxiety or social phobia, and often include the following:

- Establishing incentives for completing therapeutic homework assignments
- Establishing disincentives for failing to complete assignments or for related behavior problems
- Ignoring or otherwise extinguishing inappropriate behaviors
- Establishing set routines in the morning, evening, and weekends to encourage naturally occurring social interactions and performances before others
- Modifying parent commands to make them more succinct and effective

INCENTIVES

As a child is asked to execute somatic control exercises, practice cognitive techniques, develop social and coping skills, and participate in exposure-based assignments, the therapist and parents can design an *incentive* package to help the child engage in these procedures. Often the most useful incentives are attention-based, such as extra time with parents or the comfort of family time without pressures to interact with outside family members. However, other youths respond better to tangible rewards, so these could be offered as well. Of course, incentives would be given only *after* the child has successfully completed specific therapeutic homework assignments. For example, a child may be required to order ice cream in a public place and then be allowed to eat the ice cream (tangible reward) with his or her family members (attention-based reward).

In children with social anxiety and social phobia, rewards are often linked as well to *shaping processes* such as gradual increases in school attendance, ongoing steps in anxiety management skills, and progressive exposures to feared stimuli. A progressive reward system can be implemented, for example, in accordance with successive classes a child adds to his school schedule or with each social skill that becomes proficient. Positive reinforcement is usually a preferred consequence for anxious children. This is so because a child's anxiety may have been ignored, stigmatized, ridiculed, or otherwise punished for some time with little benefit. In addition, encouraging approach behaviors is often more agreeable to parents than using threats.

DISINCENTIVES

Failure to complete therapeutic homework assignments may also be met with *disincentives*, though care and restraint should be employed. If a child is noncompliant with respect to a therapeutic homework assignment, then the therapist should *first* explore whether the assignment was simply too difficult for the child and whether other (e.g., school-based) obstacles were present. If the child could have completed the assignment but still did not, then mild punishment in the form of early bedtime or expression of disappointment may be used. Harsher punishments are not generally recommended for this population, though may be necessary when severe behavior problems (e.g., school refusal behavior) are comorbid with a child's social phobia.

For younger children, a *token economy with response cost* may be a desirable way of meting out incentives and disincentives. This involves a formal system of giving a child tokens (or tangible markers such as stickers) or points for appropriate behavior (Kerr & Nelson, 2002). For example, a child may earn a token or certain number of points for demonstrating a predetermined socially acceptable behavior. At a later point, perhaps at the end of that day or week, the child may exchange his or her tokens/points for tangible rewards that increase in value the more tokens/points are accrued. Token economies are generally more effective with a response cost component, or loss of some tokens/points for inappropriate behaviors such as disruptiveness, noncompliance, or avoidance (Gelfand & Hartmann, 1984). Token economies for problematic behaviors may be implemented at home, but are often amenable to school classrooms as well.

EXTINCTION

Relatedly, parents may be taught to engage in *extinction*, or withholding attention or tangible rewards from children who act inappropriately. Such acts include, among others, unnecessary avoidance, noncompliance, temper tantrums, whining, crying, pouting, refusing to move, dirty looks, withdrawal, mean-spirited statements, complaints about treatment, or other regressive or disruptive behaviors to force parental acquiescence. *Time-out* may be an effective form of extinction for younger children. For older children and adolescents, parents should generally ignore and "work through" minor inappropriate behaviors and strictly adhere to commands to their children to engage in appropriate behaviors. More severe inappropriate behaviors may be met with formal punishments.

Extinction is particularly useful for *excessive reassurance-seeking behavior*, or a constant barrage of questions or statements to parents to alleviate distress or avoid obligation (e.g., "Are you sure it will be okay?" "What if X happens?" "Do I have to?"). Often these questions or statements surround social- and performance-based events, school and therapy attendance, and whether parents will be at a certain place and time to retrieve or "rescue" a child (e.g., "Be sure to be there at 3:15 *exactly*, Mom"). In these cases, shaping is generally recommended. For example, parents are allowed to answer the child's first question (e.g., "Do I *have* to go?") in a succinct, calm, and therapy-relevant way (e.g., "Yes, you *are* going to the birthday party"). Subsequent questions or related statements can then be ignored for a certain time period (e.g., one hour) and then answered once again.

ROUTINES

Another common contingency management practice for this population is to develop set *routines* for a family that increase natural occurrences of social interaction and performances before others. Many cases of childhood social phobia involve family members who have reinforced a child's avoidant behavior for long periods of time. Therefore, parents must often learn to pay attention to, and reward, even minor child behaviors that are approach-oriented and more socially appropriate in nature.

In the morning, for example, children may be asked to engage in a set routine as they prepare for school, which includes conversations with others at the breakfast table, greetings to a school bus driver or peers when arriving at school, and questions to and conversations with others about the upcoming day. During the evening and weekends, youths may be asked to answer the telephone or door, greet others in casual settings, ask someone for help or directions, call an acquaintence or friend regarding homework or a social gathering, order food in a restaurant, perform somehow (e.g., play a musical instrument) before relatives or others, or be assertive when necessary. Compliance to these day-to-day expectations should be rewarded as well. Structuring routines is also a key aspect of treating many youths with social phobia with concurrent school refusal behavior.

COMMANDS

Contingency management procedures for this population may also involve modifying parent *commands* toward greater brevity and effectiveness. Many parents who are frustrated with their child's behavior use commands that are dominated by criticism, lectures, vague statements, and blame. If so for a youth with social phobia, then parents can be educated about the negative effects of such commands on their relationship with their child, prospects for compliance, and eventual resolution of avoidant behaviors. Instead, parents may be taught to provide brief, clear commands to which a child may or may not respond. Appropriate responses are then rewarded and inappropriate responses or avoidance are then punished if desirable. Parent commands and statements may also be altered to encourage appropriate social behaviors in a child, guide a child gently through an assigned exposure, remind a child of different techniques that are useful in anxiety-provoking situations, and offer suitable comfort and support during therapy.

During the course of therapy, parents should continually engage in an active contingency management process to enhance other therapeutic techniques and to address noncompliant behaviors. Obstacles to such treatment include inconsistent application of the procedures, marital discord, fears about "pushing" a child in therapy, and resistance to change in what is sometimes perceived as a "child-only" problem. In these cases, working closely with parents, if even by telephone, is highly recommended. Reiterating treatment rationales and goals may be necessary as well. In other cases, especially those where the parents have social phobia or other psychopathology themselves, concurrent or referred treatment may be necessary.

CONTINGENCY CONTRACTING

Another commonly used technique for youths with social phobia is *contingency contracting*. Contingency contracting refers essentially to written contracts between parents and a child regarding commitment to the therapy process, therapeutic homework assignments, and related issues such as chores and other responsibilities (e.g., curfew). Contracts may apply most to adolescent cases of social phobia or cases where contingency management procedures are not fully applicable.

The development of contracts often coincides with communication and problem-solving skills training. The general goal of these treatments is to improve a family's ability to define problems, negotiate solutions to these problems, and evaluate the effectiveness of the solutions. Contracts are initially developed in-session under the direction of the therapist, who usually serves as mediator. The first contract involves a general statement whereby all parties commit to the therapy process. In addition, this contract may include simple requirements such as completing an initial therapeutic homework assignment (e.g., practicing somatic control exercises) and accompanying incentives and disincentives for compliance or noncompliance, respectively.

Subsequent contracts may address compliance to more detailed therapeutic procedures as well as behavior problems other than social phobia (especially school refusal behavior). As therapy progresses, family members can hold meetings at home to design and implement contracts more independently. In addition, a therapist can blend contracts with communication skills training and other methods of problem-solving training. Family members can, for example, practice conversational skills as they develop a contract.

Common obstacles to contracts include insufficient strength of incentives and disincentives, noncompliance, and disingenuous agreement to a contract. The latter may result from a desire to avoid or escape the problem resolution process, or may result from one party pressuring another to sign a contract. I recommend contacting each party soon after a contract has been developed to reconfirm everyone's commitment to it and to assess for desired changes. Contracts may also have to be tweaked or simplified with respect to type and strength of responsibilities and consequences.

SAMPLE CASE: JULIANNA

A sample case is provided here and throughout Chapters 8 and 9 to further illustrate treatment procedures. Julianna was a 13-year-old multiracial (Hispanic and Caucasian) female referred to a university-based clinic for youths with general behavior problems. Her parents and school counselor had referred her based on recent problems at school. Specifically, Julianna had a two-year history of sporadic school absences as well as recently declining grades. In fact, Julianna was in danger of not passing eighth grade.

A therapist met individually with Julianna and her parents. Julianna reportedly felt unwell at her middle school and constantly pressured by all of the demands there. In particular, she was overwhelmed by the presence of new peers and diverse academic assignments. Julianna skipped school and classes on days when she had to participate in large group settings such as basketball games in physical education class, assemblies, and oral presentations during English class. In addition, she dreaded tests, eating in the cafeteria, walking down a hallway and into class, and riding the school bus. Her anxiety in these situations was so intense that she rarely enjoyed herself at school and was considering dropping out altogether. She also felt sad and tearful, had no friends, and wanted to stay home with her parents and younger siblings.

Julianna's parents largely echoed their daughter's report but also provided a more historical view of her problems. Julianna was described as a shy child who often wanted to stay close to home. She did have some friends in elementary school but did not initiate extensive contact with them. Instead, she usually waited for others to invite her to parties or to other social gatherings. Her parents also reported that Julianna was traditionally a good student at school and generally preferred solitary activities such as playing the piano or family activities such as trips.

Unfortunately, many of Julianna's earlier friends moved to other schools, leaving her quite isolated in middle school. Over the course of seventh grade and much of the current academic year, Julianna became more agitated, withdrawn, and depressed. In fact, Julianna's recent mood had worsened in recent weeks to the point where she was crying often and had even talked about hurting herself so she would not have to attend school. Julianna's school counselor confirmed these reports and said that Julianna would often try to stay in the counselor's office during key times such as lunch.

In addition to these general interviews, assessment consisted of (1) child self-report questionnaires surrounding depression, general and social anxiety, school refusal behavior, and self-esteem, (2) parent- and teacher-based measures of general internalizing and externalizing behavior problems, and (3) ADIS-IV: C/P sections regarding social phobia and depression. School counselor observations and self-monitoring of mood were utilized as well. The therapist, after reviewing all relevant information, concluded that Julianna primarily met criteria for social phobia and had subclinical depression. Both problems were closely related to her school refusal behavior, which was found to be largely maintained by a desire to escape aversive social and/or evaluative situations.

The first formal treatment session included consultation and psychoeducation. Julianna and her parents were given a summary of the assessment findings, and all agreed that the general clinical picture portrayed by the therapist was accurate. The therapist then discussed the nature of social anxiety and the impairments that Julianna experienced as a result (e.g., declining grades, poor mood, social isolation). In addition, the therapist noted that Julianna's social skills were good but not excellent, as she bowed her head when speaking to others and often could not be heard audibly.

The psychoeducation process also focused on Julianna's sequences of symptoms in anxiety-provoking situations. Julianna's most anxiety-provoking situations were entering school and class, eating at lunchtime, performing on tests and other academic assignments before others, and playing sports during physical education class. Although the sequence of anxiety symptoms sometimes changed, Julianna said she often experienced nervousness in her stomach, shaking, trembling, and headaches during these times. These physical symptoms usually triggered thoughts about possible consequences, including vomiting and failure and subsequent ridicule and humiliation. Julianna would then engage in *overt* avoidance such as skipping class or *covert* avoidance such as going to her counselor's office, participating on the fringes during physical education and other classes, and bowing her head in the hallway at school to avoid eye contact with others.

The therapist explained how the proposed treatment regimen would target each of these anxiety responses. Julianna and her parents agreed that the treatment regimen seemed reasonable. Julianna was asked to continue to record various aspects of her anxious episodes, including details of physical symptoms, troublesome thoughts, and all types of avoidant behaviors. Julianna's parents were also encouraged to reinforce Julianna for completing her self-monitoring and the upcoming somatic control exercises. During the next session, Julianna engaged in relaxation training and breathing retraining and was instructed to practice these techniques at least twice per day and during anxiety-provoking times at school. Finally, an initial written contract was designed to provide reinforcements for appropriate school attendance with the provision that Julianna could go to the counselor's office when feeling overwhelmed.

CHAPTER 8

TREATING YOUTHS WITH SOCIAL ANXIETY AND SOCIAL PHOBIA

DEVELOPING ADVANCED SKILLS

The previous chapter described initial procedures that are commonly used to lay the groundwork for treating youths with social anxiety and social phobia. Techniques such as psychoeducation, self-monitoring, somatic control exercises, contingency management, and contingency contracting are generally designed to help youths understand the goals and rationales of treatment, control anxious physical feelings, and provide incentives for completing therapeutic homework assignments and engaging in other appropriate behaviors. In addition, these foundational techniques set the stage for more advanced skills training, most notably *cognitive therapy* and *social skills training*. Both procedures are designed to help youths manage anxiety in key social and/or performance situations and engage in more adaptive behaviors with others. In turn, these procedures help set the stage for later exposure-based practices (see Chapter 9).

Cognitive therapy is specifically designed to help youths recognize and modify irrational cognitions that instigate or maintain anxiety in a given situation. Social skills training is specifically designed to teach a child to interact with, or perform before, others in more effective ways and/or increase the frequency of already skilled behaviors. These therapies are discussed separately in this chapter, but are often combined and administered in conjunction with exposure-based practices. An extension of the sample case from Chapter 7 (Julianna) is provided as well.

COGNITIVE THERAPY

Cognitive therapy includes a variety of procedures that can be tailored to the needs of a particular child. Indeed, many youths are especially responsive to one or two specific cognitive therapy techniques than several in combination. Other youths, however, do require a more comprehensive cognitive therapy approach and still others do not respond at all to this approach. Recall from Chapters 3 and 6 that cognitive procedures for youths with social phobia remain controversial and may produce changes in irrational thoughts but *not necessarily* changes in anxious behaviors. Therefore, cognitive therapy for this population may be most effective for (1) older children or adolescents, (2) youths with social phobia *clearly* maintained by irrational cognitions, and (3) youths highly motivated with respect to self-monitoring and modifying thoughts.

Cognitive therapy techniques that are applicable to socially anxious children include psychoeducation, examining evidence for and against specific thoughts, decatastrophizing, cognitive self-control, decentering, reattribution training, reframing/relabeling, behavioral experiments, self-instructional training, and cognitive rehearsal. Each is described separately, though overlap is often present during implementation.

Psychoeducation for Cognitive Therapy

Psychoeducation in this context refers to instructing youths about (1) the basis for and importance of cognitive therapy, and (2) various cognitive distortions that are common to this population. These aspects are described separately next.

Basis for and Importance of Cognitive Therapy

Cognitive therapy may begin by instructing youths and their parents, if applicable and desirable, of the major assumptions surrounding the use of this therapy for social phobia. The following assumptions are adapted from Antony and Swinson (2000):

- Specific negative emotions such as anxiety, anger, and sadness often result from a person's specific interpretation of a given event. For example, a youth may interpret the fact that he or she did not receive an invitation to an acquaintance's birthday party as an omen of isolation at school that leads to anxiety, a deliberate harmful practice that leads to anger, or a sign of personal rejection that leads to sadness. One's *interpretation* of an event and *not the event per se* leads to social anxiety, and this interpretation can be changed. Interpretation of events about the self, world, and future are particularly important (Beck, Rush, Shaw, & Emery, 1979).

- When someone views a situation as *threatening or dangerous*, anxiety is likely to result. From the previous scenario, for example, the youth may worry that others at the party believe him or her to be stupid, unattractive, or clumsy and thus unworthy of inclusion. Related to this is the idea that having a thought does not necessarily mean the thought is true, and this should be conveyed as well.
- A person is his or her own *expert* regarding thoughts. As such, a youth, especially an older one, can be given free rein to identify and describe his or her most troublesome thoughts. This helps validate a youth's experiences, but he or she must also understand that the therapist will help him or her recognize and modify problematic or unrealistic thoughts.
- Cognitive therapy is designed to help a person think more *realistically*, not necessarily more positively. The therapist must convey that the purpose of cognitive therapy is not to "think happy thoughts" but rather to fundamentally alter the way in which one evaluates a given situation (i.e., by using evidence). From the previous scenario, for example, a youth may realize that party invitations may have been sent only to a few close friends and not all acquaintances.
- Youths who are socially anxious tend to pay more attention to negative events that confirm their negative beliefs more so than positive or neutral events that disconfirm them. As such, youths are encouraged to examine *all* of the evidence of a given situation to glean a balanced and realistic appraisal of what is happening. In doing so, a problem-solving orientation will be developed for a youth.

As a therapist explains these assumptions, specific examples from a child's formal assessment may be used for illustrative purposes. Woven into this discussion should also be a description of anxiety sequences that are specific to the child and that contain irrational cognitions as triggers or maintaining factors. A youth should eventually understand that irrational thoughts are potentially destructive or counterproductive but also that they can be modified within a grand plan to reduce social anxiety.

Cognitive Distortions

The next psychoeducational step for cognitive therapy is to help a youth identify different types of cognitive distortions that trigger or maintain his or her social anxiety. Cognitive distortions have been out-lined by many scientists and practitioners (e.g., Beck, Emery, & Greenberg, 1985; Beck et al., 1979; Burns, 1999; Persons, 1989; Wilkes, Belsher, Rush, Frank, & Associates, 1994), and primarily include the following:

- *Absolutist or all-or-nothing or black-and-white thinking*: evaluating events in highly dichotomous or radical ways such as good or bad or never or always
- *Arbitrary inference or jumping to conclusions*: making a conclusion not supported by evidence or making a conclusion contrary to support-ing evidence
- *Catastrophization*: assuming irrationally terrible and uncontrollable negative consequences from an event
- *Fortune-telling*: predicting future events, often as negative, without sufficient evidence to do so
- *Labeling*: defining a situation or someone's personality by one event or behavior
- *Magnification*: evaluating a situation as much worse than is true
- *Mind Reading*: mistakenly assuming what others are thinking in gen-eral and about oneself in particular
- *Minimization or discounting the positive*: evaluating a positive or neu-tral situation as negative, trivial, or one to be dismissed
- *Negative filtering or dark glasses*: Focusing much more on the negative than the neutral or positive aspects of a situation
- *Overestimating*: expecting that the chances of a negative outcome in an event are much higher than is true
- *Overgeneralization*: making an overall conclusion from one and not many events
- *Personalization*: mistakenly assuming that external events are caused by oneself, which may lead to self-blame for events not within one's control
- *Selective abstraction*: selectively attending to or remembering one, possibly negative or trivial detail and ignoring the context or "big picture" of a situation
- *Should statements*: mistaken assumptions about the way the world should work or the way one should be, which may create needlessly high standards of behavior

When self-monitoring, a youth can be asked to provide a list of his or her thoughts in anxiety-provoking situations. From this list, which can be augmented by formal assessment material, a therapist can help the youth match thoughts to different cognitive distortion categories. With practice, the youth should be able to categorize his or her thoughts and identify which distortions, if any, are being made. Negative but *realistic* thoughts should not be altered. Youths with more limited cognitive development will, of course, require greater help from the therapist during these procedures. For example, a child could be shown a cartoon of children interacting and asked to complete thought bubbles above their heads. Once a youth is generally proficient at identifying distortions, the following procedures to control or modify such distortions can be implemented.

Examining the Evidence for and Against Specific Thoughts

A common technique for modifying the cognitive distortions of socially anxious youths is to examine the actual evidence for and against specific thoughts (Beck et al., 1979; Friedberg & McClure, 2002). To do so, a therapist may write a child's thought on paper or a writing board and draw two columns: evidence for and evidence against. The therapist and youth then explore pieces of *actual* evidence that do or do not support the thought. Important questions in this process are "What is the evidence?" and "What other evidence might there be?" Socratic questioning in this and other cognitive therapy techniques is common.

For example, a child may enter a room, see others snickering, and assume that the others are laughing at him and dislike him. The therapist may begin by asking "What is the evidence for your thought that the others were laughing at you and dislike you?" Supporting evidence may be found in the proximity of the two events: the child entered the room and the others happened to be laughing at the same time. The next question could be "What other evidence might there be, or what other reasons might the boys have been laughing?" The youth may initially need some help answering the question, but alternative explanations include a coincidence, the others were laughing at a joke or something else in the room, or the others were just being silly. In addition, very weak beliefs such as the one that others necessarily dislike the child should be fully exposed and dissected.

Decatastrophizing

Related to examining evidence is the technique of *decatastrophizing*, or assuming the worst-case scenario and fully exploring whether the scenario is as bad as the youth believes (Beck et al., 1979; Eisen & Kearney, 1995; Friedberg & McClure, 2002). In the above example, the child may believe that because others are laughing, he or she will experience substantial embarrassment and social isolation as a result. By asking, "What if this did happen?," the therapist explores the core issues of the child's social fear and exposes them as less stressful then the child might think. For example, even if the child did feel substantial embarrassment, all people have this experience at some time and the feeling is usually manageable and temporary. The child's past feelings of embarrassment can be helpful for illustrative purposes as well. Regarding the child's other thought: even if the other youths truly did not like him or her, he or she can still develop friendships with many of the other hundreds of children at school.

Dispute handles, or questions that a child can ask internally when anxious, may be used when examining evidence and decatastrophizing. Examples adapted from Kearney and Albano (2000) include:

- Am I absolutely sure this will happen?
- What is the worst/best/most realistic thing that will happen?
- Do I really know what that person is thinking?
- Have I been in a situation like this one before, and was it really that bad?
- If I am not perfect in this situation, then so what?
- Am I the only person that has ever had to deal with this situation?

Over time, the child practices this technique in anxiety-provoking situations to habitually examine all relevant explanations for a given event and not simply negative ones. In addition, methods of coping with potentially disastrous situations should be explored and perhaps integrated with social skills training (see below) and exposure-based practices (see Chapter 9). As such, a child can realize that negative consequences are not as durable or catastrophic as he or she initially believed.

COGNITIVE SELF-CONTROL

Cognitive self-control procedures are often used in conjunction with the above techniques and similarly focus on identifying problematic cognitions and using covert verbalizations to control anxious apprehension. Two popular cognitive self-control models have been developed. One is Kendall and colleagues' (1992) FEAR technique:

- F—*Feeling* frightened? (child recognizes anxious physical feelings in a given situation)
- E—*Expecting* bad things to happen? (child recognizes anxious apprehension and problematic thoughts)
- A—*Actions and attitudes* that will help (child considers different problem-solving-oriented coping behaviors and statements to manage anxiety)

- R—*Results and rewards* (child evaluates his or her anxiety management in the situation and engages in self-reinforcement as appropriate)

Another is Silverman and colleagues' (Silverman & Kurtines, 1996) STOP technique:

- S—Are you feeling *Scared*? (child recognizes fear or anxiety in a given situation)
- T—What are you *Thinking*? (child identifies problematic thoughts)
- O—*Other*, helpful coping thoughts? (child generates coping thoughts and behaviors)
- P—*Praise* and *Plan* for next time (child evaluates his or her anxiety management in the situation, engages in self-reinforcement as appropriate, and considers changes for the next time)

Both approaches may be used to organize cognitive therapy with youths. In addition, both are highly applicable to younger children who may not fully grasp formal examination of evidence and decatastrophization.

DECENTERING

Youths with social phobia often focus heavily on their anxiety-based physical feelings and thoughts and assume that others can readily note their nervousness. In essence, they become highly egocentric about their anxiety and worry that others are judging them harshly. To counter this belief, two decentering practices may be useful (Corsini & Wedding, 2000). The first involves discussions with a youth about how he or she perceives others in social or performance-based situations. For example, the youth can be asked about how he or she perceives or judges someone who makes a mistake during a speech, slips a bit at a music recital, or drops a spoon while eating in a restaurant. Typically, most youths say they pay little attention to these things, forget them rather quickly, or attribute the behaviors to common nervousness that passes. The point to be made is that others are likely judging the youth in a similar, benign fashion.

During this process, the point should also be emphasized that anxiety-based physical feelings and thoughts are not generally visible to others. Sometimes decentering can be integrated with real-life examples such as walking across a school campus or eating in a restaurant. While doing so with the child, the therapist can highlight how others are mostly engrossed in their own activities and are paying relatively little attention to the child. Videotaping an audience during some performance by the child and then showing their general lack of reaction may also be helpful in this regard.

A second decentering practice is to have a child view situations from a different perspective. For example, the child could be asked about what he or she might say to someone who was nervous during and after an oral presentation. Most children say they would probably comfort the other child, tell him or her that the anxiety was not all that noticeable, point out that other people did not care too much about the anxiety, and tell the person that he or she likely did better than believed. Other children say they would share their own anxiety experiences and explain that everyone gets nervous at some time. Most children, especially those with social phobia, are not critical of others. Of course, the general point to this practice is to have the child understand that these comforting statements are generally what *others* are thinking when the *child* is in certain social or performance situations.

REATTRIBUTION TRAINING

Reattribution training may also be helpful for some youths with social phobia. This technique, often used for youths with depression, initially involves identifying attributions of failure in a given situation that are internal, global, and stable in nature (Braswell & Kendall, 1988; Carr, 2002). A youth may perform poorly during an oral presentation, for example, and subsequently attribute perceived failure to internal (e.g., "I am stupid"), global (e.g., "I cannot speak well in front of *anyone*"), and stable (e.g., "I'll *never* be able to do this") factors that maintain social anxiety.

Alternative, more optimistic attributions can then be developed. Specifically, a child could be encouraged to identify evidence that fits external, specific, and unstable attributions. Regarding the above example, a child could recognize external factors that contributed to the problem (e.g., "I was not given enough time to finish"), evidence of specificity (e.g., "This was just one presentation, and I have done well in others"), and the possibility or likelihood of instability (e.g., "I know I can do better next time"). Of course, reattributions should only be encouraged when evidence truly warrants them.

REFRAMING/RELABELING

Reframing or relabeling involves substituting more adaptive contexts, definitions, or explanations of a given situation for maladaptive or negative ones (Wilkes et al., 1994). This often involves using a positive way to describe a situation or goal rather than a negative way. This technique is common to family therapy, such as when a child's temper tantrums (negative construct) are reframed or relabeled as a means of communicating or seeking attention from parents (positive construct). The technique is also common to therapy for youths with disruptive behavior, such as redefining a "negative" treatment goal such as decreasing out-of-seat behavior to a "positive" one such as increasing in-seat behavior. More specifically for youths with social phobia, for example, mistakes or difficulty in a social or performance situation could be reframed or relabeled as "a good try," "important exposure practice," "normal behavior," or a prelude to "a better performance next time."

BEHAVIORAL EXPERIMENTS

Behavioral experiments are useful for testing the validity of distortions related to overestimating negative events (Kendall et al., 1992). Initially, a child may be asked to state the probability that some predefined negative event will occur in a certain situation. For example, the child may be asked to gauge the probability that an acquaintance will hang up during a telephone conversation. For some youths with social phobia, these probabilities are grossly inflated and sometimes in the range of 70–100%. The therapist then responds with his or her own estimate, which may be around 0–5%. One must ensure, of course, that the true probability of the negative event is not all that high.

The child then engages in some therapeutic homework assignment to test his or her probability (e.g., an actual telephone conversation). The child also reports back to the therapist the outcome of the experiment. Over time and with repetition, the child should realize that his or her estimates of disaster are inflated, and many youths begin to provide estimates that are progressively lower and closer to reality. Of course, the child should also understand that negative events *could* happen. However, the probability is low and the child can likely cope with whatever negative event might take place. Behavioral experiments are especially useful during decentering and exposure-based practices.

SELF-INSTRUCTIONAL TRAINING

Self-instructional training has been utilized for several populations and can be adapted for youths with social phobia by enhancing anxiety management or social skills (Braswell & Kendall, 1988; Meichenbaum, 1977). The therapist may begin this process by modeling coping methods regarding different social and/or performance-based situations. As therapy progresses, the therapist gently prompts the child's appropriate responses through whispers or hand gestures. As therapy progresses even further, children should internalize these prompts by using self-speech or self-instruction.

For example, a child may be quite nervous about entering a classroom full of other children. During early stages of treatment, a therapist can fully describe and prompt the use of somatic control and cognitive exercises to manage anxiety. During middle stages of treatment, the therapist can use subtle hand gestures or index cards with written cues to prompt the child. During later stages of treatment, the child should engage in self-statements that surround what needs to be done (e.g., "I need to breathe regularly"), concentration on the task at hand (e.g., "I need to focus on going to my seat"), handling distractions (e.g., "I must ignore the others and sit down"), and self-reinforcement (e.g., "I did a good job") (adapted from Carr, 2002). This method should begin with low anxiety-provoking situations and progress to more difficult ones, and can be integrated with other anxiety management practices as appropriate.

Cognitive Rehearsal

Cognitive skills should be rehearsed within the context of other techniques for treating social phobia (Eisen & Kearney, 1995). Cognitive skills, for example, can be integrated with somatic control exercises, role plays in social skills training (see below), and exposure-based practices as a child learns to manage anxiety. Such integration must be done, of course, in accordance with a child's cognitive development and motivation.

GROUP AND INDIVIDUAL COGNITIVE THERAPY

Cognitive therapy may be conducted in group settings, and often involves the active participation of members who help identify and modify distortions and develop coping strategies. However, cognitive therapy is not always recommended for group settings because children progress at different paces and because some are often reluctant to share personal thoughts before others. As such, individual cognitive therapy may be best for some youths.

Even within individual therapy, however, many youths have trouble generating thoughts and need considerable help from a therapist. If a youth *is* amenable to cognitive therapy, however, then he or she should be assigned regular homework tasks. These tasks may include identifying and categorizing distortions, utilizing cognitive and behavioral coping methods in anxiety-provoking situations, and rehearsing the cognitive techniques described here.

SOCIAL SKILLS TRAINING

As mentioned in Chapter 2, many youths with social phobia have deficient social skills as a result of avoidance or peer exclusion. These youths subsequently experience failure in key social and performance situations and thus avoid even more. Therefore, social skills training is an important treatment component for this population. In this section, the essential elements of social skills training are presented. These elements most commonly include *modeling and coaching, rehearsal and feedback*, and *practice in real-life situations* (Cartledge & Milburn, 1995).

Social skills training should be tailored to a child's exact problems, which may involve failure to *acquire* many social skills, failure to *refine* social skills, or failure to *perform* existing social skills (Gresham, 1998). A specific listing of a child's social skills deficits from formal assessment should be available, and training usually progresses from easier to more difficult or complex skills. In addition, a treatment rationale should be provided to the child and parents, especially with respect to the fact that social skills will result in reinforcement from others, increased friendships, and better quality of life. Good social skills are also an excellent means of coping with stressful situations, and this may be conveyed as well.

Modeling and Coaching

Modeling or vicarious learning is an essential aspect of social skills training, especially for youths who have not acquired many social skills. The therapist, or peers close to a child's age, may serve as a model for key skills such as greeting others, smiling, starting and maintaining conversations and friendships, listening to others, establishing eye contact and articulation, joining groups, being assertive, speaking on the telephone, performing before others, exiting social situations gracefully, maintaining appropriate appearance, and minimizing inappropriate behaviors (Beidel & Turner, 1998; Eisen & Kearney, 1995). However, other skills that are unique to a particular youth would obviously be targeted as well.

The process begins by having a youth observe a live model execute a specific social or performance behavior, although symbolic modeling methods may be used as well (Cartledge & Milburn, 1995). A detailed discussion of the modeled skill should follow, and the youth may be encouraged to ask and answer questions about various aspects of the enactment. Such modeling may recur several times so the youth fully understands what is being emphasized and expected. In fact, different models may be introduced to show different nuances and methods of successfully executing a specific skill.

For children who have social skills that need refinement, *coaching* may be a useful procedure. Instead of establishing a live or symbolic model, the therapist uses verbal instruction to coach a child to alter his or her behavior in subtle ways. A child who mumbles during a formal presentation, for example, can be instructed to articulate better and establish more eye contact with the audience. Use of social skills board games can also be helpful in this regard.

Rehearsal and Feedback

The fundamental component of social skills training is behavior *rehearsal*. This requires a youth to actually practice the social or performance skill that has been modeled or coached. However, such practice should be done in a protective therapeutic setting that is controlled by the therapist and not subject to negative consequences (Gresham, 1998). Rehearsal may take the form of *covert responding* in which a child imagines engaging in certain appropriate social behaviors, *verbal responding* in which he or she states aloud what appropriate social behaviors should be displayed, and *motor responding* in which he or she physically practices or role plays a specific social or performance skill (Bandura, 1977). Regarding youths with social phobia, the latter should be emphasized.

As the child rehearses key social and performance behaviors, the therapist and relevant others provide *feedback* about which behaviors need modification and additional practice. Audiotaping or videotaping behavior rehearsals is invaluable in this regard as a therapist can illustrate areas that need improvement on a frame-by-frame basis. An important aspect of feedback is to give the child extensive reinforcement for his or her efforts and improvement. In addition, questions can be asked of the child about what happened during the role play, and youths should be able to engage in self-evaluation and identify and correct problems more readily over time. In general, one social skill per session should be emphasized, although that particular social skill can be practiced in different settings and across different scenarios (Beidel & Turner, 1998).

Practice in Real-Life Situations

Once a child becomes proficient at a particular social or performance skill, he or she may be asked to practice the skill outside of the office during a therapy session or to complete homework assignments designed to practice the skill in more natural situations. Regarding the former, for example, we often bring a child to nearby places and require him or her to practice a particular skill on unwitting others. The child may, for example, be required to ask others for directions, order food in a restaurant, greet others during a walk, engage in small talk with someone in line, or deliberately make mistakes when purchasing something and then skillfully correct the mistake. This process is repeated often and can progress to more difficult and independent scenarios over time.

Homework assignments may also be given so that the child must practice a particular social or performance skill in settings more representative of his or her daily life. Examples include telephoning acquaintances, answering the door at home, or giving an oral presentation before a class at school. Often these homework assignments are integrated with exposure-based practices, so the child may not engage in this step until he or she is ready for such exposures. Homework assignments are graduated so that easier ones precede more difficult ones. During each treatment session, the child reports back to the therapist about successes as well as problems that need to be addressed.

Generalization of social skills training must also take place and requires the use of varied settings and circumstances as well as practice in difficult situations. For example, a child could practice handling a situation where others are truly laughing at his or her mistake. Hypothetical scenarios could also be presented to the child to see whether he or she develops appropriate responses. Finally, specific areas of concern that the child expects in the near future can be discussed. Many children, for example, are particularly worried about the start of a new school year. Extensive practice of social and performance skills that are pertinent to this scenario (e.g., asking for help, initiating conversations and small talk, making friends) can then be emphasized.

Contingency management (see Chapter 7) should be closely linked to social skills training and later generalization. For example, parents should reward a child for engaging in new social skills, practicing these skills in different situations, and complying with parent requests to complete daily activities that require greater social interaction and performance before others. Parents can also discourage or even punish behaviors that compete with adaptive social interactions. Examples include avoidance, escape, noncompliance, and aggression.

GROUP AND INDIVIDUAL SOCIAL SKILLS TRAINING

Social skills training is especially amenable to group settings because all members can actively participate as observers, models, and actors in role plays. Potential problems, however, include differential skill levels among participants, rigid cognitive styles, excessive avoidance, and failure to develop and generalize a particular skill (Beidel & Turner, 1998). As such, groups may be kept small and targeted skills should be tailored closely to each child's individual deficits.

Individual therapy may be preferred when a child has severe social phobia. In fact, individual therapy may be a useful prelude to group therapy. If individual therapy is preferred, then treatment should still involve others who are familiar and unfamiliar to the child. In addition, an emphasis should be placed on extensive role plays outside of the office and integration with exposure-based practices.

SAMPLE CASE: JULIANNA

Recall from Chapter 7 that Julianna was diagnosed with social phobia and had concurrent subclinical depression and school refusal behavior. Her most anxiety-provoking situations were entering school and class, eating at lunchtime, performing on tests and other academic assignments before others, and playing sports during physical education class. In addition to physical feelings of anxiety, Julianna often had thoughts about possible negative consequences in key situations, especially about vomiting and failure and subsequent ridicule and humiliation. This led to overt and covert avoidance of the activities listed above. Julianna also had good but not excellent social skills, as she bowed her head when speaking to others and often could not be heard audibly.

In conjunction with the procedures mentioned in the previous chapter, Julianna's therapist concentrated on cognitive therapy and social skills training. Much of Julianna's cognitive therapy surrounded a logical examination of evidence regarding possible negative consequences as well as decatastrophization and behavioral experiments. For example, the therapist focused on Julianna's fear of vomiting while in the school cafeteria. Julianna provided evidence for this fear by explaining that she often felt nervous and occasionally nauseous when eating alone there. However, the therapist encouraged Julianna to provide detailed evidence against this fear, which included the fact that she had never vomited in public before, that she would likely be able to make it to the restroom in time even if she was about to vomit (given that she sat near the exit), and that she generally ate foods that were not greasy or prone to be regurgitated.

Julianna also engaged in decatastrophization with the therapist and explored what would happen even if the worst-case scenario came true. Julianna reported that she would feel extremely embarrassed and humiliated, so the therapist concentrated on the fact that such embarrassment would be temporary and manageable. In addition, the therapist engaged in some decentering, asking Julianna how she would feel if she saw some-one else vomit. Julianna said she would feel sympathetic and perhaps help the person to the nurse's office. Although not all youths would react in this way, Julianna did come to understand that many people in the cafe-teria would probably view her with sympathy if she did indeed vomit. Using behavioral experiments, the therapist also asked Julianna to esti-mate the likelihood that she would vomit in the cafeteria on a particular day. As expected, Julianna's percentage estimates were initially inflated but decreased over time. These procedures were later integrated with ex-posures in which Julianna was required to sit in the center of the cafeteria rather than the edge. Cognitive therapy techniques were also extended to Julianna's exaggerated fears of failure when entering school and class and when performing before others.

The therapist also engaged in moderate social skills training to alter some of Julianna's interfering behaviors. For example, she was coached during several in-session role plays to keep her head up and to express herself clearly with proper volume when addressing others. The thera-pist brought in several clinic staff members so that Julianna could practice conversing with different people in this manner. She quickly became profi-cient and was able to maintain a conversation for longer periods of time. As therapy progressed, Julianna was expected to complete homework assign-ments designed to generalize these skills to school activities. For example, Julianna was required to initiate and maintain conversations with acquain-tances and to use appropriate affect.

CHAPTER 9

TREATING YOUTHS WITH SOCIAL ANXIETY AND SOCIAL PHOBIA

EXPOSURE-BASED PRACTICES

The previous two chapters covered the primary techniques designed to facilitate the most critical psychological treatment element for youths with social anxiety and social phobia: *exposure-based practices*. By the time a child reaches this point in therapy, he or she should be proficient at monitoring anxiety-based symptoms, managing aversive physical feelings, identifying and modifying irrational thoughts (if applicable), and practicing social and assertiveness skills with ease (at least within a comfortable therapeutic environment). In addition, parents should be proficient in contingency management procedures, and all relevant family members should clearly understand the rationale and nature of treatment. Proficiency at other skills, such as communication or contract development, may also be necessary by this point. Insufficient development of any of these key skills may seriously impair the effectiveness of exposure-based practices. Therefore, an in-depth evaluation of treatment progress, necessary refinement of skills, and careful minimization of treatment obstacles are recommended at this time.

The purpose of this chapter is to describe the primary aspects of exposure-based practices for youths with social anxiety and social phobia. Exposure in this context essentially refers to confronting social and/or evaluative stimuli that a child fears, or is otherwise distressed by, and that a child avoids or escapes. In doing so, the child is expected to practice the skills described previously to manage anxiety. In this chapter, the potential mechanisms of action, forms, and steps regarding exposure-based practices are described. Individual and group exposure therapy is also discussed, and obstacles to exposure treatment are covered throughout. An extension of the sample case from Chapter 7 (Julianna) is provided as well.

MECHANISMS OF ACTION OF EXPOSURE

The mechanisms of action traditionally thought to underlie exposure primarily include habituation, extinction, and reciprocal inhibition. In the context of phobia treatment, *habituation* refers to a weakened fear/anxiety response to a stimulus when that stimulus is presented repeatedly (Mackintosh, 1987). For example, a person's physiological arousal around dogs may decrease as he or she frequently comes into contact with dogs. In related fashion, *extinction* in this context refers to a weakened fear/anxiety response to a stimulus when that stimulus is linked to a lack of aversive consequences (Mowrer, 1960). For example, a person's fear of dogs may decrease when his or her fear is no longer associated with negative outcomes when around dogs for an extended period of time. *Reciprocal inhibition* refers to a weakened fear/anxiety response to a stimulus when some antagonistic response is learned and practiced during the response (Wolpe, 1990). For example, a person's fear of dogs may decrease as he or she practices relaxation training in the presence of dogs.

These and other explanations for exposure mechanisms of action remain popular, but have been criticized on several grounds, including the prominent fact that many people experience fear even with repeated exposures to a stimulus (Craske, 1999). Newer mechanism of action theories surround a person's *beliefs* that a certain stimulus is dangerous, that anxious responses to the stimulus will persist and increase indefinitely, and that horrible outcomes will occur when faced with the stimulus (see also Chapter 3). Successful exposure thus provides *new* information that is incompatible with these perceptions and expectancies: the stimulus is not dangerous, anxiety reactions are time-limited and manageable, and horrible outcomes will not occur.

Exposure may provide some short-term anxiety reduction via habituation. In the long run, however, successful exposure treatment may require the development of more *realistic* perceptions or expectancies and beneficial emotional processing that facilitates a return to normal functioning (Bouchard, Mendlowitz, Coles, & Franklin, 2004; Foa & Kozak, 1986; Rachman, 1980). *Perceived self-efficacy*, or a confident understanding that one can successfully cope with a feared stimulus, is likely crucial for successful exposure treatment as well (Bandura, 1977). Exposure for treating social phobia, therefore, may concentrate on habituation, development of new associations between social/evaluative stimuli and positive or realistic expectancies/outcomes, constructive emotional processing, and a heightened sense of self-efficacy in social/evaluative situations.

FORMS OF EXPOSURE

Mechanisms of action of exposure are quite varied, and so are its forms. These forms primarily include spaced versus massed, assisted versus independent, and imaginal versus in vivo exposure. *Spaced exposure* refers to periodically confronting a feared stimulus along a graded hierarchy, whereas *massed exposure* or flooding refers to confronting a feared stimulus at a high intensity level for one extended period of time (e.g., Marshall, 1985). Massed exposure is less time-consuming, of course, but not always the best choice for young children, those with extreme anxiety, those with chronic anxiety problems, or those with anxieties about social/evaluative situations (Kearney & Albano, 2000). Therefore, spaced exposure is emphasized in this chapter.

Assisted or *modeled exposure* refers to having a child confront a stimulus with someone else. Typically, the other person is a therapist, parent, older relative, or friend. Assisted exposure allows children to receive support and feedback from someone they trust and to observe an effective model who manages a difficult situation with calm and aplomb (Ritter, 1968). Assisted exposures are generally recommended in the early sessions of exposure-based treatment for children. Assisted *interoceptive* exposure, where one confronts anxiety-provoking *internal* stimuli, may be helpful for some youths as well.

Effective treatment in the long run, however, will likely require more *independent exposures*, or having children practice exposures by themselves. This method accelerates the child's edification that various social/evaluative stimuli are not dangerous, that anxiety reactions can be controlled, that aversive outcomes are not always present, and that avoidance is unnecessary for fear reduction. In addition, this method requires children to practice behaviors that facilitate a return to normal functioning, such as going to school or speaking with peers. In addition, perceived self-efficacy is likely enhanced most during successful independent exposures.

Finally, *imaginal exposure* refers to confronting a stimulus through visual imagery, perhaps as a child discusses his or her fear/anxiety or as a therapist reads an anxiety-provoking story or hypothetical scenario (e.g., Bornstein & Knapp, 1981). Imaginal exposure is typically conducted in-session, directed closely by a therapist, and designed as a prelude to in vivo exposure. *In vivo exposure* refers to confronting an actual stimulus either in-session or in external settings (e.g., Stableford, 1979). Successful exposure treatment, particularly for youths with social phobia, will almost necessarily have to include some degree of in vivo exposure (Garcia-Lopez, Olivares, Turner, et al., 2002).

STEPS OF EXPOSURE

When conducting exposure-based treatment for youths with social anxiety and social phobia, several general steps are typically employed, with some variation. Major steps include psychoeducation about exposure, development of an anxiety/avoidance hierarchy and rating scale, imaginal exposure, assisted or modeled in vivo exposure, and independent in vivo exposure. These steps are described in turn.

PSYCHOEDUCATION ABOUT EXPOSURE

Although a general treatment description and rationale was likely presented early in therapy, providing a new and more detailed summary regarding exposure-based practices is highly recommended at this point. This is because the "heavy lifting" part of therapy is about to begin and will require considerable effort from the child and his or her parents. A complete understanding of why a child must now enter and stay in difficult situations to confront feared/anxious stimuli will facilitate motivation and compliance to do so.

The technical mechanisms of action regarding exposure can be es-chewed in favor of an approach that draws an analogy to skills that the child has already developed. Most children, by the time they enter therapy, have developed basic skills such as riding a bicycle, swimming in a pool, playing a simple song on a musical instrument, or even skiing down a small hill. A discussion with the child about these skills can begin with a description of how he or she performed during the initial stages of learning. Most children report that they fell down frequently, made constant mistakes, and experienced a sense of frustration. Follow-up questioning by the therapist, however, can lead a child to describe the process by which he or she eventually became proficient at the skill. Most of the time, of course, this involved extensive practice, support and feedback from others, and modeling of others prior to independent functioning.

As the child discusses several of these examples, an analogy can be drawn to exposure-based practices. The therapist may convey that managing one's anxiety in different situations is a skill not unlike others mentioned by the child. In fact, the therapist can remind the child that he or she has already learned different skills (e.g., somatic control, cognitive, social) to manage such anxiety, but must now put these skills to use in the "real world." However, just like riding a bicycle, the child will necessarily feel awkward and frustrated in the beginning. Therefore, the therapist and the child's parents will provide substantial support and feedback during early exposure sessions. However, just as the child eventually tried to ride a bicycle independently of others, so too will he or she have to practice managing anxiety alone in key social and evaluative situations.

Questions can be addressed at this point, and the child should understand that exposure will be a gradual process that will proceed at a regular but not overwhelming pace. However, the therapist should also convey that the child will be nudged forward on occasion and will be expected to eventually manage even difficult situations more independently over time. In addition, the therapist can remind the child and parents of the final goals of therapy and indicate that the final steps are now approaching. Expected improvements in the child's/family's quality of life (e.g., more friends, less fear and conflict, full-time school attendance) should be emphasized as well. Extensive rapport, encouragement, and contact with the child at this time are strongly recommended.

DEVELOP AN ANXIETY/AVOIDANCE HIERARCHY
AND RATING SCALE

Following this psychoeducation process, the therapist and child can work together to develop an anxiety/avoidance hierarchy and accompanying rating scale. An *anxiety/avoidance hierarchy* is a list of key social and evaluative situations that range from least to most anxiety-provoking in nature. Items for the hierarchy, which will serve as *targets for the exposures*, can be derived from the child's formal assessment material, daily logbooks, recent verbal statements and areas of avoidance, or a child's endorsement of a list of many hypothetical social and evaluative situations (see Chapter 2 for examples). The hierarchy, the form of which may change several times during therapy, may initially consist of about 5–20 items with a preferred number of about 10.

The child must understand that each item is one that he or she will eventually confront in various forms, including independently. However, many children often need reassurance that their most feared items will not be encountered immediately. Although such reassurance can be given, the child should be reminded that all situations will be confronted in time. Questions about the hierarchy may then be addressed, and any necessary modifications can be made.

To help organize these items, children can employ a rating scale that is developmentally appropriate for them. A common rating scale is 0–10 where 0 = none, 2 = mild, 4 = moderate, 6 = intense, 8 = severe, and 10 = extreme anxiety or avoidance. A thermometer-type scale for younger children may also be helpful. Condensed scales (e.g., 1–3 or 1–5) may also be used but tend to restrict the number of clearly defined hierarchy items. Extended scales (e.g., 0–100) are likely better for adolescents than children. The rating scale used for the hierarchy is often similar to that used for the child's daily logbooks.

Youths are then asked to rate their anxiety level for each item on the hierarchy as well as their level of avoidance, or how often they avoid or wish to avoid a given situation. The therapist then draws the hierarchy along various columns and presents the final version to the youth and his or her parents for review and confirmation of accuracy. An example of an anxiety/avoidance hierarchy for Julianna, the case discussed in previous chapters and later in this chapter, is presented in Table 9.1.

The anxiety/avoidance hierarchy may need extensive modification throughout treatment. Many children, for example, progress well along a hierarchy until one particular item leads to strong resistance. For example, a child may successfully engage in many exposures outside of session and school, but balk when school attendance is required. In these cases, items can be subdivided into smaller steps. For example, some children respond better to a part-time school attendance schedule before proceeding to hierarchy items that require formal performance before others in school. In still other cases, children have multiple facets of social phobia that demand more than one hierarchy. Some, for example, have great difficulties interacting with others *and* performing before others. In this situation, dual hierarchies may be developed to address each element.

IMAGINAL EXPOSURES

Once the hierarchy or hierarchies have been developed, the formal exposure process may begin. As mentioned earlier, *imaginal exposure* is often a prelude to later in vivo exercises. Imaginal exposure is largely a therapist-child interaction, though others can be present as appropriate. To conduct imaginal exposures, the therapist prepares various scenarios that are closely linked to the hierarchy items. The process begins by having the child listen to a scenario closely linked to a low-level hierarchy item. Imaginal exposure is not generally recommended for youths under age 10 years, although imagery training procedures may be helpful for some of these children (Beidel & Turner, 1998).

The scenario chosen by the therapist should be brief but also graphic, detailed, and comprehensive. Worst-case scenarios regarding a particular hierarchy item are emphasized as well so a child fully processes all possible sources and consequences of anxiety. If necessary, however, the therapist may also include statements of the child's ability to effectively cope and manage anxiety and remain in the situation. The goal of imaginal exposure is to have a child listen to an entire anxiety scene and fully process the scene without stopping. An example of an imaginal scene from Julianna's hierarchy follows:

> You are sitting in the school cafeteria for lunch, and the room is crowded with noisy, talkative, and even disruptive students. You were not able to get a seat close to the exit, so you have to sit about three rows away from the exit. You wanted to be alone but instead had to squeeze between two other people. As you try to eat your lunch and read your book, you start to feel nervous about what others are doing and how they might disrupt your lunch. For example, your stomach begins to tighten, you feel a bit sweaty and dizzy, and your heart is beating faster. You start to think about all the bad things that could happen in this situation, including other people watching you and making comments, laughing at the way you are sitting and bowing your head, preventing you from reading your book, and making you feel humiliated, nauseous, and tempted to throw up in the cafeteria. You just want the whole period to end, so you start to eat a little too quickly. As you do, a couple of kids bump into you as they are getting to their seat and the people next to you give you dirty looks. You are feeling really nervous now, and the cafeteria food is greasy and makes your stomach churn. The people around you snicker and you suddenly feel very queasy and sick. You get up quickly to leave but trip over the seat and fall down. By now, everyone is laughing loudly and you become so dizzy that you have trouble standing up. Instead, your stomach heaves and you begin to vomit all over the floor and on people's backpacks. Now, everyone is screaming and yelling at you to leave, which only makes you more nauseous. You feel like you just can't get away from the situation, and start to feel sick again.

Imaginal exposure may begin with somatic control exercises to relax the child and to set the stage for practicing these exercises prior to real-life anxiety-provoking situations. Audiotaping the process is a good idea so the child can practice the imaginal exposures at home. The therapist also explains that the child may raise a hand if his or her anxiety level rises above a certain point on the rating scale previously developed. If the child raises a hand during the exposure, then the therapist temporary halts the description and helps the child lower arousal via somatic control exercises, other relevant therapy skills, and/or thoughts about more pleasant scenes.

Therapists must use good clinical judgment when deciding what anxiety level would halt an exposure, but a rating of 3+ on a 1–5 scale or 6+ on a 0–10 scale may be useful. Once a child's anxiety abates, the therapist can resume describing the imaginal scene. Throughout the scene, the therapist may periodically (e.g., every 30 seconds) ask for anxiety ratings from the youth. This helps the therapist and child later process the exposure, and hopefully provides the youth with evidence that longer endurance in an anxiety-provoking scenario results in greater anxiety reduction. If this is not the case, then easier scenarios may be necessary. If the child does endure the entire scenario, then somatic control exercises may be used to end the session on a relaxing note. Of course, extensive encouragement and praise should be employed throughout this process.

As therapy progresses, the child confronts more difficult, complicated, or anxiety-provoking scenarios that are linked to higher-ranking hierarchy items. In addition, the child can be asked to tolerate increasingly higher levels of anxiety before raising a hand and stopping the procedure. Homework assignments to practice these exposures at home must also be emphasized. Many children progress through imaginal exposures with only occasional difficulty, but others require more time. At least one scenario per session should be completed, but more may be done as feasible and appropriate.

ASSISTED/MODELED IN VIVO EXPOSURES

Once a child has mastered imaginal exposures, then controlled in-session in vivo exposures may be done with the help of a therapist and relevant others such as parents. For younger children, "relevant others" may also include their favorite superheroes who team with them to "attack" anxiety (i.e., *emotive imagery*) (Lazarus & Abramovitz, 1962). As with imaginal exposure, assisted or modeled exposures are initially conducted for easier hierarchy items and later more difficult ones. In my experience, such in-session exposures are often closely linked as well with social skills training goals (see Chapter 8).

Assisted or modeled in vivo exposures may be conducted in stages. Initially, a child may be asked to simply observe a therapist or relevant others perform a task and successfully practice skills to manage anxiety. The next stage requires the child and relevant others to practice the task *together*. Common tasks include introducing oneself, initiating and maintaining a conversation, being assertive, joining a group, entering a room full of people, speaking on the telephone, listening to others, and performing in some way before others (e.g., making an oral presentation, eating, playing a musical instrument). As a child progresses through these team-oriented exposures, he or she may be asked to do so more independently, but with considerable support, feedback, and praise from trusted others. The child is also reminded to use appropriate social and anxiety management skills during these tasks as necessary and appropriate.

Out-of-office assisted/modeled exposures may also be conducted, and often include the therapist and the child attending different places and practicing together various tasks and social and anxiety management skills. Task examples include asking others for directions, handling mistakes when purchasing something, and striking up conversations with strangers. In these early exposures, the child often relies heavily on the therapist or others for support, guidance, and feedback. The child may stop the exposure if anxiety is excessive, but therapists should encourage a child to remain in the situation and practice appropriate skills for as long as possible. Finally, including same-age peers may also be helpful during this process, which makes group therapy often advantageous in this regard. Whatever the format, however, assisted/modeled exposures are usually closely supervised and controlled so that the child likely experiences success.

Homework assignments in this regard are also assigned. Typically, parents are asked to engage in exposures with their child that mimic those conducted in-session. Critical to this process, however, is the parents' understanding that the child should not be rescued from the exposure prematurely. Instead, parents should demonstrate to the child (as the therapist did) how to handle the anxiety-provoking situation *without* protecting the child from anxiety. In fact, parents may need to be reminded that the child's experience of anxiety is necessary for exposure to work. If helpful, parents can be reminded as well of the original rationale and mechanism of action for exposure.

Interoceptive exposure may also be integrated with assisted/modeled exposures. Interoceptive exposure refers to confronting fearful *internal* stimuli such as heart palpitations, dizziness, and shortness of breath (Craske et al., 2000). In this procedure, a person is exposed to internal stimuli in-session and then asked to lower arousal via somatic control exercises. Exposure examples include running up a flight of stairs to increase heart rate, spinning in a swivel chair to induce dizziness, and breathing through a coffee straw to produce shortness of breath. In each case, the person learns that the symptoms are not dangerous and that they can be controlled. While not used extensively for anxious children, interoceptive conditioning may be particularly useful for adolescents with clearly defined panic attacks in social and/or evaluative situations.

In general, assisted or modeled exposures are especially useful for children who are younger, cannot tolerate a faster therapy pace, and/or have extreme levels of anxiety. In addition, assisted/modeled exposures are usually a good prelude to independent in vivo exposures or as a "bridge" between imaginal and independent in vivo exposures. The exposures are also useful for very difficult hierarchy items that a child strongly resists confronting. As with imaginal exposure, however, assisted/modeled exposures may need to be subdivided as necessary for a child to proceed systematically.

INDEPENDENT IN VIVO EXPOSURES

Once a child has successfully navigated through various assisted or modeled exposures, more *independent in vivo exposures* are conducted. This step involves having the child independently confront various anxiety-provoking social and evaluative tasks from his or her hierarchy. In many cases, independent in vivo exposures are first aligned with assisted or modeled exposures. For example, a child may ask a stranger for directions without help from the therapist, who is still several steps away. However, *later* independent in vivo exposures will necessarily involve *contrived* tasks that cannot or should not include a therapist's presence (e.g., oral presentation in a school classroom; eating in the cafeteria) and *non-contrived* tasks that develop without warning (e.g., accidentally bumping into someone in a hallway; spontaneous conversations with peers).

As with previous exposures, independent in vivo exposures must involve active practice of social and anxiety management skills. Because a child must practice these skills *and* confront a situation independently, initial exposures should involve ones that have a very high probability of success (i.e., little desire for escape). In this way, the child's motivation and perceived self-efficacy are enhanced. Movement up different treatment hierarchies can then proceed. In addition, all appropriate efforts during exposures should be amply rewarded by others, although the child should be encouraged to engage in substantial *self-reinforcement* as well upon a successful exposure. Children should also be encouraged to linger in an exposure even several minutes *after* anxiety has completely abated to ensure its effectiveness and to build self-efficacy. Extensive practice and repetition of exposures is also recommended for complete emotional processing.

As a child engages in independent exposures, he or she should supply ratings of anxiety and desired avoidance every 30–60 seconds. This information is then shared with the therapist to process whether anxiety is truly declining during the exposure. If so, the child is praised and shown again that remaining in a difficult situation and handling it appropriately will lower anxiety and is a better approach than avoidance or escape. However, problems may occur. Some children, for example, report declining anxiety levels to simply escape a given situation. Conversely, some children report *increasing* levels of anxiety or *spikes* of anxiety at intermittent times of the exposure. Here, the child either is not ready for exposure treatment, in which case previous techniques should be reemphasized, or the child is not ready for that particular hierarchy item. If the latter is so, then designing a slightly less challenging exposure may be in order. Once a child masters this less challenging exposure, however, he or she is expected to proceed as before.

Between-session homework assignments are obviously crucial for independent in vivo exposures, and should involve as many situations as possible to ensure generalization of treatment effects. As treatment progresses, increasingly difficult and complicated tasks are assigned. In general, at least one exposure task per session can be completed, although more can be addressed as appropriate. In addition, near the end of therapy, a child may be asked to respond to hypothetical anxiety-provoking scenarios to evaluate his or her anxiety management skills and to anticipate any future problems.

For all exposure-based practices, but especially independent in vivo exposures, *safety signals and subtle avoidance behaviors must be eliminated.* Some youths, for example, will attend school as long as their best friend is with them. Tasks to eliminate this safety signal might thus involve attending classes without that friend and developing new friendships. Recall from Julianna's case that one of her subtle avoidance behaviors was sitting near an exit in case she felt nauseous. A good exposure here might thus include sitting in the middle of the cafeteria surrounded by others. All *distractions* that a child uses for subtle avoidance must be identified and eliminated during exposure treatment as well to enhance full emotional processing. Distraction examples include switching scenes during imaginal exposure or repeating irrelevant words silently to oneself during in vivo exposure.

INDIVIDUAL VERSUS GROUP EXPOSURE

Exposure-based practices may be conducted in individual or group format. A clear advantage of group therapy, of course, is that similar-aged peers are readily available for formal and informal (e.g., break time) exposures. As mentioned in Chapter 6, the process of *double exposures*, whereby youths with social phobia participate in exposures designed for other youths with social phobia (Albano & Barlow, 1996), is a key group treatment ingredient for this population. A potential risk of group-based exposure therapy, however, is that some members will not progress at the same rate as their groupmates and will feel even more isolated as a result.

In addition, for some children, particularly those with more severe or co-morbid symptomatology such as depression/suicidality or school refusal behavior, individual exposure therapy may be more appropriate. However, successful therapy in this regard will still require comprehensive exposures that involve many social interactions and performances before others.

SAMPLE CASE: JULIANNA

Julianna had progressed well during her early stages of therapy, but was clearly very nervous about the upcoming exposure-based practices. As a result, her therapist devoted one entire session to psychoeducation and addressing Julianna's concerns. Her main concern was having to progress quickly, which she felt would happen given that her parents were pressuring her daily to resume full-time school attendance. The therapist secured an agreement from Julianna's parents and school guidance counselor, however, that a measured exposure regimen would be satisfactory. Still, Julianna was reminded that she was expected to fully complete the exposures at a systematic and adequate pace.

Julianna and her therapist then designed *two* anxiety/avoidance hierarchies. The first (see Table 9.1) involved the primary social/evaluative activities that made Julianna most anxious, and these were arranged from least to most anxiety- and avoidance-provoking in nature. Interestingly, Julianna's ratings did not completely match with what she had said during

TABLE 9.1. Julianna's Initial Anxiety and Avoidance Hierarchy

Situations or places that scare me	Anxiety rating	Avoidance rating
Eating lunch in the school cafeteria	9	9
Playing sports in physical education class	9	8
Starting conversations with others	9	8
Calling someone unknown on the telephone	8	8
Oral presentations before others in class	8	7
Taking tests in class	8	7
Walking along a crowded hallway at school	7	6
Walking into class	7	5
Walking into the school building	7	5
Maintaining conversations with others	5	5
Going to assemblies at school	4	4
Riding the school bus to and from school	3	3
Calling someone known on the telephone	2	2
Answering the door at home	2	1
Speaking to extended relatives at home	1	1

the earlier assessment, which often happens among youths. For example, eating in the cafeteria was now rated worse than playing sports in physical education class. In addition, Julianna added some items such as starting conversations with others and calling someone unknown on the telephone. Also interesting was the fact that *maintaining* conversations with others was rated as less anxiety- and avoidance-provoking than *starting* conversations with others. As the therapist later discovered, however, this was primarily due to a subtle avoidance behavior on Julianna's part.

Exposure treatment began imaginally, but Julianna handled various scenarios with ease. Treatment then shifted quickly to assisted/modeled exposures that initially intersected with her social skills training. For example, Julianna was asked to repeat in-session what she had learned earlier, especially with respect to using good eye contact and voice volume when speaking with or to others. Once this mini-review was complete, the therapist enlisted a few clinic staff members to listen to Julianna's oral presentations. With practice, she was gradually able to handle more people in the room as well as people who were instructed to behave somewhat rudely during her presentation.

Julianna was also expected to have conversations with same-age peers who were presented by the therapist to speak with her. The therapist noted two interesting facts. First, Julianna had enormous difficulty making small talk to initiate a conversation, so considerable practice was placed on this skill as well as proper introductions, smiling, and anxiety control when doing so. Second, the therapist saw that Julianna maintained her conversations with others by simply asking questions about the other person and deflecting attention away from herself. This subtle avoidance behavior was identified for Julianna, who did not realize what she was doing, and she was instructed to engage in more conversation about herself or a neutral topic.

In-session assisted/modeled exposures also required Julianna to walk into the clinic alone, walk in clinic hallways when other people were present, and walk into a room full of people who then looked at her. Julianna was also asked to call clinic staff members on the telephone. Throughout these exposures, the therapist gently guided Julianna to practice whatever skill was most appropriate for that situation. Often this involved subtle control of physical anxiety symptoms and extensive cognitive restructuring to stay in a certain situation. Outside the office, Julianna and her therapist also engaged in exposures that involved riding a bus, playing a pick-up basketball game at a local playground, and sitting in a large crowd (to simulate assemblies).

Julianna's second anxiety/avoidance hierarchy involved number of classes attended at school, and this overlapped with the beginning of independent in vivo exposures. Julianna was asked to pick three school classes that were easiest for her to attend. She did so and successfully attended those classes. In doing so, Julianna practiced many of the tasks on her hierarchy, such as walking into school and class. Each subsequent week, Julianna was told to add one class to her schedule. Not surprisingly, she chose those classes that involved little chance of having to perform before others. Physical education and English classes and lunchtime were the last to be added.

Working closely with the teachers, the therapist established methods for gradually reintroducing Julianna to these latter classes. During physical education class, for example, Julianna initially observed games that were being played, then participated in one-on-one games, and later participated in larger groups. During English class, Julianna was permitted to conduct makeup oral presentations before the teacher only, but was later expected to present orally before her peers. During lunchtime, Julianna was asked to sit one row closer to the middle of the cafeteria per week until she could sit without anxiety in the center of the room. During each exposure, Julianna practiced her anxiety management and social skills and provided anxiety ratings for the therapist. Although several exposures were less than successful, Julianna eventually experienced a general decline in her anxiety in these situations. Her sense of self-efficacy and mood improved greatly as well.

When full-time school attendance was achieved, Julianna wanted to end the therapy program. However, the therapist pointed out that long-term treatment effectiveness would depend heavily on Julianna's ability to develop and maintain some close friendships. Therefore, she was given a list of extracurricular activities and asked to choose at least three to join. With some reluctance, Julianna chose a choir group, a swim club, and a tutoring program where she could help peers with homework. Although her swim club attendance was problematic, she did faithfully attend the other groups and develop a few close friends as a result.

Chapter 10

PREVENTION, DIFFICULT CASES, AND FUTURE DIRECTIONS

Previous chapters concentrated on important clinical processes that occur following the identification of youths with social anxiety or social phobia. In this chapter, however, a summary is presented of the emerging field of prevention with respect to childhood anxiety disorders in general and social phobia in particular. Specifically, an emphasis will be placed on general and relapse prevention. In addition, recommendations are made for addressing difficult cases of childhood social phobia, including cases that involve extensive comorbidity, intense symptomatology, noncompliance, and desires for early termination. Finally, future directions are covered in the area of childhood anxiety disorders in general and social phobia in particular.

GENERAL PREVENTION OF CHILDHOOD ANXIETY DISORDERS AND SOCIAL PHOBIA

To address childhood social anxiety and social phobia, most researchers have focused on intevention, but some investigators have begun to explore prevention-based efforts as well. Evolving prevention efforts in this area will likely focus on key risk factors for anxiety, including genetic predisposition, behavioral inhibition and other temperaments, threat-based cognitions, anxious-resistant attachment, parental psychopathology

169

and certain childrearing behaviors, stressful life events, poor social support and coping skills, and salient sociocultural factors, among others (Donovan & Spence, 2000) (see also Chapter 3). In related fashion, Spence (2001) outlined several groups that seem to be at particular risk for developing anxiety disorders. These groups include children with emerging anxiety symptomatology, children born to parents with anxiety and/or faulty childrearing styles, children with problematic attachment and temperaments (i.e., behavioral inhibition and/or negative affect/neuroticism and/or low effortful control), and children exposed to frequent trauma and/or difficult life transitions.

Spence (1994, 2001) outlined as well an integrated developmental model for preventing childhood anxiety disorders, with special emphasis on tailoring various techniques to different phases of an at-risk child's lifespan. Some prevention techniques could apply to *all* phases of a child's lifespan, of course, and may include counseling during problematic times (e.g., trauma, divorce), developing coping skills, and preparing a child for upcoming difficult events (e.g., movement to a new school). Prevention techniques during pre-birth and infancy periods would obviously concentrate on parents and could include training to improve parenting skills as well as treatment for existing parental psychopathology. For older children and adolescents, prevention efforts may focus on parent-based contingency management, family-based communication and problem-solving skills training, environment-based reduction of trauma, and child-based techniques for enhancing adjustment to new situations, understanding the difference between dangerous and nondangerous situations, and managing somatic, cognitive, and behavioral aspects of anxiety.

Investigators have begun to explore early intervention and prevention programs for youths with anxiety disorders. A prominent example was a controlled trial conducted by Dadds and colleagues (1997), who initially screened 1786 youths aged 7–14 years via child self-report measures and teacher information. Later screening was done to exclude youths with disruptive behaviors and, via structured diagnostic interview, to identify youths with subclinical features of an anxiety disorder. A minority of youths had features of social phobia. Youths were then assigned to an intervention (n = 61) or a simple monitoring/control (n = 67) group.

The intervention consisted of 10 group sessions held weekly at the childrens' schools, and included child-based cognitive-behavioral techniques to manage somatic, cognitive, and behavioral anxiety responses as well as parent-based psychoeducation, contingency management procedures, and strategies to manage parental anxiety. Youths in the prevention program progressed toward a formal anxiety disorder in only 16% of cases compared to 54% in the control group. These results did not translate well to changes on child self-report measures, however. At two-year follow-up, Dadds and colleagues (1999) reported that formal anxiety disorder was present in 20% of the intervention group and 39% of the control group. The authors concluded that a brief intervention for youths with mild to moderate anxiety symptoms can be effective for preventing more debilitating future problems.

Prevention efforts such as this one have largely focused on children with a wide variety of anxiety symptoms and not youths with specific features of one disorder per se. Some have successfully targeted very young children with *anxious-withdrawn* behavior using parent-based strategies (e.g., LaFreniere & Capuano, 1997), but future work will need to target youths with features of social phobia. Such work will likely parallel the general cognitive-behavioral child- and parent-based procedures described in this book and elsewhere. Several authors have outlined other areas of future preventative work as well, including the need to examine (1) universal prevention strategies (as opposed to secondary, at-risk approaches), (2) children of various ages and developmental levels, (3) multivaried sources of information, (4) techniques that are tailored to individual child characteristics, (5) cost-effectiveness, (6) utility and funding of prevention versus intervention, (7) various prevention targets (e.g., anxiety versus many behavior problems), and (8) appropriate assessment devices to identify youths most in need of prevention programs (Barrett & Turner, 2004; Donovan & Spence, 2000; Ferdinand, Barrett, & Dadds, 2004; Spence, 2001).

RELAPSE PREVENTION OF CHILDHOOD ANXIETY DISORDERS AND SOCIAL PHOBIA

Although much work remains with respect to *general* prevention of anxiety in children, more attention has been paid to *relapse* prevention for individual cases. Relapse prevention in this context refers to techniques designed to help youths and parents maintain the skills they have learned in therapy to appropriately address future anxiety-provoking situations and to prevent regression to a poor level of functioning. Again, work in this area has generally targeted youths with anxiety disorders in general and less so youths with social phobia per se. As with general prevention, however, parallels between these two populations can be drawn for relapse prevention.

Relapse prevention efforts generally occur late in the therapy process as a child and family members approach their final treatment goals. However, children and parents should be relatively proficient at whatever skills were emphasized during treatment prior to detailed discussions of relapse prevention and termination. For example, the child should be functioning at a high level that involves managing anxiety effectively, demonstrating good social skills, and entering and remaining in many difficult social and evaluative situations. As mentioned in Chapter 9, however, relapse prevention efforts can overlap in some cases with later exposures from a child's anxiety/avoidance hierarchy. Pertinent relapse prevention techniques for youths with social phobia include:

- Addressing slips and relapse
- Presenting hypothetical scenarios of future problematic situations
- Issuing formal reminders of skills to manage anxiety
- Developing structured routines and activities
- Monitoring social anxiety regularly
- Providing booster sessions

ADDRESSING SLIPS AND RELAPSE

Slips refer to small problems that may spawn minor regression from final treatment status and limited interference in daily functioning (Brownell, Marlatt, Lichtenstein, & Wilson, 1986). *Relapse*, however, refers to substantial regression from final treatment status and severe interference in daily functioning (Kearney, 2001). For youths with social phobia, slips can involve spiked anxiety during one or more social or evaluative situations, overwhelming physical symptoms or irrational cognitions that instigate minor avoidance or escape, temporary refusal to attend school, mild depression, moderate disruptive behaviors to test parental resolve, or transient distance from friends. Given the frequent ebbs and flows of emotions and events in childhood and adolescence, slips are expected and common. As slips become more frequent and intense, however, the risk of formal relapse becomes greater. Family members should be educated about the difference between slips and relapse prior to termination.

The most important way for youths and parents to address slips is to redouble their efforts to practice the therapy skills they learned to manage anxiety and maintain progress. Periodic contact with the therapist for several months after the end of treatment is often helpful in this regard. In addition, reframing may be beneficial. Instead of focusing on the child's new deficits, for example, a therapist can remind family members that some social anxiety is normal and can help them understand that new challenges offer everyone the chance to "brush up" on key aspects of treatment. These key aspects will likely include somatic control exercises, cognitive therapy techniques, further practice of social and assertiveness skills, and more thorough entry into various social and evaluative situations. Should relapse occur, however, then resuming formal treatment may be the best option.

PRESENTING HYPOTHETICAL SCENARIOS OF FUTURE PROBLEMATIC SITUATIONS

Near the end of treatment, a therapist can also introduce hypothetical anxiety-provoking scenarios to see whether youths and/or family members develop appropriate plans to manage anxiety and deter avoidance (see also Chapter 9). These scenarios could involve transitions or special events that will certainly occur in the near future (e.g., new school year, final examinations), but they could also involve new situations that may or may not occur soon (e.g., asking someone on a date). As with imaginal exposure, the therapist can describe a particular situation, ask the child and/or family members to visualize the scene, and solicit general and specific ideas about how everyone would address that situation. Of course, family members would hopefully give detailed answers that are heavily based on the skills they learned in therapy. If someone struggles with the scenario, however, then further practice of skills may be necessary prior to termination.

ISSUING FORMAL REMINDERS OF SKILLS TO MANAGE ANXIETY

Researchers have also designed more formal methods for helping youths remember skills to manage anxiety. Kendall and colleagues (1992), for example, discussed the concept of videotaping a child who has completed treatment and who describes his or her success and methods for managing anxiety and resisting avoidance. In doing so, the child may concentrate on treatment components that were most helpful to him or her. The child can also use the videotape in the future as a formal reminder of what needs to be done in anxiety-provoking situations.

Other methods in this regard involve photographing youths during successful exposures and placing the pictures in an album. This serves as a reminder of what the child has accomplished and increases perceived self-efficacy. In addition, instructions for managing anxiety and avoidance can be written and placed in an obvious spot in the house (e.g., refrigerator door), or reminders can be placed on index cards that the child carries surreptitiously. Of course, the index cards per se must not serve as safety signals to help a child cope with anxiety-provoking situations.

Developing Structured Routines and Activities

Relapse prevention is generally enhanced for this population when a child is on a fairly regular (though not rigid) daily routine. This is especially pertinent to youths with social phobia *and* school refusal behavior. In general, youths should maintain a regular bedtime and morning routine, even on weekends and during vacation times, to reduce the stress associated with new transitions such as going back to school. These routines can also be linked to contingency management procedures so that parents continue to practice appropriate ways of addressing compliance and noncompliance.

Another good method for preventing slips and relapse in this population is to have a child practice social and anxiety management skills in day-to-day situations and during extracurricular activities. Parents may, for example, ask a child to regularly answer the telephone or door, order food in a restaurant, or approach peers at a mall for information. In addition, the child could enroll in various activities that are fun and that require interaction or cooperation with, or performance before, peers and others. In this way, therapy-based skills and exposures are continually practiced, natural social reinforcement from others is received, and friendships will hopefully be developed.

Monitoring Social Anxiety Regularly

For effective relapse prevention, key behaviors should continue to be monitored daily. For youths with social phobia, this may involve general ratings of social anxiety, time missed from school, and severity of somatic complaints, among others. Daily or weekly behavior reports from teachers, as well as observations from relevant others about attempted avoidance or escape, would also be helpful. In this way, spikes in anxiety or other difficulties can be addressed before they create greater problems. Any sudden changes in behavior or attitude may be noteworthy as well.

Providing Booster Sessions

Relapse prevention may be enhanced as well by a therapist's provision of booster sessions during particularly stressful times for a child. Booster sessions allow a therapist to review and enhance key skills learned in treatment and allow a child to articulate his or her current concerns in a comfortable setting. Booster sessions may be conducted individually or with others and can be either very focused on a child's specific concerns at that point or broader in nature to include a more general review of social and anxiety management skills. Booster sessions can be linked to specific stressors that a child is facing (e.g., entry into a new school, SAT) and can even be combined with upcoming, inadvertent exposures (e.g., tour of a new school, practice test). These sessions are particularly useful for reducing anticipatory anxiety, improving perceived self-efficacy, and short-circuiting regression to old patterns of avoidance and escape.

DIFFICULT CASES

Although the procedures described in this book largely pertain to prototypical examples of childhood social phobia, many cases of social and performance anxiety are difficult, severe ones that involve extensive comorbidity, intense symptomatology, treatment noncompliance, and/or desires for early termination. These areas of concern are discussed in turn.

EXTENSIVE COMORBIDITY

Common comorbidities were covered in Chapter 2, but therapists treating youths with social phobia should be especially watchful of concurrent school refusal behavior, depression and suicidality, and substance abuse. In these cases, many of the treatment techniques described in this book can be tailored to some extent to simultaneously address social/performance anxiety *and* these comorbid problems.

With respect to school refusal behavior, for example, anxiety about school attendance can be managed using the techniques described previously, and reentry into school can be done on a gradual basis in conjunction with an anxiety/avoidance hierarchy. The urgency of ameliorating school refusal behavior, however, often demands a fast therapy pace. Therefore, therapists are urged to consult with school officials about school-based areas (e.g., library, main office) that a child can attend without necessarily having to confront extremely stressful stimuli (e.g., classroom). If a child with social phobia and school refusal behavior displays considerable attention-seeking behavior, then parent-based contingency management procedures may be emphasized. If a child is refusing school for tangible rewards outside of school, then family-based procedures (e.g., contracts) to increase incentives for school attendance may be helpful. More detailed procedures for addressing school refusal behavior are available elsewhere (Kearney, 2001; Kearney & Albano, 2000).

With respect to comorbid depression and suicidality, therapists may need to concentrate on cognitive therapies and behavioral activation within the context of general social phobia treatment. Addressing safety and crisis issues must, of course, supercede other treatment procedures, and therapists may have to adopt a very slow approach in these cases. With respect to substance abuse, therapists may need to increase parental monitoring and supervision, mandate regular drug testing as necessary and appropriate, identify triggers to substance abuse, and develop a child's strategies to better cope with stressors and negative emotions. Such treatment can also address a youth's desire to medicate his or her anxiety symptoms (see Chapter 2).

INTENSE SYMPTOMATOLOGY

Intense symptomatology can also deter treatment progress for youths with social phobia. Examples include very severe or unusual somatic complaints, rigid cognitions or obsessions or delusions, and more overt behaviors that lead to intransigent avoidance. In these cases, therapists are encouraged to make referrals to a pediatrician and psychiatrist to rule out or address organic problems and to consider the use of medication to lower excess levels of arousal. In addition, a very slow psychosocial therapy approach may be needed, which may involve widely spaced exposures over a long period of time. Coordination with school officials is typically necessary in these cases, and changes to a child's educational plan to accommodate these slow therapeutic steps may need to be pursued. Other reasons for a child's extreme symptomatology, such as recent traumatic experiences and/or maltreatment, should be identified and addressed as well.

TREATMENT NONCOMPLIANCE

Noncompliance is a common threat to psychotherapy effectiveness in general, but is quite damaging to the treatment of childhood social phobia in particular. For example, failure to practice therapy-based procedures between sessions will likely result in poor social and anxiety management skill development, limited generalization of treatment effects, and high risk of future relapse. Sporadic therapy attendance will likely produce uneven treatment effects, laziness, and backsliding as well. Even less severe noncompliance, such as failure to maintain daily logbook information, can indicate a lack of motivation and commitment to the therapy process.

To address noncompliance in this population, its reasons should be clearly understood and addressed as early as possible. Noncompliance may result from fixable problems such as confusion about daily measures or treatment rationales, overly difficult therapeutic homework assignments, resistance from school officials regarding a certain therapy step, lack of sufficient rapport with the therapist, and inconvenient scheduling of sessions. However, noncompliance may also result from intractable problems such as serious lack of motivation regarding treatment, refusal of key family members to participate in treatment, family exigencies that mandate long breaks from therapy, and deliberate treatment sabotage. In these circumstances, family members may not be adequately prepared for treatment, which may have to be delayed. In other cases, severe behavioral problems must be addressed prior to social phobia symptoms.

DESIRE FOR EARLY TERMINATION

Another key problem when treating youths with social phobia is premature therapy termination once major crises have passed. Family members, for example, may press for treatment termination (or simply stop coming) when a child has returned to school full-time, completed all makeup work, experienced temporary anxiety reduction, or joined a social group. Unfortunately, the child may not yet have fully grasped the skills needed to manage social and performance anxiety, or may not have fully progressed along his or her anxiety/avoidance hierarchy. In these cases, an extensive discussion with family members should be held to inform them of the risks of premature therapy withdrawal. In doing so, an analogy may be drawn to the use of antibiotic treatment for a bacterial infection: although outward symptoms may disappear, underlying problems likely remain and may worsen if treatment (antibiotic or psychosocial) ends before it should. If family members continue to insist on termination, however, then periodic follow-up contact may be pursued as appropriate.

FUTURE DIRECTIONS

Much has been accomplished with respect to understanding, assessing, and treating childhood anxiety disorders in general and social phobia in particular, but much more work remains. With respect to childhood anxiety disorders in general, key areas of future work include a clearer understanding of normal and abnormal anxiety, developmental factors that influence diagnoses/clinical symptom presentation and assessment and treatment, long-term treatment and developmental outcomes, maintaining factors, parent roles for treating anxious children and adolescents, variables that influence effective therapist-child relationships, medications and their treatment utility, new and positive psychosocial treatment components, individual treatment component effectiveness, and outcome evaluations based on normative data (Kashdin & Herbert, 2001; Kendall & Ollendick, 2004).

These key areas of future work for childhood anxiety disorders apply, of course, to childhood social phobia research as well. Beidel, Morris, and Turner (2004), however, articulated several *additional* directions for future work regarding childhood social phobia per se. One important research direction involves examining daily social experiences of youths with social phobia to obtain a detailed functional analysis of their anxiety. This would include data from children with social phobia and their parents, peers, and clinicians from multiple settings, both natural and in-session. A second important research direction involves family-based methods of transferring anxiety from parents and other family members to children. A third important research direction involves transferring known, effective treatments such as in vivo exposure from specialized urban clinics to more widespread familial, academic, community, and rural venues.

FINAL COMMENTS

Knowledge regarding the conceptualization, diagnosis, assessment, and treatment of youths with social anxiety and social phobia has advanced in leaps and bounds in recent years, though much work remains. This book, while a thorough summary of research conducted so far, presents work that is simply a prelude of the much more sophisticated models and techniques to come. As such, professionals are encouraged to aggressively maintain their knowledge base in this area. In this regard, I invite future comments from readers regarding this book or this population.

REFERENCES

Achenbach, T.M., & Edelbrock, C.S. (1983). *Manual for the Child Behavior Checklist and Revised Child Behavior Profile*. Burlington, VT: University of Vermont.

Achenbach, T.M., & Rescorla, L.A. (2001). *Manual for the ASEBA school-age forms & profiles*. Burlington, VT: University of Vermont Research Center for Children, Youth, & Families.

Albano, A.M. (1995). Treatment of social anxiety in adolescents. *Cognitive and Behavioral Practice, 2*, 271–298.

Albano, A.M. (2003). Treatment of social anxiety disorder. In M.A. Reinecke, F.M. Datillio, & A. Freeman (Eds.), *Cognitive therapy with children and adolescents: A casebook for clinical practice* (pp. 128–161). New York: Guilford.

Albano, A.M., & Barlow, D.H. (1996). Breaking the vicious cycle: Cognitive-behavioral group treatment for socially anxious youth. In E.D. Hibbs & P.S. Jensen (Eds.), *Psychosocial treatments for child and adolescent disorders: Empirically based strategies for clinical practice* (pp. 43–62). Washington, DC: American Psychological Association.

Albano, A.M., Chorpita, B.F., & Barlow, D.H. (2003). Childhood anxiety disorders. In E.J. Mash & R.A. Barkley (Eds.), *Child psychopathology* (2nd.ed.) (pp. 279–329). New York: Guilford.

Albano, A.M., & Detweiler, M.F. (2001). The developmental and clinical impact of social anxiety and social phobia in children and adolescents. In S.G. Hofmann & P.M. DiBartolo (Eds.), *From social anxiety to social phobia: Multiple perspectives* (pp. 162–178). Needham Heights, MA: Allyn and Bacon.

Albano, A.M., Detweiler, M.F., & Logsdon-Conradsen, S. (1999). Cognitive-behavioral interventions with socially phobic children. In S.W. Russ & T.H. Ollendick (Eds.), *Handbook of psychotherapies with children and families* (pp. 255–280). New York: Kluwer Academic/Plenum.

Albano, A.M., DiBartolo, P.M., Heimberg, R.G., & Barlow, D.H. (1995). Children and adolescents: Assessment and treatment. In R.G. Heimberg, M.R. Liebowitz,

D.A. Hope, & F.R. Schneier (Eds.), *Social phobia: Diagnosis, assessment, and treatment* (pp. 387–425). New York: Guilford.

Albano, A.M., & Hayward, C. (2004). Social anxiety disorder. In T.H. Ollendick & J.S. March (Eds), *Phobic and anxiety disorders in children and adolescents: A clinician's guide to effective psychosocial and pharmacological interventions* (pp. 198–235). New York: Oxford University Press.

Albano, A.M., & Kendall, P.C. (2002). Cognitive behavioural therapy for children and adolescents with anxiety disorders: Clinical research advances. *International Review of Psychiatry, 14,* 129–134.

Albano, A.M., Marten, P.A., & Holt, C.S. (1991). *Therapist's manual: Cognitive-behavioral group treatment of adolescent social phobia.* Unpublished manuscript.

Albano, A.M., Marten, P.A., Holt, C.S., Heimberg, R.G., & Barlow, D.H. (1995). Cognitive-behavioral group treatment for social phobia in adolescents: A preliminary study. *Journal of Nervous and Mental Disease, 183,* 649–656.

Alfano, C.A., Beidel, D.C., & Turner, S.M. (2002). Cognition in childhood anxiety: Conceptual, methodological, and developmental issues. *Clinical Psychology Review, 22,* 1209–1238.

Allport, G.W., & Odbert, H.S. (1936). Trait-names: A psycholexical study. *Psychological Monographs, 47,* 474.

Ambrose, B., & Rholes, W.S. (1993). Automatic cognitions and symptoms of depression and anxiety in children and adolescents: An examination of the content specificity hypothesis. *Cognitive Therapy and Research, 17,* 289–308.

American Academy of Child and Adolescent Psychiatry. (1997). Practice parameters for the assessment and treatment of children and adolescents with anxiety disorders. *Journal of the American Academy of Child and Adolescent Psychiatry, 36,* 69S–84S.

American Psychiatric Association. (1952). *Diagnostic and Statistical Manual of Mental Disorders.* Washington, DC: American Psychiatric Press.

American Psychiatric Association. (1968). *Diagnostic and Statistical Manual of Mental Disorders* (2nd.ed.). Washington, DC: American Psychiatric Press.

American Psychiatric Association. (1980). *Diagnostic and Statistical Manual of Mental Disorders* (3rd.ed.). Washington, DC: American Psychiatric Press.

American Psychiatric Association. (1987). *Diagnostic and Statistical Manual of Mental Disorders* (3rd.ed., rev.). Washington, DC: American Psychiatric Press.

American Psychiatric Association. (1994). *Diagnostic and Statistical Manual of Mental Disorders* (4th.ed.). Washington, DC: American Psychiatric Press.

American Psychiatric Association. (2000). *Diagnostic and Statistical Manual of Mental Disorders* (4th.ed., text revision). Washington, DC: American Psychiatric Press.

Anderson, J.C., Williams, S., McGee, R., & Silva, P.A. (1987). DSM-III disorders in preadolescent children. *Archives of General Psychiatry, 44,* 69–76.

Andrews, G., Stewart, G., Allen, R., & Henderson, A.S. (1990). The genetics of six neurotic disorders: A twin study. *Journal of Affective Disorders, 19,* 23–29.

Angold, A., & Costello, E.J. (2000). The Child and Adolescent Psychiatric Assessment (CAPA). *Journal of the American Academy of Child and Adolescent Psychiatry, 39,* 39–48.

Antony, M.M., & Swinson, R.P. (2000). *The shyness & social anxiety workbook: Proven techniques for overcoming your fears*. Oakland, CA: New Harbinger.

Arbelle, S., Benjamin, J., Golin, M., Kremer, I., Belmaker, R.H., & Ebstein, R.P. (2003). Relation of shyness in grade school children to the genotype for the long form of the serotonin transporter promotor region polymorphism. *American Journal of Psychiatry, 160*, 671–676.

Argyropoulos, S.V., Bell, C.J., & Nutt, D.J. (2001). Brain function in social anxiety disorder. *Psychiatric Clinics of North America, 24*, 707–722.

Arrindell, W.A., Emmelkamp, P.M.G., Monsma, A., & Brilman, E. (1983). The role of perceived parental rearing practices in the aetiology of phobic disorders: A controlled study. *British Journal of Psychiatry, 143*, 183–187.

Arrindell, W.A., Kwee, M.G.T., Methorst, G.J., van der Ende, J., Pol. E., & Moritz, B.J.M. (1989). Perceived parental rearing styles of agoraphobic and socially phobic in-patients. *British Journal of Psychiatry, 155*, 526–535.

Asendorpf, J.B. (1990a). Beyond social withdrawal: Shyness, unsociability and peer avoidance. *Human Development, 33*, 250–259.

Asendorpf, J.B. (1990b). The development of inhibition during childhood: Evidence for situational specificity and a two-factor model. *Developmental Psychology, 26*, 721–730.

Asendorpf, J.B. (1994). The malleability of behavioral inhibition: A study of individual developmental functions. *Developmental Psychology, 30*, 912–919.

Asendorpf, J.B., & Meier, G.H. (1993). Personality effects on children's speech in everyday life: Sociability-mediated exposure and shyness-mediated reactivity to social situations. *Journal of Personality and Social Psychology, 64*, 1072–1083.

Austin, A.A., & Chorpita, B.F. (2004). Temperament, anxiety, and depression: Comparisons across five ethnic groups of children. *Journal of Clinical Child and Adolescent Psychology, 33*, 216–226.

Baker-Morissette, S.L., Gulliver, S.B., Wiegel, M., & Barlow, D.H. (2004). Prevalence of smoking in anxiety disorders uncomplicated by comorbid alcohol or substance abuse. *Journal of Psychopathology and Behavioral Assessment, 26*, 107–112.

Bandura, A. (1977). *Social learning theory*. Englewood Cliffs, NJ: Prentice-Hall.

Barkley, R.A. (1998). *Attention-deficit hyperactivity disorder: A handbook for diagnosis and treatment* (2nd. ed.). New York: Guilford.

Barlow, D.H. (2000). Unraveling the mysteries of anxiety and its disorders from the perspective of emotion theory. *American Psychologist, 55*, 1247–1263.

Barlow, D.H. (2002). *Anxiety and its disorders: The nature and treatment of anxiety and panic* (2nd.ed.). New York: Guilford.

Barrett, P.M. (2000). Treatment of childhood anxiety: Developmental aspects. *Clinical Psychology Review, 20*, 479–494.

Barrett, P.M., Dadds, M.R., & Rapee, R.M. (1996). Family treatment of childhood anxiety: A controlled trial. *Journal of Consulting and Clinical Psychology, 64*, 333–342.

Barrett, P.M., Duffy, A.L., Dadds, M.R., & Rapee, R.M. (2001). Cognitive-behavioral treatment of anxiety disorders in children: Long-term (6-year) follow-up. *Journal of Consulting and Clinical Psychology, 69*, 135–141.

Barrett, P.M., Rapee, R.M., Dadds, M.M., & Ryan, S.M. (1996). Family enhancement of cognitive style in anxious and aggressive children. *Journal of Abnormal Child Psychology, 24*, 187–203.

Barrett, P.M., & Turner, C.M. (2004). Prevention strategies. In T.L. Morris & J.S. March (Eds.), *Anxiety disorders in children and adolescents* (2nd.ed.) (pp. 371–386). New York: Guilford.

Battaglia, M., Ogliari, A., Zanoni, A., Villa, F., Citterio, A., Binaghi, F., Fossati, A., & Maffei, C. (2004). Children's discrimination of expressions of emotions: Relationship with indices of social anxiety and shyness. *Journal of the American Academy of Child and Adolescent Psychiatry, 43*, 358–365.

Beck, A.T., Emery, G., & Greenberg, R.L. (1985). *Anxiety disorders and phobias: A cognitive perspective.* New York: Basic.

Beck, A.T., Rush, A.J., Shaw, B.F., & Emery, G. (1979). *Cognitive therapy of depression.* New York: Guilford.

Beidel, D.C. (1989). Assessing anxious emotions: A review of psychophysiological assessment in children. *Clinical Psychology Review, 9*, 717–736.

Beidel, D.C. (1991). Social phobia and overanxious disorder in school age children. *Journal of the American Academy of Child and Adolescent Psychiatry, 30*, 545–552.

Beidel, D.C. (1998). Social anxiety disorder: Etiology and early clinical presentation. *Journal of Clinical Psychiatry, 59*, 27–31.

Beidel, D.C., Christ, M.A.G., & Long, P.J. (1991). Somatic complaints in anxious children. *Journal of Abnormal Child Psychology, 19*, 659–670.

Beidel, D.C., Ferrell, C., Alfano, C.A., & Yeganeh, R. (2001). The treatment of childhood social anxiety disorder. *Psychiatric Clinics of North America, 24*, 831–846.

Beidel, D.C., & Morris, T.L. (1993). Avoidant disorder of childhood and social phobia. *Child and Adolescent Psychiatric Clinics of North America, 2*, 623–638.

Beidel, D.C., & Morris, T.L. (1995). Social phobia. In J.S. March (Ed.), *Anxiety disorders in children and adolescents* (pp. 181–211). New York: Guilford.

Beidel, D.C., Morris, T.L., & Turner, M.W. (2004). Social phobia. In T.L. Morris & J.S. March (Eds.), *Anxiety disorders in children and adolescents* (2nd.ed.) (pp. 141–163). New York: Guilford.

Beidel, D.C., Neal, A.M., & Lederer, A.S. (1991). The feasibility and validity of a daily diary for the assessment of anxiety in children. *Behavior Therapy, 22*, 505–517.

Beidel, D.C., & Turner, S.M. (1988). Comorbidity of test anxiety and other anxiety disorders in children. *Journal of Abnormal Child Psychology, 16*, 275–287.

Beidel, D.C., & Turner, S.M. (1997). At risk for anxiety: I. Psychopathology in the offspring of anxious parents. *Journal of the American Academy of Child and Adolescent Psychiatry, 36*, 918–924.

Beidel, D.C., & Turner, S.M. (1998). *Shy children, phobic adults: Nature and treatment of social phobia.* Washington, DC: American Psychological Association.

Beidel, D.C., & Turner, S.M. (1999). The natural course of shyness and related syndromes. In L.A. Schmidt & J. Schulkin (Eds.), *Extreme fear, shyness, and social phobia* (pp. 203–223). New York: Oxford University Press.

Beidel, D.C., Turner, S.M., & Dancu, C.V. (1985). Physiological, cognitive and be-havioral aspects of social anxiety. *Behaviour Research and Therapy, 23,* 109–117.

Beidel, D.C., Turner, S.M., & Fink, C.M. (1996). Assessment of childhood social phobia: Construct, convergent, and discriminative validity of the Social Phobia and Anxiety Inventory for Children (SPAI-C). *Psychological Assessment, 8,* 235–240.

Beidel, D.C., Turner, S.M., Hamlin, K., & Morris, T.L. (2000). The Social Phobia and Anxiety Inventory for Children (SPAI-C): External and discriminative validity. *Behavior Therapy, 31,* 75–87.

Beidel, D.C., Turner, S.M., & Morris, T.L. (1995). A new inventory to assess child-hood social anxiety and phobia: The Social Phobia and Anxiety Inventory for Children. *Psychological Assessment, 7,* 73–79.

Beidel, D.C., Turner, S.M., & Morris, T.L. (1999). Psychopathology of childhood social phobia. *Journal of the American Academy of Child and Adolescent Psychiatry, 38,* 643–650.

Beidel, D.C., Turner, S.M., & Morris, T.L. (2000a). *Social Phobia and Anxiety Inven-tory for Children (SPAI-C): User's manual.* North Tonawanda, NY: Multi-Health Systems.

Beidel, D.C., Turner, S.M., & Morris, T.L. (2000b). Behavioral treatment of childhood social phobia. *Journal of Consulting and Clinical Psychology, 68,* 1072–1080.

Beidel, D.C., Turner, M.W., & Trager, K.N. (1994). Test anxiety and childhood anxiety disorders in African American and White school children. *Journal of Anxiety Disorders, 8,* 169–179.

Bell-Dolan, D.J. (1995). Social cue interpretation of anxious children. *Journal of Child Clinical Psychology, 24,* 1–10.

Bell-Dolan, D.J., Last, C.G., & Strauss, C.C. (1990). Symptoms of anxiety disorders in normal children. *Journal of the American Academy of Child and Adolescent Psychiatry, 29,* 759–765.

Benjamin, R.S., Costello, E.J., & Warren, M. (1990). Anxiety disorders in a pediatric sample. *Journal of Anxiety Disorders, 4,* 293–316.

Bergman, R.L., Piacentini, J., & McCracken, J.T. (2002). Prevalence and description of selective mutism in a school-based sample. *Journal of the American Academy of Child and Adolescent Psychiatry, 41,* 938–946.

Berman, S.L., Weems, C.F., Silverman, W.K., & Kurtines, W.M. (2000). Predictors of outcome in exposure-based cognitive and behavioral treatments for phobic and anxiety disorders in children. *Behavior Therapy, 31,* 713–731.

Bernstein, G.A., Massie, E.D., Thuras, P.D., Perwien, A.R., Borchardt, C.M., & Crosby, R.D. (1997). Somatic symptoms in anxious-depressed school refusers. *Journal of the American Academy of Child and Adolescent Psychiatry, 36,* 661–668.

Biederman, J., Faraone, S.V., Hirshfeld-Becker, D.R., Friedman, D., Robin, J.A., & Rosenbaum, J.F. (2001). Patterns of psychopathology and dysfunction in high-risk children of parents with panic disorder and major depression. *American Journal of Psychiatry, 158,* 49–57.

Biederman, J. Hirshfeld-Becker, D.R., Rosenbaum, J.F., Herot, C., Friedman, D., Snidman, N., Kagan, J., & Faraone, S.V. (2001). Further evidence of association between behavioral inhibition and social anxiety in children. *American Journal of Psychiatry, 158,* 1673–1679.

Biederman, J., Rosenbaum, J.F., Bolduc-Murphy, E.A., Faraone, S.V., Chaloff, J., Hirshfeld, D.R., & Kagan, J. (1993). A 3-year follow-up of children with and without behavioral inhibition. *Journal of the American Academy of Child and Adolescent Psychiatry, 32,* 814–821.

Biederman, J., Rosenbaum, J.F., Hirshfeld, D.R., Faraone, S.V., Bolduc, E.A., Gersten, M., Meminger, S.R., Kagan, J., Snidman, N., & Reznick, J.S. (1990). Psychiatric correlates of behavioral inhibition in young children of parents with and without psychiatric disorders. *Archives of General Psychiatry, 47,* 21–26.

Birbaumer, N., Grodd, W., Diedrich, O., Klose, U., Erb, M., Lotze, M., Schneider, F., Weiss, U., & Flor, H. (1998). fMRI reveals amygdala activation to human faces in social phobics. *NeuroReport, 9,* 1223–1226.

Birmaher, B., Axelson, D.A., Monk, K., Kalas, C., Clark, D. B., Ehmann, M., Bridge, J., Heo, J., & Brent, D.A. (2003). Fluoxetine for the treatment of childhood anxiety disorders. *Journal of the American Academy of Child and Adolescent Psychiatry, 42,* 415–423.

Birmaher, B., Brent, D.A., Chiappetta, L., Bridge, J., Monga, S., & Baugher, M. (1999). Psychometric properties of the Screen for Child Anxiety Related Emotional Disorders (SCARED): A replication study. *Journal of the American Academy of Child and Adolescent Psychiatry, 38,* 1230–1236.

Birmaher, B., Khetarpal, S., Brent, D., Cully, M., Balach, L., Kaufman, J., & Neer, S.M. (1997). The Screen for Child Anxiety Related Emotional Disorders (SCARED): Scale construction and psychometric characteristics. *Journal of the American Academy of Child and Adolescent Psychiatry, 36,* 545–553.

Birmaher, B., & Ollendick, T.H. (2004). Childhood-onset panic disorder. In T.H. Ollendick & J.S. March (Eds), *Phobic and anxiety disorders in children and adolescents: A clinician's guide to effective psychosocial and pharmacological interventions* (pp. 306–333). New York: Oxford University Press.

Birmaher, B., Waterman, G.S., Ryan, N., Cully, M., Balach, L., Ingram, J., & Brodsky, M. (1994). Fluoxetine for childhood anxiety disorders. *Journal of the American Academy of Child and Adolescent Psychiatry, 33,* 993–999.

Black, B., & Uhde, T.W. (1995). Psychiatric characteristics of children with selective mutism: A pilot study. *Journal of the American Academy of Child and Adolescent Psychiatry, 34,* 847–856.

Blonk, R.W.B., Prins, P.J.M., Sergeant, J.A., Ringrose, J., & Brinkman, A.G. (1996). Cognitive-behavioral group therapy for socially incompetent children: Short-term and maintenance effects with a clinical sample. *Journal of Clinical Child Psychology, 25,* 215–224.

Bogels, S.M., Snieder, N., & Kindt, M. (2003). Specificity of dysfunctional thinking in children with symptoms of social anxiety, separation anxiety and generalised anxiety. *Behaviour Change, 20,* 160–169.

Bogels, S.M., van Oosten, A., Muris, P., & Smulders, D. (2001). Familial correlates of social anxiety in children and adolescents. *Behaviour Research and Therapy, 39,* 273–287.

Bogels, S.M., & Zigterman, D. (2000). Dysfunctional cognitions in children with social phobia, separation anxiety disorder, and generalized anxiety disorder. *Journal of Abnormal Child Psychology, 28*, 205–211.

Bond, F.W., & Dryden, W. (2002). *Handbook of brief cognitive behaviour therapy*. New York: Wiley.

Boone, M.L., McNeil, D.W., Masia, C.L., Turk, C.L., Carter, L.E., Ries, B.J., & Lewin, M.R. (1999). Multimodal comparisons of social phobia subtypes and avoidant personality disorder. *Journal of Anxiety Disorders, 13*, 271–292.

Bornstein, P.H., & Knapp, M. (1981). Self-control desensitization with a multi-phobic boy: A multiple baseline design. *Journal of Behavior Therapy and Experimental Psychiatry, 12*, 281–285.

Bouchard, S., Mendlowitz, S.L., Coles, M.E., & Franklin, M. (2004). Considerations in the use of exposure with children. *Cognitive and Behavioral Practice, 11*, 56–65.

Boyd, R.C., Ginsburg, G.S., Lambert, S.F., Cooley, M.R., & Campbell, K.D.M. (2003). Screen for Child Anxiety Related Emotional Disorders (SCARED): Psychometric properties in an African-American parochial high school sample. *Journal of the American Academy of Child and Adolescent Psychiatry, 42*, 1188–1196.

Brady, E.U., & Kendall, P.C. (1992). Comorbidity of anxiety and depression in children and adolescents. *Psychological Bulletin, 111*, 244–255.

Braswell, L., & Kendall, P.C. (1988). Cognitive-behavioral methods with children. In K.S. Dobson (Ed.), *Handbook of cognitive-behavioral therapies* (pp. 167–213). New York: Guilford.

Briesmeister, J.M., & Schaefer, C.E. (1998). *Handbook of parent training: Parents as co-therapists for children's behavior problems* (2nd. ed.). New York: Wiley.

Brown, T.A., DiNardo, P.A., & Barlow, D.H. (1994). *Anxiety Disorders Interview Schedule for DSM-IV (ADIS-IV)*. San Antonio, TX: Psychological Corporation/Graywind Publications.

Brownell, K.D., Marlatt, G.A., Lichtenstein, E., & Wilson, G.T. (1986). Understanding and preventing relapse. *American Psychologist, 41*, 765–776.

Bruch, M.A. (1989). Familial and developmental antecedents of social phobia: Issues and findings. *Clinical Psychology Review, 9*, 37–47.

Bruch, M.A., & Cheek, J.M. (1995). Developmental factors in childhood and adolescent shyness. In R.G. Heimberg, M.R. Liebowitz, D.A. Hope, & F.R. Schneier (Eds.), *Social phobia: Diagnosis, assessment, and treatment* (pp. 163–182). New York: Guilford.

Bruch, M.A., & Heimberg, R.G. (1994). Differences in perceptions of parental and personal characteristics between generalized and nongeneralized social phobics. *Journal of Anxiety Disorders, 8*, 155–168.

Bruch, M.A., Heimberg, R.G., Berger, P., & Collins, T.M. (1989). Social phobia and perceptions of early parental and personal characteristics. *Anxiety Research, 2*, 57–65.

Bruch, M.A., Rivet, K.M., Heimberg, R.G., Hunt, A., & McIntosh, B. (1999). Shyness and sociotropy: Additive and interactive relations in predicting interpersonal concerns. *Journal of Personality, 67*, 373–406.

Burgess, K.B., Rubin, K.H., Cheah, C.S.L., & Nelson, L.J. (2001). Behavioral inhibition, social withdrawal, and parenting. In W.R. Crozier & L.E. Alden (Eds.), *International handbook of social anxiety: Concepts, research, and interventions relating to the self and shyness* (pp. 137–158). New York: Wiley.

Burns, D.D. (1999). *The feeling good handbook* (revised edition). New York: Plume.

Buss, A.H. (1986). A theory of shyness. In W.H. Jones, J.M. Cheek, & S.R. Briggs (Eds.), *Shyness: Perspectives on research and treatment* (pp. 39–46). New York: Plenum.

Buss, A.H., & Plomin, R. (1984). *Temperament: Early developing personality traits.* Hillsdale, NJ: Erlbaum.

Cantwell, D.P., & Baker, L. (1989). Stability and natural history of DSM-III childhood diagnoses. *Journal of the American Academy of Child and Adolescent Psychiatry, 28,* 691–700.

Carr, A. (2002). Child and adolescence problems. In F.W. Bond & W. Dryden (Eds.), *Handbook of brief cognitive behaviour therapy* (pp. 207–238). New York: Wiley.

Cartledge, G., & Milburn, J.F. (1995). *Teaching social skills to children and youth: Innovative approaches* (3rd.ed.). Boston, MA: Allyn and Bacon.

Caspi, A., Moffitt, T.E., Newman, D.L., & Silva, P.A. (1996). Behavioral observations at age 3 years predict adult psychiatric disorders: Longitudinal evidence from a birth cohort. *Archives of General Psychiatry, 53,* 1033–1039.

Caspi, A., & Silva, P.A. (1995). Temperamental qualities at age three predict personality traits in young adulthood: Longitudinal evidence from a birth cohort. *Child Development, 66,* 486–498.

Caster, J.B., Inderbitzen, H.M., & Hope, D. (1999). Relationship between youth and parent perceptions of family environment and social anxiety. *Journal of Anxiety Disorders, 13,* 237–251.

Cattell, R.B. (1966). *The scientific analysis of personality.* Baltimore: Penguin.

Cattell, R.B. (1973). *Personality and mood by questionnaire.* San Francisco: Jossey-Bass.

Chansky, T.E., & Kendall, P.C. (1997). Social expectancies and self-perceptions in anxiety-disordered children. *Journal of Anxiety Disorders, 11,* 347–363.

Chartier, M.J., Walker, J.R., & Stein, M.B. (2001). Social phobia and potential childhood risk factors in a community sample. *Psychological Medicine, 31,* 307–315.

Cheek, J.M., & Briggs, S.R. (1990). Shyness as a personality trait. In W.R. Crozier (Ed.), *Shyness and embarrassment: Perspectives from social psychology* (pp. 315–337). Cambridge: Cambridge University Press.

Cheek, J.M., & Krasnoperova, E. (1999). Varieties of shyness in adolescence and adulthood. In L.A. Schmidt & J. Schulkin (Eds.), *Extreme fear, shyness, and social phobia: Origins, biological mechanisms, and clinical outcomes* (pp. 224–250). New York: Oxford University Press.

Chen, X., Rubin, K.H., Li, B., & Li, D. (1999). Adolescent outcomes of social functioning in Chinese children. *International Journal of Behavioral Development, 23,* 199–223.

Chorpita, B.F. (2001). Control and the development of negative emotion. In M.W. Vasey & M.R. Dadds (Eds.), *The developmental psychopathology of anxiety* (pp. 112–142). New York: Oxford University Press.

Chorpita, B.F. (2002). The tripartite model and dimensions of anxiety and depression: An examination of structure in a large school sample. *Journal of Abnormal Child Psychology, 30*, 177–190.

Chorpita, B.F., Albano, A.M., & Barlow, D.H. (1996). Cognitive processing in children: Relationship to anxiety and family influences. *Journal of Clinical Child Psychology, 25*, 170–176.

Chorpita, B.F., Albano, A.M., & Barlow, D.H. (1998). The structure of negative emotions in a clinical sample of children and adolescents. *Journal of Abnormal Psychology, 107*, 74–85.

Chorpita, B.F., & Barlow, D.H. (1998). The development of anxiety: The role of control in the early environment. *Psychological Bulletin, 124*, 3–21.

Chorpita, B.F., & Daleiden, E.L. (2002). Tripartite dimensions of emotion in a child clinical sample: Measurement strategies and implications for clinical utility. *Journal of Consulting and Clinical Psychology, 70*, 1150–1160.

Chorpita, B.F., Plummer, C.M., & Moffitt, C.E. (2000). Relations of tripartite dimensions of emotion to childhood anxiety and mood disorders. *Journal of Abnormal Child Psychology, 28*, 299–310.

Christoff, K.A., Scott, W.O.N., Kelley, M.L., Schlundt, D., Baer, G., & Kelly, J.A. (1985). Social skills and social problem-solving training for shy young adolescents. *Behavior Therapy, 16*, 468–477.

Clark, D.B., Turner, S.M., Beidel, D.C., Donovan, J.E., Kirisci, L., & Jacob, R.G. (1994). Reliability and validity of the Social Phobia and Anxiety Inventory for adolescents. *Psychological Assessment, 6*, 135–140.

Clark, D.M., & McManus, F. (2002). Information processing in social phobia. *Biological Psychiatry, 51*, 92–100.

Clark, L.A., & Watson, D. (1991). Tripartite model of anxiety and depression: Psychometric evidence and taxonomic implications. *Journal of Abnormal Psychology, 100*, 316–336.

Cobham, V.E., Dadds, M.R., & Spence, S.H. (1998). The role of parental anxiety in the treatment of childhood anxiety. *Journal of Consulting and Clinical Psychology, 66*, 893–905.

Compton, S.N., Grant, P.J., Chrisman, A.K., Gammon, P.J., Brown, V.L., & March, J.S. (2001). Sertraline in children and adolescents with social anxiety disorder: An open trial. *Journal of the American Academy of Child and Adolescent Psychiatry, 40*, 564–571.

Compton, S.N., Nelson, A.H., & March, J.S. (2000). Social phobia and separation anxiety symptoms in community and clinical samples of children and adolescents. *Journal of the American Academy of Child and Adolescent Psychiatry, 39*, 1040–1046.

Conners, C.K. (1997). *Conners Rating Scales-Revised*. North Tonawanda, NY: Multi-Health Systems.

Cooper, P.J., & Eke, M. (1999). Childhood shyness and maternal social phobia: A community study. *British Journal of Psychiatry, 174*, 439–443.

Corsini, R.J., & Wedding, D. (2000). *Current psychotherapies* (6th.ed.). Itasca, IL: F.E. Peacock.

Costello, E.J. (1989). Child psychiatric disorders and their correlates: A primary care pediatric sample. *Journal of the American Academy of Child and Adolescent Psychiatry, 28,* 851–855.

Costello, E.J., & Angold, A. (1995). Epidemiology. In J.S. March (Ed.), *Anxiety disorders in children and adolescents* (pp. 109–124). New York: Guilford.

Costello, E.J., Costello, A.J., Edelbrock, C., Burns, B.J., Dulcan, M.K., Brent, D., & Janiszewski, S. (1988). Psychiatric disorders in pediatric primary care: Prevalence and risk factors. *Archives of General Psychiatry, 45,* 1107–1116.

Costello, E.J., Mustillo, S., Erkanli, A., Keeler, G., & Angold, A. (2003). Prevalence and development of psychiatric disorders in childhood and adolescence. *Archives of General Psychiatry, 60,* 837–844.

Cowan, P.A., Cohn, D.A., Pape-Cowan, C.P., & Pearson, J.L. (1996). Parents' attachment histories and children's externalizing and internalizing behaviors. *Journal of Consulting and Clinical Psychology, 64,* 53–63.

Craske, M.G. (1999). *Anxiety disorders: Psychological approaches to theory and treatment.* Boulder, CO: Westview.

Craske, M.G., Barlow, D.H., & Meadows, E.A. (2000). *Mastery of your anxiety and panic: Third edition (MAP-3): Therapist guide for anxiety, panic, and agoraphobia.* San Antonio, TX: Psychological Corporation.

Cretekos, C.J.G. (1977). Some techniques in rehabilitating the school phobic adolescent. *Adolescence, 12,* 237–246.

Crick, N.R., & Ladd, G.W. (1993). Children's perceptions of their peer experiences: Attributions, loneliness, social anxiety, and social avoidance. *Developmental Psychology, 29,* 244–254.

Dadds, M.R., Barrett, P.M., Rapee, R.M., & Ryan, S. (1996). Family process and child anxiety and aggression: An observational analysis. *Journal of Abnormal Child Psychology, 24,* 715–734.

Dadds, M.R., Davey, G.C.L., & Field, A.P. (2001). Developmental aspects of conditioning processes in anxiety disorders. In M.W. Vasey & M.R. Dadds (Eds.), *The developmental psychopathology of anxiety* (pp. 205–230). New York: Oxford University Press.

Dadds, M.R., Holland, D.E., Laurens, K.R., Mullins, M., Barrett, P.M., & Spence, S.H. (1999). Early intervention and prevention of anxiety disorders in children: Results at 2-year follow-up. *Journal of Consulting and Clinical Psychology, 67,* 145–150.

Dadds, M.R., & Roth, J.H. (2001). Family processes in the development of anxiety problems. In M.W. Vasey & M.R. Dadds (Eds.), *The developmental psychopathology of anxiety* (pp. 278–303). New York: Oxford University Press.

Dadds, M.R., Spence, S.H., Holland, D.E., Barrett, P.M., & Laurens, K.R. (1997). Prevention and early intervention for anxiety disorders: A controlled trial. *Journal of Consulting and Clinical Psychology, 65,* 627–635.

Daleiden, E.L., & Vasey, M.W. (1997). An information-processing perspective on childhood anxiety. *Clinical Psychology Review, 17,* 407–429.

Daniels, D., & Plomin, R. (1985). Origins of individual differences in infant shyness. *Developmental Psychology, 21,* 118–121.

Davidson, J.R.T., Hughes, D.L., George, L.K., & Blazer, D.G. (1993). The epidemiology of social phobia: Findings from the Duke Epidemiological Catchment Area Study. *Psychological Medicine, 23*, 709–718.

Davidson, J.R.T., Krishnan, K.R.R., Charles, H.C., Boyko, O., Potts, N.L.S., Ford, S.M., & Patterson, L. (1993). Magnetic resonance spectroscopy in social phobia: Preliminary findings. *Journal of Clinical Psychiatry, 54*, 19–25.

Davidson, R.J., Marshall, J.R., Tomarken, A.J., & Henriques, J.B. (2000). While a phobic waits: Regional brain electrical and autonomic activity in social phobics during anticipation of public speaking. *Biological Psychiatry, 47*, 85–95.

Dekovic, M., & Janssens, J.M.A.M. (1992). Parents' child-rearing style and child sociometric status. *Developmental Psychology, 28*, 925–932.

Dell'Osso, L., Saettoni, M., Papasogli, A., Rucci, P., Ciapparelli, A., Di Poggio, A.B., Ducci, F., Hardoy, C., & Cassano, G.B. (2002). Social anxiety spectrum: Gender differences in Italian high school students. *Journal of Nervous and Mental Disease, 190*, 225–232.

Delprato, D.J., & McGlynn, F.D. (1984). Behavioral theories of anxiety disorders. In S.M. Turner (Ed.), *Behavioral treatment of anxiety disorders* (pp. 63–122). New York: Plenum.

DeWit, D.J., Ogborne, A., Offord, D.R., & MacDonald, K. (1999). Antecedents of the risk of recovery from DSM-III-R social phobia. *Psychological Medicine, 29*, 569–582.

DiBartolo, P.M., Albano, A.M., Barlow, D.H., & Heimberg, R.G. (1998). Cross-informant agreement in the assessment of social phobia in youth. *Journal of Abnormal Child Psychology, 26*, 213–220.

DiLalla, L.F., Kagan, J., & Reznick, J.S. (1994). Genetic etiology of behavioral inhibition among 2-year-old children. *Infant Behavior and Development, 17*, 405–412.

DiNardo, P.A., Brown, T.A., & Barlow, D.H. (1994). *Anxiety Disorders Interview Schedule for DSM-IV: Lifetime Version (ADIS-IV-L)*. San Antonio, TX: Psychological Corporation/Graywind Publications.

DiNardo, P.A., O'Brien, G.T., Barlow, D.H., Waddell, M.T., & Blanchard, E.B. (1983). Reliability of DSM-III anxiety disorder categories using a new structured interview. *Archives of General Psychiatry, 40*, 1070–1074.

Dong, Q., Yang, B., & Ollendick, T.H. (1994). Fears in Chinese children and adolescents and their relations to anxiety and depression. *Journal of Child Psychology and Psychiatry, 35*, 351–363.

Donovan, C.L., & Spence, S.H. (2000). Prevention of childhood anxiety disorders. *Clinical Psychology Review, 20*, 509–531.

Dow, S.P., Sonies, B.C., Scheib, D., Moss, S.E., & Leonard, H.L. (1995). Practical guidelines for the assessment and treatment of selective mutism. *Journal of the American Academy of Child and Adolescent Psychiatry, 34*, 836–846.

Dumas, J.E., LaFreniere, P.J., & Serketich, W.J. (1995). "Balance of power": A transactional analysis of control in mother-child dyads involving socially competent, aggressive, and anxious children. *Journal of Abnormal Psychology, 104*, 104–113.

Dummit, E.S., Klein, R.G., Tancer, N.K., Asche, B., Martin, J., & Fairbanks, J.A. (1997). Systematic assessment of 50 children with selective mutism. *Journal of the American Academy of Child and Adolescent Psychiatry, 36*, 653–660.

Eaves, L.J., Eysenck, H.J., & Martin, N.G. (1989). *Genes, culture and personality: An empirical approach.* New York: Academic.

Egger, H.L., Costello, E.J., & Angold, A. (2003). School refusal and psychiatric disorders: A community study. *Journal of the American Academy of Child and Adolescent Psychiatry, 42,* 797–807.

Ehrenreich, J.T., & Gross, A.M. (2002). Biased attentional behavior in childhood anxiety: A review of theory and current empirical investigation. *Clinical Psychology Review, 22,* 991–1008.

Eisen, A.R., & Kearney, C.A. (1995). *Practitioner's guide to treating fear and anxiety in children and adolescents: A cognitive-behavioral approach.* Northvale, NJ: Jason Aronson.

Eisen, A.R., Spasaro, S.A., Brien, L.K., Kearney, C.A., & Albano, A.M. (2004). Parental expectancies and childhood anxiety disorders: Psychometric properties of the Parental Expectancies Scale. *Journal of Anxiety Disorders, 18,* 89–109.

Eley, T.C. (2001). Contributions of behavioral genetics research: Quantifying genetic, shared environmental and nonshared environmental influences. In M.W. Vasey & M.R. Dadds (Eds.), *The developmental psychopathology of anxiety* (pp. 45–59). New York: Oxford University Press.

Elizur, Y., & Perednik, R. (2003). Prevalence and description of selective mutism in immigrant and native families: A controlled study. *Journal of the American Academy of Child and Adolescent Psychiatry, 42,* 1451–1459.

Emde, R., Gaensbauer, T., & Harmon, R. (1976). Emotional expression in infancy: A biobehavioral study. *Psychological Issues Monograph, Vol. 10* (No. 37). New York: International Universities Press.

Emmelkamp, P.M.G., & Scholing, A. (1997). Behavioral treatment strategies for panic disorder, social phobia, and obsessive-compulsive disorder. In J.A. den Boer (Ed.), *Clinical management of anxiety* (pp. 79–108). New York: Dekker.

Epkins, C.C. (1996a). Affective confounding in social anxiety and dysphoria in children: Child, mother, and father reports of internalizing behaviors, social problems, and competence domains. *Journal of Social and Clinical Psychology, 15,* 449–470.

Epkins, C.C. (1996b). Cognitive specificity and affective confounding in social anxiety and dysphoria in children. *Journal of Psychopathology and Behavioral Assessment, 18,* 83–101.

Epkins, C.C. (2002). A comparison of two self-report measures of children's social anxiety in clinic and community samples. *Journal of Clinical Child and Adolescent Psychology, 31,* 69–79.

Essau, C.A., Conradt, J., & Petermann, F. (1999). Frequency and comorbidity of social phobia and social fears in adolescents. *Behaviour Research and Therapy, 37,* 831–843.

Essau, C.A., Conradt, J., & Petermann, F. (2000). Frequency, comorbidity, and psychosocial impairment of anxiety disorders in German adolescents. *Journal of Anxiety Disorders, 14,* 263–279.

Essau, C.A., Conradt, J., & Petermann, F. (2002). Course and outcome of anxiety disorders in adolescents. *Journal of Anxiety Disorders, 16,* 67–81.

Essau, C.A., & Petermann, F. (2001). *Anxiety disorders in children and adolescents: Epidemiology, risk factors and treatment.* New York: Brunner-Routledge.

Eysenck, H.J., & Eysenck, S.B.G. (1969). *Personality structure and measurement.* New York: Routledge and Kegan Paul.

Eysenck, S.B.G., & Eysenck, H.J. (1963). The validity of questionnaire and rating assessments of extraversion and neuroticism, and their factorial stability. *British Journal of Psychology, 54,* 51–62.

Ferdinand, R.F., Barrett, P.M., & Dadds, M.R. (2004). Anxiety and depression in childhood: Prevention and intervention. In T.H. Ollendick & J.S. March (Eds), *Phobic and anxiety disorders in children and adolescents: A clinician's guide to effective psychosocial and pharmacological interventions* (pp. 459–475). New York: Oxford University Press.

Fergusson, D.M., Horwood, J., & Lynskey, M.T. (1993). Prevalence and comorbidity of DSM-III-R diagnoses in a birth cohort of 15 year olds. *Journal of the American Academy of Child and Adolescent Psychiatry, 32,* 1127–1134.

Ferrell, C.B., Beidel, D.C., & Turner, S.M. (2004). Assessment and treatment of socially phobic children: A cross cultural comparison. *Journal of Clinical Child and Adolescent Psychology, 33,* 260–268.

Field, A.P., Hamilton, S.J., Knowles, K.A., & Plews, E.L. (2003). Fear information and social phobic beliefs in children: A prospective paradigm and preliminary results. *Behaviour Research and Therapy, 41,* 113–123.

Flannery-Schroeder, E.C., & Kendall, P.C. (2000). Group and individual cognitive-behavioral treatments for youth with anxiety disorders: A randomized clinical trial. *Cognitive Therapy and Research, 24,* 251–278.

Foa, E.B., & Kozak, M.J. (1986). Emotional processing of fear: Exposure to corrective information. *Psychological Bulletin, 99,* 20–35.

Ford, M.A., Sladeczek, I.E., Carlson, J., & Kratochwill, T.R. (1998). Selective mutism: Phenomenological characteristics. *School Psychology Quarterly, 13,* 192–227.

Ford, T., Goodman, R., & Meltzer, H. (2003). The British child and adolescent mental health survey 1999: The prevalence of DSM-IV disorders. *Journal of the American Academy of Child and Adolescent Psychiatry, 42,* 1203–1211.

Fordham, K., & Stevenson-Hinde, J. (1999). Shyness, friendship quality, and adjustment during middle childhood. *Journal of Child Psychology and Psychiatry, 40,* 757–768.

Fox, N.A., Henderson, H.A., Rubin, K.H., Calkins, S.D., & Schmidt, L.A. (2001). Continuity and discontinuity of behavioral inhibition and exuberance: Psychophysiological and behavioral influences across the first four years of life. *Child Development, 72,* 1–21.

Francis, G., Last, C.G., & Strauss, C.C. (1992). Avoidant disorder and social phobia in children and adolescents. *Journal of the American Academy of Child and Adolescent Psychiatry, 31,* 1086–1089.

Francis, G., & Radka, D.F. (1995). Social anxiety in children and adolescents. In M.B. Stein (Ed.), *Social phobia: Clinical and research perspectives* (pp. 119–143). Washington, DC: American Psychiatric Press.

Friedberg, R.D., & McClure, J.M. (2002). *Clinical practice of cognitive therapy with children and adolescents: The nuts and bolts.* New York: Guilford.

Fyer, A.J., Mannuzza, S., Chapman, T.F., Liebowitz, M.R., & Klein, D.F. (1993). A direct interview family study of social phobia. *Archives of General Psychiatry, 50,* 286–293.

Gallagher, H.M., Rabian, B.A., & McClosky, M.S. (2004). A brief group cognitive-behavioral intervention for social phobia in childhood. *Journal of Anxiety Disorders, 18,* 459–479.

Garcia-Lopez, L.J., Olivares, J., Hidalgo, M.D., Beidel, D.C., & Turner, S.M. (2001). Psychometric properties of the Social Phobia and Anxiety Inventory, the Social Anxiety Scale for Adolescents, the Fear of Negative Evaluation Scale, and the Social Avoidance and Distress Scale in an adolescent Spanish-speaking sample. *Journal of Psychopathology and Behavioral Assessment, 23,* 51–59.

Garcia-Lopez, L.J., Olivares, J., Turner, S.M., Beidel, D.C., Albano, A.M., & Sanchez-Meca, J. (2002). Results at long-term among three psychological treatments for adolescents with generalized social phobia (II): Clinical significance and effect size. *Psicologia Conductual, 10,* 371–385.

Garcia-Lopez, L.J., Olivares, J., & Vera-Villarroel, P.E. (2003). Fobia social: Revision de los instrumentos de evaluacion validados para poblacion de lengua espanola. *Revista Latinoamericana de Psicologia, 35,* 151–160.

Gelfand, D.M., & Hartmann, D.P. (1984). *Child behavior analysis and therapy* (2nd. ed.). New York: Pergamon.

Gilbert, P. (2001). Evolution and social anxiety: The role of attraction, social competition, and social hierarchies. *Psychiatric Clinics of North America, 24,* 723–751.

Ginsburg, G.S., La Greca, A.M., & Silverman, W.K. (1998). Social anxiety in children with anxiety disorders: Relation with social and emotional functioning. *Journal of Abnormal Child Psychology, 26,* 175–185.

Ginsburg, G.S., & Silverman, W.K. (1996). Phobic and anxiety disorders in Hispanic and Caucasian youth. *Journal of Anxiety Disorders, 10,* 517–528.

Ginsburg, G.S., & Walkup, J.T. (2004). Specific phobia. In T.H. Ollendick & J.S. March (Eds), *Phobic and anxiety disorders in children and adolescents: A clinician's guide to effective psychosocial and pharmacological interventions* (pp. 175–197). New York: Oxford University Press.

Glickman, A.R., & La Greca, A.M. (2004). The Dating Anxiety Scale for Adolescents: Scale development and associations with adolescent functioning. *Journal of Clinical Child and Adolescent Psychology, 33,* 566–578.

Goldsmith, H.H., & Lemery, K.S. (2000). Linking temperamental fearfulness and anxiety symptoms: A behavior-genetic perspective. *Biological Psychiatry, 48,* 1199–1209.

Gresham, F.M. (1998). Social skills training with children: Social learning and applied behavioral analytic approaches. In T.S. Watson & F.M. Gresham (Eds.), *Handbook of child behavior therapy* (pp. 475–497). New York: Plenum.

Gresham, F.M., & Evans, S. (1987). Conceptualization and treatment of social withdrawal in the schools. *Special Services in the Schools, 3,* 37–51.

Guastello, S.J. (1993). A two-(and-a-half)-tiered trait taxonomy. *American Psychologist, 48,* 1298–1299.

Guida, F.V., & Ludlow, L.H. (1989). A cross-cultural study of test anxiety. *Journal of Cross-Cultural Psychology, 20,* 178–190.

Gullone, E., & King, N.J. (1997). Three-year follow-up of normal fear in children and adolescents aged 7 to 18 years. *British Journal of Developmental Psychology, 15,* 97–111.

Hayward, C., Killen, J.D., Kraemer, H.C., & Taylor, C.B. (1998). Linking self-reported childhood behavioral inhibition to adolescent social phobia. *Journal of the American Academy of Child and Adolescent Psychiatry, 37,* 1308–1316.

Hayward, C., Varady, S., Albano, A.M., Thienemann, M., Henderson, L., & Schatzberg, A.F. (2000). Cognitive-behavioral group therapy for social phobia in female adolescents: Results of a pilot study. *Journal of the American Academy of Child and Adolescent Psychiatry, 39,* 721–726.

Heimberg, R.G., Holt, C.S., Schneier, F.R., Spitzer, R.C., & Liebowitz, M.R. (1993). The issue of subtypes in the diagnosis of social phobia. *Journal of Anxiety Disorders, 7,* 249–269.

Heimberg, R.G., Hope, D.A., Dodge, C.S., & Becker, R.E. (1990). DSM-III-R subtypes of social phobia: Comparison of generalized social phobics and public speaking phobics. *Journal of Nervous and Mental Disease, 178,* 172–179.

Heiser, N.A., Turner, S.M., & Beidel, D.C. (2003). Shyness: Relationship to social phobia and other psychiatric disorders. *Behaviour Research and Therapy, 41,* 209–221.

Henderson, L., & Zimbardo, P. (2001b). Shyness, social anxiety, and social phobia. In S.G. Hofmann & P.M. DiBartolo (Eds.), *From social anxiety to social phobia: Multiple perspectives* (pp. 46–64). Needham Heights, MA: Allyn and Bacon.

Henderson, L., & Zimbardo, P.G. (2001a). Shyness as a clinical condition: The Stanford model. In W.R. Crozier & L.E. Alden (Eds.), *International handbook of social anxiety: Concepts, research, and interventions relating to the self and shyness* (pp. 431–447). New York: Wiley.

Hirsch, C.R., Clark, D.M., Mathews, A., & Williams, R. (2003). Self-images play a causal role in social phobia. *Behaviour Research and Therapy, 41,* 909–921.

Hirshfeld, D.R., Biederman, J., Brody, L., Faraone, S.V., & Rosenbaum, J.F. (1997). Associations between expressed emotion and child behavioral inhibition and psychopathology: A pilot study. *Journal of the American Academy of Child and Adolescent Psychiatry, 36,* 205–213.

Hirshfeld, D.R., Rosenbaum, J.F., Biederman, J., Bolduc, E.A., Faraone, S.V., Snidman, N., Reznick, J.S., & Kagan, J. (1992). Stable behavioral inhibition and its association with anxiety disorder. *Journal of the American Academy of Child and Adolescent Psychiatry, 31,* 103–111.

Hirshfeld-Becker, D.R., Biederman, J., & Rosenbaum, J.F. (2004). Behavioral inhibition. In T.L. Morris & J.S. March (Eds.), *Anxiety disorders in children and adolescents* (2nd.ed.) (pp. 27–58). New York: Guilford.

Hodges, K., McKnew, D., Cytryn, L., Stern, L., & Kline, J. (1982). The Child Assessment Schedule (CAS) diagnostic interview: A report on reliability and validity. *Journal of the American Academy of Child and Adolescent Psychiatry, 21,* 468–473.

Hofmann, S.G. (2000). Self-focused attention before and after exposure treatment of social phobia. *Behaviour Research and Therapy, 38,* 717–725.

Hofmann, S.G., Albano, A.M., Heimberg, R.G., Tracey, S., Chorpita, B.F., & Barlow, D.H. (1999). Subtypes of social phobia in adolescents. *Depression and Anxiety, 9*, 15–18.

Hofmann, S.G., & Barlow, D.H. (2002). Social phobia (social anxiety disorder). In D.H. Barlow, *Anxiety and its disorders: The nature and treatment of anxiety and panic* (2nd.ed.) (pp. 454–476). New York: Guilford.

Hofmann, S.G., Newman, M.G., Ehlers, A., & Roth, W.T. (1995). Psychophysiological differences between subgroups of social phobia. *Journal of Abnormal Psychology, 104*, 224–231.

Hope, D.A., Heimberg, R.G., Juster, H.R., & Turk, C.L. (2000). *Managing social anxiety: A cognitive-behavioral therapy approach: Client workbook*. San Antonio, TX: The Psychological Corporation.

Hope, D.A., Rapee, R.M., Heimberg, R.G., & Dombeck, M.J. (1990). Representations of the self in social phobia: Differences among sociometric status groups and rejected subgroups. *Cognitive Therapy and Research, 14*, 177–189.

Horwath, E., Wolk, S.I., Goldstein, R.B., Wickramaratne, P., Sobin, C., Adams, P., Lish, J.D., & Weissman, M.M. (1995). Is the comorbidity between social phobia and panic disorder due to familial cotransmission or other factors? *Archives of General Psychiatry, 52*, 574–582.

Houston, B.K., Fox, J.E., & Forbes, L. (1984). Trait anxiety and children's state anxiety, cognitive behaviors, and performance under stress. *Cognitive Therapy and Research, 8*, 631–641.

Hudson, J.L., Kendall, P.C., Coles, M.E., Robin, J.A., & Webb, A. (2002). The other side of the coin: Using intervention research in child anxiety disorders to inform developmental psychopathology. *Development and Psychopathology, 14*, 819–841.

Hudson, J.L., & Rapee, R.M. (2000). The origins of social phobia. *Behavior Modification, 24*, 102–129.

Inderbitzen, H.M., Walters, K.S., & Bukowski, A.L. (1997). The role of social anxiety in adolescent peer relations: Differences among sociometric status groups and rejected subgroups. *Journal of Clinical Child Psychology, 26*, 338–348.

Inderbitzen-Nolan, H., Davies, C.A., & McKeon, N.D. (2004). Investigating the construct validity of the SPAI-C: Comparing the sensitivity of the SPAI-C and the SAS-A. *Journal of Anxiety Disorders, 18*, 547–560.

Inderbitzen-Nolan, H.M., & Walters, K.S. (2000). Social Anxiety Scale for Adolescents: Normative data and further evidence of construct validity. *Journal of Clinical Child Psychology, 29*, 360–371.

Inderbitzen-Pisaruk, H., Clark, M.L., & Solano, C.H. (1992). Correlates of loneliness in midadolescence. *Journal of Youth and Adolescence, 21*, 151–167.

Ishiyama, F.I. (1984). Shyness: Anxious social sensitivity and self-isolating tendency. *Adolescence, 19*, 902–911.

John, O.P, & Srivastava, S. (1999). The big five trait taxonomy: History, measurement, and theoretical perspectives. In L.A. Pervin & O.P. John (Eds.), *Handbook of personality: Theory and research* (pp. 102–138). New York: Guilford.

Johnson, J.G., Cohen, P., Pine, D.S., Klein, D.F., Kasen, S., & Brook, J.S. (2000). Association between cigarette smoking and anxiety disorders during adolescence and early adulthood. *Journal of the American Medical Association, 284*, 2348–2351.

Joiner, T.E., Catanzaro, S.J., & Laurent, J. (1996). Tripartite structure of positive and negative affect, depression, and anxiety in child and adolescent psychiatric inpatients. *Journal of Abnormal Psychology, 105*, 401–409.

Jung, C.G. (1921/1971). *Psychological types.* Collected works (Vol. 6). Princeton, NJ; Princeton University Press.

Kagan, J. (1994). *Galen's prophecy.* New York: Basic.

Kagan, J. (1997). Temperament and the reactions to unfamiliarity. *Child Development, 68*, 139–143.

Kagan, J. (2001). Temperamental contributions to affective and behavioral profiles in childhood. In S.G. Hofmann & P.M. DiBartolo (Eds.), *From social anxiety to social phobia: Multiple perspectives* (pp. 216–234). Needham Heights, MA: Allyn and Bacon.

Kagan, J., Reznick, J.S., & Snidman, N. (1988). Biological bases of childhood shyness. *Science, 240*, 167–171.

Kagan, J., & Snidman, N. (1999). Early childhood predictors of adult anxiety disorders. *Biological Psychiatry, 46*, 1536–1541.

Kagan, J., Snidman, N., McManis, M., & Woodward, S. (2001). Temperamental contributions to the affect family of anxiety. *Psychiatric Clinics of North America, 24*, 677–688.

Kashani, J.H., & Orvaschel, H. (1990). A community study of anxiety in children and adolescents. *American Journal of Psychiatry, 147*, 313–318.

Kashara, Y. (1988). Social phobia in Japan. *Transcultural Psychiatric Research Review, 25*, 145–150.

Kashdan, T.B., & Herbert, J.D. (2001). Social anxiety disorder in childhood and adolescence: Current status and future directions. *Clinical Child and Family Psychology Review, 4*, 37–61.

Kaslow, N.J., Stark, K.D., Printz, B., Livingston, R., & Tsai, S.L. (1992). Cognitive Triad Inventory for Children: Development and relation to depression and anxiety. *Journal of Clinical Child Psychology, 21*, 339–347.

Kaufman, J., Birmaher, B., Brent, D., Rao, U., Flynn, C., Moreci, P., Williamson, D., & Ryan, N. (1997). Schedule for Affective Disorders and Schizophrenia for School-Age Children-Present and Lifetime Version (K-SADS-PL): Initial reliability and validity data. *Journal of the American Academy of Child and Adolescent Psychiatry, 36*, 980–988.

Kazdin, A.E. (1990). Evaluation of the Automatic Thoughts Questionnaire: Negative cognitive processes and depression among children. *Psychological Assessment, 2*, 73–79.

Kearney, C.A. (2001). *School refusal behavior in youth: A functional approach to assessment and treatment.* Washington, DC: American Psychological Association.

Kearney, C.A. (2002). Identifying the function of school refusal behavior: A revision of the School Refusal Assessment Scale. *Journal of Psychopathology and Behavioral Assessment, 24,* 235–245.

Kearney, C.A. (2003). Bridging the gap among professionals who address youths with school absenteeism: Overview and suggestions for consensus. *Professional Psychology: Research and Practice, 34,* 57–65.

Kearney, C.A., & Albano, A.M. (2000). *When children refuse school: A cognitive-behavioral therapy approach: Therapist guide.* San Antonio, TX: Psychological Corporation.

Kearney, C.A., & Albano, A.M. (2004). The functional profiles of school refusal behavior: Diagnostic aspects. *Behavior Modification, 28,* 147–161.

Kearney, C.A., Albano, A.M., Eisen, A.R., Allan, W.D., & Barlow, D.H. (1997). The phenomenology of panic disorder in youngsters: An empirical study of a clinical sample. *Journal of Anxiety Disorders, 11,* 49–62.

Kearney, C.A., Drabman, R.S., & Beasley, J.F. (1993). The trials of childhood: The development, reliability, and validity of the Daily Life Stressors Scale. *Journal of Child and Family Studies, 2,* 371–388.

Kearney, C.A., & Drake, K. (2002). Social phobia. In M. Hersen (Ed.), *Clinical behavior therapy: Adults and children* (pp. 326–344). New York: Wiley.

Kearney, C.A., & Silverman, W.K. (1992). Let's not push the "panic" button: A critical analysis of panic and panic disorder in adolescents. *Clinical Psychology Review, 12,* 293–305.

Kearney, C.A., & Silverman, W.K. (1996). The evolution and reconciliation of taxonomic strategies for school refusal behavior. *Clinical Psychology: Science and Practice, 3,* 339–354.

Kearney, C.A., & Silverman, W.K. (1998). A critical review of pharmacotherapy for youth with anxiety disorders: Things are not as they seem. *Journal of Anxiety Disorders, 12,* 83–102.

Kearney, C.A., Sims, K.E., Pursell, C.R., & Tillotson, C.A. (2003). Separation anxiety disorder in young children: A longitudinal and family analysis. *Journal of Clinical Child and Adolescent Psychology, 32,* 593–598.

Kendall, P.C. (1994). Treating anxiety disorders in children: Results of a randomized clinical trial. *Journal of Consulting and Clinical Psychology, 62,* 100–110.

Kendall, P.C., & Chansky, T.E. (1991). Considering cognition in anxiety-disordered children. *Journal of Anxiety Disorders, 5,* 167–185.

Kendall, P.C., Chansky, T.E., Kane, M.T., Kim, R.S., Kortlander, E., Ronan, K.R., Sessa, F.M., & Siqueland, L. (1992). *Anxiety disorders in youth: Cognitive-behavioral interventions.* Boston, MA: Allyn and Bacon.

Kendall, P.C., Flannery-Schroeder, E., Panichelli-Mindel, S.M., Southam-Gerow, M., Henin, A., & Warman, M. (1997). Therapy for youths with anxiety disorders: A second randomized clinical trial. *Journal of Consulting and Clinical Psychology, 65,* 366–380.

Kendall, P.C., & Ollendick, T.H. (2004). Setting the research and practice agenda for anxiety in children and adolescence: A topic comes of age. *Cognitive and Behavioral Practice, 11,* 65–74.

Kendall, P.C., & Southam-Gerow, M.A. (1996). Long-term follow-up of a cognitive-behavioral therapy for anxiety-disordered youth. *Journal of Consulting and Clinical Psychology, 64*, 724–730.

Kendall, P.C., & Warman, M.J. (1996). Anxiety disorders in youth: Diagnostic consistency across DSM-III-R and DSM-IV. *Journal of Anxiety Disorders, 10*, 453–463.

Kendler, K.S., Karkowski, L.M., & Prescott, C.A. (1999). Fears and phobias: Reliability and heritability. *Psychological Medicine, 29*, 539–553.

Kendler, K.S., Neale, M.C., Kessler, R.C., Heath, A.C., & Eaves, L.J. (1992). The genetic epidemiology of phobias in women: The interrelationship of agoraphobia, social phobia, situational phobia, and simple phobia. *Archives of General Psychiatry, 49*, 273–281.

Kernberg, P.F., Weiner, A.S., & Bardenstein, K.K. (2000). *Personality disorders in children and adolescents*. New York: Basic.

Kerr, M.M., & Nelson, C.M. (2002). *Strategies for addressing behavior problems in the classroom* (4th. ed.). Upper Saddle River, NJ: Prentice-Hall.

Kessler, R.C., Foster, C.L., Saunders, W.B., & Stang, P.E. (1995). Social consequences of psychiatric disorders, I: Educational attainment. *American Journal of Psychiatry, 152*, 1026–1032.

Kessler, R.C., Stein, M.B., & Berglund, P. (1998). Social phobia subtypes in the National Comorbidity Survey. *American Journal of Psychiatry, 155*, 613–619.

Kindt, M., Bogels, S., & Morren, M. (2003). Processing bias in children with separation anxiety disorder, social phobia and generalised anxiety disorder. *Behaviour Change, 20*, 143–150.

King, N.J. (1994). Physiological assessment. In T.H. Ollendick, N.J. King, & W. Yule (Eds.), *International Handbook of Phobic and Anxiety Disorders in Children and Adolescents* (pp. 365–379). New York: Plenum.

King, N., Murphy, G.C., & Heyne, D. (1997). The nature and treatment of social phobia in youth. *Counselling Psychology Quarterly, 10*, 377–387.

Klein, R.G., & Last, C.G. (1989). *Anxiety disorders in children* (Developmental clinical psychology and psychiatry series, Vol. 20). New York: Sage.

Kovacs, M. (1985). The Interview Schedule for Children (ISC). *Psychopharmacology Bulletin, 21*, 991–994.

Kovacs, M. (1992). *Children's Depression Inventory manual*. North Tonawanda, NY: Multi-Health Systems.

Kovacs, M., Gatsonis, C., Paulauskas, S.L., & Richards, C. (1989). Depressive disorders in childhood. IV. A longitudinal study of comorbidity with and risk for anxiety disorders. *Archives of General Psychiatry, 46*, 776–782.

Kroger, R.O., & Wood, L.A. (1993). Reification, "Faking," and the Big Five. *American Psychologist, 48*, 1297–1298.

Krohne, H.W., & Hock, M. (1991). Relationships between restrictive mother-child interactions and anxiety of the child. *Anxiety Research, 4*, 109–124.

LaFreniere, P.J., & Capuano, F. (1997). Preventive intervention as means of clarifying direction of effects in socialization: Anxious-withdrawn preschoolers case. *Development and Psychopathology, 9*, 551–564.

La Greca, A.M. (1998). *Social anxiety scales for children and adolescents: Manual and instructions for the SASC, SASC-R, SAS-A (adolescents), and parent versions of the scales*. Miami, FL: Author.

La Greca, A.M. (1999). The social anxiety scales for children and adolescents. *the Behavior Therapist, 22*, 133–136.

La Greca, A.M. (2001). Friends or foes? Peer influences on anxiety among children and adolescents. In W.K. Silverman & P.D.A. Treffers (Eds.), *Anxiety disorders in children and adolescents: Research, assessment and intervention* (pp. 159–186). New York: Cambridge University Press.

La Greca, A.M., Dandes, S.K., Wick, P., Shaw, K., & Stone, W.L. (1988). Development of the Social Anxiety Scale for Children: Reliability and concurrent validity. *Journal of Clinical Child Psychology, 17*, 84–91.

La Greca, A.M., & Lopez, N. (1998). Social anxiety among adolescents: Linkages with peer relations and friendships. *Journal of Abnormal Child Psychology, 26*, 83–94.

La Greca, A.M., & Santogrossi, D.A. (1980). Social skills training with elementary school students: A behavioral group approach. *Journal of Consulting and Clinical Psychology, 48*, 220–227.

La Greca, A.M., & Stone, W.L. (1993). Social Anxiety Scale for Children-Revised: Factor structure and concurrent validity. *Journal of Clinical Child Psychology, 22*, 17–27.

Lang, A.J., & Stein, M.B. (2001). Social phobia: Prevalence and diagnostic threshold. *Journal of Clinical Psychiatry, 62 (suppl. 1)*, 5–10.

Lang, P.J. (1968). Fear reduction and fear behavior: Problems in treating a construct. In J.M. Shlien (Ed.), *Research in psychotherapy* (Vol. 3) (pp. 90–102). Washington, DC: American Psychological Association.

Last, C.G. (1991). Somatic complaints in anxiety disordered children. *Journal of Anxiety Disorders, 5*, 125–138.

Last, C.G., Francis, G., Hersen, M., Kazdin, A.E., & Strauss, C.C. (1987). Separation anxiety and school phobia: A comparison using DSM-III criteria. *American Journal of Psychiatry, 144*, 653–657.

Last, C.G., Francis, G., & Strauss, C.C. (1989). Assessing fears in anxiety-disordered children with the Revised Fear Survey Schedule for Children (FSSC-R). *Journal of Clinical Child Psychology, 18*, 137–141.

Last, C.G., Hansen, C., & Franco, N. (1998). Cognitive-behavioral treatment of school phobia. *Journal of the American Academy of Child and Adolescent Psychiatry, 37*, 404–411.

Last, C.G., Hersen, M., Kazdin, A.E., Francis, G., & Grubb, H.J. (1987). Psychiatric illness in the mothers of anxious children. *American Journal of Psychiatry, 144*, 1580–1583.

Last, C.G., Hersen, M., Kazdin, A., Orvaschel, H., & Perrin, S. (1991). Anxiety disorders in children and their families. *Archives of General Psychiatry, 48*, 928–934.

Last, C.G., & Perrin, S. (1993). Anxiety disorders in African-American and White children. *Journal of Abnormal Child Psychology, 21*, 153–164.

Last, C.G., Perrin, S., Hersen, M., & Kazdin, A.E. (1992). DSM-III-R anxiety disorders in children: Sociodemographic and clinical characteristics. *Journal of the American Academy of Child and Adolescent Psychiatry, 31*, 1070–1076.

Last, C.G., Perrin, S., Hersen, M., & Kazdin, A.E. (1996). A prospective study of childhood anxiety disorders. *Journal of the American Academy of Child and Adolescent Psychiatry, 35*, 1502–1510.

Last, C.G., & Strauss, C.C. (1990). School refusal in anxiety-disordered children and adolescents. *Journal of the American Academy of Child and Adolescent Psychiatry, 29*, 31–35.

Last, C.G., Strauss, C.C., & Francis, G. (1987). Comorbidity among childhood anxiety disorders. *Journal of Nervous and Mental Disease, 175*, 726–730.

Laurent, J., & Stark, K.D. (1993). Testing the cognitive content-specificity hypothesis with anxious and depressed youngsters. *Journal of Abnormal Psychology, 102*, 226–237.

Lazarus, A.A., & Abramovitz, A. (1962). The use of "emotive imagery" in the treatment of children's phobias. *Journal of Mental Science, 108*, 191–195.

Leary, M.R. (1990). Responses to social exclusion: Social anxiety, jealousy, loneliness, depression, and low self-esteem. *Journal of Social and Clinical Psychology, 9*, 221–229.

Leary, M.R. (2001). Shyness and the self: Attentional, motivational, and cognitive self-processes in social anxiety and inhibition. In W.R. Crozier & L.E. Alden (Eds.), *International handbook of social anxiety: Concepts, research, and interventions relating to the self and shyness* (pp. 217–234). New York: Wiley.

Leitenberg, H., Yost, L.W., & Carroll-Wilson, M. (1986). Negative cognitive errors in children: Questionnaire development, normative data, and comparisons between children with and without self-reported symptoms of depression, low self-esteem, and evaluation anxiety. *Journal of Consulting and Clinical Psychology, 54*, 528–536.

Lewinsky, H. (1941). The nature of shyness. *British Journal of Psychiatry, 32*, 105–113.

Lewinsohn, P.M., Hops, H., Roberts, R.E., Seeley, J.R., & Andrews, J.A. (1993). Adolescent psychopathology: I. Prevalence and incidence of depression and other DSM-III-R disorders in high school students. *Journal of Abnormal Psychology, 102*, 133–144.

Lewinsohn, P.M., Zinbarg, R., Seeley, J.R., Lewinsohn, M., & Sack, W.H. (1997). Lifetime comorbidity among anxiety disorders and between anxiety disorders and other mental disorders in adolescents. *Journal of Anxiety Disorders, 11*, 377–394.

Lieb, R., Wittchen, H.-U., Hofler, M., Fuetsch, M., Stein, M.B., & Merikangas, K.R. (2000). Parental psychopathology, parenting styles, and the risk of social phobia in offspring: A prospective-longitudinal community study. *Archives of General Psychiatry, 57*, 859–866.

Liebowitz, M.R., Heimberg, R.G., Fresco, D.M., Travers, J., & Stein, M.B. (2000). Social phobia or social anxiety disorder: What's in a name? *Archives of General Psychiatry, 57*, 191–192.

Lindhout, I.E., Boer, F., Markus, M.T., Hoogendijk, T.H.G., Maingay, R., & Borst, S.R. (2003). Sibling relationships of anxiety disordered children – a research note. *Journal of Anxiety Disorders, 17*, 593–601.

Lonigan, C.J., & Phillips, B.M. (2001). Temperamental influences on the development of anxiety disorders. In M.W. Vasey & M.R. Dadds (Eds.), *The developmental psychopathology of anxiety* (pp. 60–91). New York: Oxford University Press.

Lonigan, C.J., Vasey, M.W., Phillips, B.M., & Hazen, R.A. (2004). Temperament, anxiety, and the processing of threat-relevant stimuli. *Journal of Clinical Child and Adolescent Psychology, 33*, 8–20.

Mackintosh, N.J. (1987). Neurobiology, psychology and habituation. *Behaviour Research and Therapy, 25*, 81–97.

Magnusdottir, I., & Smari, J. (1999). Social anxiety in adolescents and appraisal of negative events: Specificity or generality of bias? *Behavioural and Cognitive Psychotherapy, 27*, 223–230.

Mallet, P., & Rodriguez-Tome, G. (1999). Social anxiety with peers in 9- to 14-year-olds. Developmental process and relations with self-consciousness and perceived peer acceptance. *European Journal of Psychology of Education, 14*, 387–402.

Mancini, C., Van Ameringen, M., Szatmari, P., Fugere, C., & Boyle, M. (1996). A high-risk pilot study of the children of adults with social phobia. *Journal of the American Academy of Child and Adolescent Psychiatry, 35*, 1511–1517.

Manassis, K. (2001). Child-parent relations: Attachment and anxiety disorders. In W.K. Silverman & P.D.A. Treffers (Eds.), *Anxiety disorders in children and adolescents: Research, assessment and intervention* (pp. 255–272). New York: Cambridge University Press.

Mancini, C., Van Ameringen, M., Oakman, J.M., & Farvolden, P. (1999). Serotonergic agents in the treatment of social phobia in children and adolescents: A case series. *Depression and Anxiety, 10*, 33–39.

Mannuzza, S., Schneier, F.R., Chapman, T.F., Liebowitz, M.R., Klein, D.F., & Fyer, A.J. (1995). Generalized social phobia: Reliability and validity. *Archives of General Psychiatry, 52*, 230–237.

March, J. (1997). *Multidimensional Anxiety Scale for Children.* North Tonawanda, NY: Multi-Health Systems.

March, J.S., & Albano, A.M. (2002). Anxiety disorders in children and adolescents. In D.J. Stein & E. Hollander (Eds.), *Textbook of anxiety disorders* (pp. 415–427). Washington, DC: American Psychiatric Publishing.

March, J.S., & Ollendick, T.H. (2004). Integrated psychosocial and pharmacological treatment. In T.H. Ollendick & J.S. March (Eds), *Phobic and anxiety disorders in children and adolescents: A clinician's guide to effective psychosocial and pharmacological interventions* (pp. 141–172). New York: Oxford University Press.

March, J.S., Sullivan, K., & Parker, J. (1999). Test-retest reliability of the Multidimensional Anxiety Scale for Children. *Journal of Anxiety Disorders, 13*, 349–358.

Marshall, W.L. (1985). The effects of variable exposure in flooding therapy. *Behavior Therapy, 16*, 117–135.

Martin, C., Cabrol, S., Bouvard, M.P., Lepine, J.P., & Mouren-Simeoni, M.C. (1999). Anxiety and depressive disorders in fathers and mothers of anxious school-refusing children. *Journal of the American Academy of Child and Adolescent Psychiatry, 38,* 916–922.

Martin, M., Horder, P., & Jones, G.V. (1992). Integral bias in naming phobia-related words. *Cognition and Emotion, 6,* 479–486.

Masia, C.L., Klein, R.G., Storch, E.A., & Corda, B. (2001). School-based behavioral treatment for social anxiety disorder in adolescents: Results of a pilot study. *Journal of the American Academy of Child and Adolescent Psychiatry, 40,* 780–786.

Masia, C.L., & Morris, T.L. (1998). Parental factors associated with social anxiety: Methodological limitations and suggestions for integrated behavioral research. *Clinical Psychology: Science and Practice, 5,* 211–228.

Matheny, A.P. (1989). Children's behavioral inhibition over age and across situations: Genetic similarity for a trait during change. *Journal of Personality, 57,* 215–235.

McCrae, R.R., & Costa, P.T., Jr. (1986). Clinical assessment can benefit from recent advances in personality psychology. *American Psychologist, 41,* 1001–1003.

McCrae, R.R., & Costa, P.T., Jr. (1999). A five-factor theory of personality. In L.A. Pervin & O.P. John (Eds.), *Handbook of personality: Theory and research* (pp. 139–153). New York: Guilford.

McGee, R., Feehan, M., Williams, S., Partridge, F., Silva, P.A., & Kelly, J. (1990). DSM-III disorders in a large sample of adolescents. *Journal of the American Academy of Child and Adolescent Psychiatry, 29,* 611–619.

McManis, M.H., Kagan, J., Snidman, N.C., & Woodward, S.A. (2002). EEG asymmetry, power, and temperament in children. *Developmental Psychobiology, 41,* 169–177.

McNeil, D.W. (2001). Terminology and evolution of constructs in social anxiety and social phobia. In S.G. Hofmann & P.M. DiBartolo (Eds.), *From social anxiety to social phobia: Multiple perspectives* (pp. 8–19). Needham Heights, MA: Allyn and Bacon.

McNeil, D.W., Lejuez, C.W., & Sorrell, J.T. (2001). Behavioral theories of social anxiety and social phobia: Contributions of basic behavioral principles. In S.G. Hofmann & P.M. DiBartolo (Eds.), *From social anxiety to social phobia: Multiple perspectives* (pp. 235–253). Needham Heights, MA: Allyn and Bacon.

McNeil, D.W., Ries, B.J., & Turk, C.L. (1995). Behavioral assessment: Self- and other-report, physiology, and overt behavior. In R.G. Heimberg, M.R. Liebowitz, D.A. Hope, & F.R. Schneier (Eds.), *Social phobia: Diagnosis, assessment, and treatment* (pp. 202–231). New York: Guilford.

Meichenbaum, D. (1977). *Cognitive behavior modification: An integrative approach.* New York: Plenum.

Melfsen, S., Osterlow, J., & Florin, I. (2000). Deliberate emotional expressions of socially anxious children and their mothers. *Journal of Anxiety Disorders, 14,* 249–261.

Mendlowitz, S.L., Manassis, K., Bradley, S., Scapillato, D., Miezitis, S., & Shaw, B.F. (1999). Cognitive-behavioral group treatments in childhood anxiety disorders: The role of parental involvement. *Journal of the American Academy of Child and Adolescent Psychiatry, 38,* 1223–1229.

Merikangas, K.R., Avenevoli, S., Dierker, L., & Grillon, C. (1999). Vulnerability factors among children at risk for anxiety disorders. *Biological Psychiatry, 46,* 1523–1535.

Messer, S.C., & Beidel, D.C. (1994). Psychosocial correlates of childhood anxiety disorders. *Journal of the American Academy of Child and Adolescent Psychiatry, 33,* 975–983.

Mick, M.A., & Telch, M.J. (1998). Social anxiety and history of behavioral inhibition in young adults. *Journal of Anxiety Disorders, 12,* 1–20.

Money, J., & Pollitt, E. (1966). Studies in the psychology of dwarfism II: Personality maturation and response to growth hormone treatment in hypopituitary dwarfs. *Journal of Pediatrics, 68,* 381–390.

Moos, R.H., & Moos, B.S. (1986). *Family Environment Scale* manual (2nd. ed.). Palo Alto, CA: Consulting Psychologists Press.

Morris, T.L. (2001). Social phobia. In M.W. Vasey & M.R. Dadds (Eds.), *The developmental psychopathology of anxiety* (pp. 435–458). New York: Oxford University Press.

Morris, T.L., Hirshfeld-Becker, D.R., Henin, A., & Storch, E.A. (2004). Developmentally sensitive assessment of social anxiety. *Cognitive and Behavioral Practice, 11,* 13–28.

Morris, T.L., & Masia, C.L. (1998). Psychometric evaluation of the Social Phobia and Anxiety Inventory for Children: Concurrent validity and normative data. *Journal of Clinical Child Psychology, 27,* 452–458.

Moutier, C.Y., & Stein, M.B. (2001). The biological basis of social phobia. In S.G. Hofmann & P.M. DiBartolo (Eds.), *From social anxiety to social phobia: Multiple perspectives* (pp. 179–199). Needham Heights, MA: Allyn and Bacon.

Mowrer, O.H. (1960). *Learning theory and behavior.* New York: Wiley.

Muris, P., Meesters, C., Merckelbach, H., Sermon, A., & Zwakhalen, S. (1998). Worry in normal children. *Journal of the American Academy of Child and Adolescent Psychiatry, 37,* 703–710.

Muris, P., & Merckelbach, H. (2001). The etiology of childhood specific phobia: A multifactorial model. In M.W. Vasey & M.R. Dadds (Eds.), *The developmental psychopathology of anxiety* (pp. 355–385). New York: Oxford.

Muris, P., Merckelbach, H., & Damsma, E. (2000). Threat perception bias in non-referred, socially anxious children. *Journal of Clinical Child Psychology, 29,* 348–359.

Muris, P., Merckelbach, H., Gadet, B., & Moulaert, V. (2000). Fears, worries, and scary dreams in 4- to 12-year old children: Their content, developmental pattern, and origins. *Journal of Clinical Child Psychology, 29,* 43–52.

Muris, P., Merckelbach, H., Mayer, B., & Meesters, C. (1998). Common fears and their relationship to anxiety disorders symptomatology in normal children. *Personality and Individual Differences, 24,* 575–578.

Muris, P., Merckelbach, H., Schmidt, H., & Mayer, B. (1999). The revised version of the Screen for Child Anxiety Related Emotional Disorders (SCARED-R): Factor structure in normal children. *Personality and Individual Differences, 26,* 99–112.

Muris, P., Merckelbach, H., Wessel, I., & van de Ven, M. (1999). Psychopathological correlates of self-reported behavioural inhibition in normal children. *Behaviour Research and Therapy, 37*, 575–584.

Muris, P., Rapee, R., Meesters, C., Schouten, E., & Geers, M. (2003). Threat perception abnormalities in children: The role of anxiety disorders symptoms, chronic anxiety, and state anxiety. *Journal of Anxiety Disorders, 17*, 271–287.

Myers, M.G., Stein, M.B., & Aarons, G.A. (2002). Cross validation of the Social Anxiety Scale for Adolescents in a high school sample. *Journal of Anxiety Disorders, 16*, 221–232.

Nauta, M.H., Scholing, A., Emmelkamp, P.M.G., & Minderaa, R.B. (2003). Cognitive-behavioral therapy for children with anxiety disorders in a clinical setting: No additional effect of a cognitive parent training. *Journal of the American Academy of Child and Adolescent Psychiatry, 42*, 1270–1278.

Neal, J.A., & Edelmann, R.J. (2003). The etiology of social phobia: Toward a developmental profile. *Clinical Psychology Review, 23*, 761–786.

Nelson, E.C., Grant, J.D., Bucholz, K.K., Glowinski, A., Madden, P.A.F., Reich, W., & Heath, A.C. (2000). Social phobia in a population-based female adolescent twin sample: Co-morbidity and associated suicide-related symptoms. *Psychological Medicine, 30*, 797–804.

Newman, D.L., Moffitt, T.E., Caspi, A., Magdol, L., Silva, P.A., & Stanton, W.R. (1996). Psychiatric disorder in a birth cohort of young adults: Prevalence, co-morbidity, clinical significance, and new case incidence from ages 11 to 21. *Journal of Consulting and Clinical Psychology, 64*, 552–562.

Oakman, J.M., Farvolden, P., Van Ameringen, M., & Mancini, C. (2000). Challenges in the treatment of generalized social phobia: Why our treatments work, and why they don't work better. In W.R. Crozier (Ed.), *Shyness: Development, consolidation and change* (pp. 207–226). New York: Routledge.

Ohman, A. (1986). Face the beast and fear the face: Animal and social fears as prototypes for evolutionary analyses of emotion. *Psychophysiology, 23*, 123–145.

Olivares, J., & Garcia-Lopez, L.J. (2002). Aplicacion de la version espanola de la Terapia para la Eficacia Social en Adolescentes (SET-A$_{SV}$) al tratamiento de un adolescente con fobia social generalizada [Results of the Social Effectiveness Therapy for Adolescents (SET-A) in an adolescent with social phobia]. *Psicologia Conductual, 10*, 409–419.

Olivares, J., Garcia-Lopez, L.J., Beidel, D.C., Turner, S.M., Albano, A.M., & Hidalgo, M.D. (2002). Results at long-term among three psychological treatments for adolescents with generalized social phobia (I): Statistical significance. *Psicologia Conductual, 10*, 147–164.

Olivares, J., Garcia-Lopez, L.J., Hidalgo, M.D., & Caballo, V. (2004). Relationships among social anxiety measures and their invariance: A confirmatory factor analysis. *European Journal of Psychological Assessment, 20*, 172–179.

Olivares, J., Garcia-Lopez, L.J., Hidalgo, M.D., Turner, S.M., & Beidel, D.C. (1999). The Social Phobia and Anxiety Inventory: Reliability and validity in an adolescent Spanish population. *Journal of Psychopathology and Behavioral Assessment, 21*, 67–78.

Ollendick, T.H. (1983). Reliability and validity of the Revised Fear Survey Schedule for Children (FSSC-R). *Behaviour Research and Therapy, 21,* 685–692.

Ollendick, T.H. (1998). Panic disorder in children and adolescents: New developments, new directions. *Journal of Clinical Child Psychology, 27,* 234–245.

Ollendick, T.H., & Cerny, J.A. (1981). *Clinical behavior therapy with children.* New York: Plenum.

Ollendick, T.H., & Hirshfeld-Becker, D.R. (2002). The developmental psychopathology of social anxiety disorder. *Biological Psychiatry, 51,* 44–58.

Ollendick, T.H., & March, J.S. (2004). *Phobic and anxiety disorders in children and adolescents: A clinician's guide to effective psychosocial and pharmacological interventions.* New York: Oxford University Press.

Ollendick, T.H., Vasey, M.W., & King, N.J. (2001). Operant conditioning influences in childhood anxiety. In M.W. Vasey & M.R. Dadds (Eds.), *The developmental psychopathology of anxiety* (pp. 231–252). New York: Oxford University Press.

Ollendick, T.H., Yang, B., King, N.J., Dong, Q., & Akande, A. (1996). Fears in American, Australian, Chinese, and Nigerian children and adolescents: A cross-cultural study. *Journal of Child Psychology and Psychiatry, 37,* 213–220.

Olson, D.H., Portner, J., & Lavee, Y. (1987). Family Adaptability and Cohesion Evaluation Scales (FACES III). In N. Fredman & R. Sherman (Eds.), *Handbook of measurements for marriage and family therapy* (pp. 180–185). New York: Brunner Mazel.

Ost, L.-G., & Hugdahl, K. (1981). Acquisition of phobias and anxiety response patterns in clinical patients. *Behaviour Research and Therapy, 16,* 439–447.

Panella, D., & Henggeler, S.W. (1986). Peer interactions of conduct-disordered, anxious-withdrawn, and well-adjusted Black adolescents. *Journal of Abnormal Child Psychology, 14,* 1–11.

Parker, G. (1979). Reported parental characteristics of agoraphobics and social phobics. *British Journal of Psychiatry, 135,* 555–560.

Parker, G., Roussos, J., Hadzi-Pavlovic, D., Mitchell, P., Wilhelm, K., & Austin, M.-P. (1997). The development of a refined measure of dysfunctional parenting and assessment of its relevance in patients with affective disorders. *Psychological Medicine, 27,* 1193–1203.

Parkhurst, J.T., & Asher, S.R. (1992). Peer rejection in middle school: Subgroup differences in behavior, loneliness, and interpersonal concerns. *Developmental Psychology, 28,* 231–241.

Pawlak, C., Pascual-Sanchez, T., Rae, P., Fischer, W., & Ladame, F. (1999). Anxiety disorders, comorbidity, and suicide attempts in adolescence: A preliminary investigation. *European Psychiatry, 14,* 132–136.

Payne, M.A. (1988). Adolescent fears: Some Carribean findings. *Journal of Youth and Adolescence, 17,* 255–266.

Peleg-Popko, O. (2002). Children's test anxiety and family interaction patterns. *Anxiety, Stress, & Coping, 15,* 45–59.

Peleg-Popko, O., & Dar, R. (2001). Marital quality, family patterns, and children's fears and social anxiety. *Contemporary Family Therapy, 23,* 465–487.

Perrin, S., & Last, C.G. (1997). Worrisome thoughts in children clinically referred for anxiety disorder. *Journal of Clinical Child Psychology, 26*, 181–189.

Persons, J.B. (1989). *Cognitive therapy in practice: A case formulation approach.* New York: Norton.

Pilkonis, P.A. (1977). Shyness, public and private, and its relationship to other measures of social behavior. *Journal of Personality, 45*, 585–595.

Pina, A.A., & Silverman, W.K. (2004). Clinical phenomenology, somatic symptoms, and distress in Hispanic/Latino and European American youths with anxiety disorders. *Journal of Clinical Child and Adolescent Psychology, 33*, 227–236.

Pine, D.S. (2001). Affective neuroscience and the development of social anxiety disorder. *Psychiatric Clinics of North America, 24*, 689–705.

Pine, D.S., Cohen, P., Gurley, D., Brook, J., & Ma, Y. (1998). The risk for early-adulthood anxiety and depressive disorders in adolescents with anxiety and depressive disorders. *Archives of General Psychiatry, 55*, 56–64.

Plomin, R., & Daniels, D. (1986). Genetics and shyness. In W.H. Jones, J.M. Cheek, & S.R. Briggs (Eds.), *Shyness: Perspectives on research and treatment* (pp. 63–80). New York: Plenum.

Plomin, R., Emde, R., Braungart, J.M., Campos, J., Corley, R., Fulker, D.W., Kagan, J., Reznick, S., Robinson, J., Zahn-Waxler, C., & DeFries, J.C. (1993). Genetic change and continuity from 14 to 20 months: The MacArthur Longitudinal Twin Study. *Child Development, 64*, 1354–1376.

Pollack, M.H., Otto, M.W., Rosenbaum, J.F., Sachs, G.S. (1992). Personality disorders in patients with panic disorder: Association with childhood anxiety disorders, early trauma, comorbidity, and chronicity. *Comprehensive Psychiatry, 33*, 78–83.

Prins, P.J.M., Groot, M.J.M., & Hanewald, G.J.F.P. (1994). Cognition in test-anxious children: The role of on-task and coping cognition reconsidered. *Journal of Consulting and Clinical Psychology, 62*, 404–409.

Prins, P.J.M., & Hanewald, G.J.F.P. (1997). Self-statements of test-anxious children: Thought-listing and questionnaire approaches. *Journal of Consulting and Clinical Psychology, 65*, 440–447.

Prior, M., Smart, D., Sanson, A., & Oberklaid, F. (2000). Does shy-inhibited temperament in childhood lead to problems in adolescence? *Journal of the American Academy of Child and Adolescent Psychiatry, 39*, 461–468.

Quilty, L.C., Van Ameringen, M., Mancini, C., Oakman, J., & Farvolden, P. (2003). Quality of life and the anxiety disorders. *Journal of Anxiety Disorders, 17*, 405–426.

Rachman, S. (1977). The conditioning theory of fear acquisition: A critical examination. *Behaviour Research and Therapy, 15*, 375–387.

Rachman, S. (1980). Emotional processing. *Behaviour Research and Therapy, 18*, 51–60.

Radke-Yarrow, M., McCann, K., DeMulder, E., Belmont, B., Martinez, P., Richardson, D.T. (1995). Attachment in the context of high risk conditions. *Development and Psychopathology, 7*, 247–265.

Rapee, R.M. (1997). Potential role of childrearing practices in the development of anxiety and depression. *Clinical Psychology Review, 17*, 47–67.

Rapee, R.M., Barrett, P.M., Dadds, M.R., & Evans, L. (1994). Reliability of the DSM-III-R childhood anxiety disorders using structured interview: Interrater and parent-child agreement. *Journal of the American Academy of Child and Adolescent Psychiatry, 33*, 984–992.

Rapee, R.M., & Lim, L. (1992). Discrepancy between self- and observer ratings of performance in social phobics. *Journal of Abnormal Psychology, 101*, 728–731.

Reich, J., & Yates, W. (1988). Family history of psychiatric disorders in social phobia. *Comprehensive Psychiatry, 29*, 72–75.

Reinecke, M.A., Dattilio, F.M., & Freeman, A. (2003). *Cognitive therapy with children and adolescents: A casebook for clinical practice* (2nd. ed.). New York: Guilford.

Rende, R., Warner, V., Wickramarante, P., & Weissman, M.M. (1999). Sibling aggregation for psychiatric disorders in offspring at high and low risk for depression: 10-year follow-up. *Psychological Medicine, 29*, 1291–1298.

Research Unit on Pediatric Psychopharmacology Anxiety Study Group. (2001). Fluvoxamine for the treatment of anxiety disorders in children and adolescents. *New England Journal of Medicine, 344*, 1279–1285.

Research Units on Pediatric Psychopharmacology Anxiety Study Group (2002). The Pediatric Anxiety Rating Scale (PARS): Development and psychometric properties. *Journal of the American Academy of Child and Adolescent Psychiatry, 41*, 1061–1069.

Reynolds, C.R., & Richmond, B.O. (1985). *Revised Children's Manifest Anxiety Scale manual*. Los Angeles, CA: Western Psychological Services.

Rheingold, A.A., Herbert, J.D., & Franklin, M.E. (2003). Cognitive bias in adolescents with social anxiety disorder. *Cognitive Therapy and Research, 27*, 639–655.

Riley, A.W., Ensminger, M.E., Green, B., & Kang, M. (1998). Social role functioning by adolescents with psychiatric disorders. *Journal of the American Academy of Child and Adolescent Psychiatry, 37*, 620–628.

Ritter, B. (1968). The group treatment of children's snake phobias using vicarious and contact desensitization procedures. *Behaviour Research and Therapy, 6*, 1–6.

Robinson, J.L., Kagan, J., Reznick, J.S., & Corley, R. (1992). The heritability of inhibited and uninhibited behavior: A twin study. *Developmental Psychology, 28*, 1030–1037.

Rodriguez, J.O., Alcazar, A.I.R., Caballo, V.E., Garcia-Lopez, L.J., Amoros, M.O., & Lopez-Gollonet, C. (2003). El tratamiento de la fobia social en ninos y adolescentes: Una revision meta-analitica. *Psicologia Conductual, 11*, 599–622.

Rodriguez, J.O., Caballo, V.E., Garcia-Lopez, L.J., Alcazar, A.I.R., & Lopez-Gollonet, C. (2003). Una revision de los estudios epidemiologicos sobre fobia social en poblacion infantil, adolescente y adulta. *Psicologia Conductual, 11*, 405–427.

Rodriguez, J.O., & Garcia-Lopez, L.J. (2001). Un neuvo tratamiento multicomponente para la poblacion adolescente con fobia social generalizada: Resultados de un estudio piloto [A new multicomponent treatment for adolescents with generalized social phobia: Results of a pilot study]. *Psicologia Conductual, 9*, 247–254.

Ronan, K.R., Kendall, P.C., & Rowe, M. (1994). Negative affectivity in children: Development and validation of a self-statement questionnaire. *Cognitive Therapy and Research, 18,* 509–528.

Rose, R.J., & Ditto, W.B. (1983). A developmental-genetic analysis of common fears from early adolescence to early adulthood. *Child Development, 54,* 361–368.

Rosenbaum, J.F., Biederman, J., Gersten, M., Hirshfeld, D.R., Meminger, S.R., Herman, J.B., Kagan, J., Reznick, J.S., & Snidman, N. (1988). Behavioral inhibition in children of parents with panic disorder and agoraphobia: A controlled study. *Archives of General Psychiatry, 45,* 463–470.

Rosenbaum, J.F., Biederman, J., Hirshfeld, D.R., Bolduc, E.A., Faraone, S.V., Kagan, J., Snidman, N., & Reznick, J.S. (1991). Further evidence of an association between behavioral inhibition and anxiety disorders: Results from a family study of children from a non-clinical sample. *Journal of Psychiatry Research, 25,* 49–65.

Rosenbaum, J.F., Biederman, J., Hirshfeld-Becker, D.R., Kagan, J., Snidman, N., Friedman, D., Nineberg, A., Gallery, D.J., & Faraone, S.V. (2000). A controlled study of behavioral inhibition in children of parents with panic disorder and depression. *American Journal of Psychiatry, 157,* 2002–2010.

Rosenstein, D.S., & Horowitz, H.A. (1996). Adolescent attachment and psychopathology. *Journal of Consulting and Clinical Psychology, 64,* 244–253.

Roth, D.A., & Heimberg, R.G. (2001). Cognitive-behavioral models of social anxiety disorder. *Psychiatric Clinics of North America, 24,* 753–771.

Rothbart, M.K., & Mauro, J.A. (1990). Temperament, behavioral inhibition, and shyness in childhood. In H. Leitenberg (Ed.), *Handbook of social and evaluation anxiety* (pp. 139–160). New York: Plenum.

Rowe, D.C., Stever, C., Gard, J.M.C., Cleveland, H.H., Sanders, M.L., Abramowitz, A., Kozol, S., Mohr, J.H., Sherman, S.L., & Waldman, I.D. (1998). The relation of the dopamine transporter gene (DATI) to symptoms of internalizing disorders in children. *Behavior Genetics, 28,* 215–225.

Rubin, K.H., & Asendorpf, J. (1993). *Social withdrawal, inhibition, and shyness in childhood.* Hillsdale, NJ: Erlbaum.

Rubin, K.H., Burgess, K.B., & Coplan, R. (2002). Social withdrawal and shyness. In P.K. Smith & C. Hart (Eds.), *Blackwell handbook of childhood social development* (pp. 329–352). London: Blackwell.

Rubin, K.H., Burgess, K.B., & Hastings, P.D. (2002). Stability and social-behavioral consequences of toddlers' inhibited temperament and parenting behaviors. *Child Development, 73,* 483–495.

Rubin, K.H., Burgess, K.B., Kennedy, A.E., & Stewart, S.L. (2003). Social withdrawal in childhood. In E.J. Mash & R.A. Barkley, (Eds.), *Child psychopathology* (2nd. ed.) (pp. 372–406). New York: Guilford.

Rubin, K.H., Hastings, P.D., Stewart, S.L., Henderson, H.A., & Chen, X. (1997). The consistency and concomitants of inhibition: Some of the children, all of the time. *Child Development, 68,* 467–483.

Rubin, K.H., LeMare, L.J., & Lollis, S. (1990). Social withdrawal in childhood: Developmental pathways to peer rejection. In S.R. Asher & J.D. Coie (Eds.), *Peer rejection in childhood* (pp. 217–249). New York: Cambridge.

Rubin, K.H., Nelson, L.J., Hastings, P., & Asendorpf, J. (1999). The transaction between parents' perceptions of their children's shyness and their parenting styles. *International Journal of Behavioral Development, 23*, 937–958.

Russo, M.F., & Beidel, D.C. (1994). Comorbidity of childhood anxiety and externalizing disorders: Prevalence, associated characteristics, and validation issues. *Clinical Psychology Review, 14*, 199–221.

Sarason, S.B., Davidson, K.S., Lighthall, F.F., Waite, R.R., & Ruebush, B.K. (1960). *Anxiety in elementary school children.* New York: Wiley.

Saudino, K.J. (2001). Behavioral genetics, social phobia, social fears, and related temperaments. In S.G. Hofmann & P.M. DiBartolo (Eds.), *From social anxiety to social phobia: Multiple perspectives* (pp. 200–215). Needham Heights, MA: Allyn and Bacon.

Scarpa, A., Raine, A., Venables, P.H., & Mednick, S.A. (1995). The stability of inhibited/uninhibited temperament from ages 3 to 11 years in Mauritian children. *Journal of Abnormal Child Psychology, 23*, 607–618.

Schlenker, B.R., & Leary, M.R. (1982). Social anxiety and self-presentation: A conceptualization and model. *Psychological Bulletin, 92*, 641–669.

Schmidt, L.A. (1999). Frontal brain electrical activity in shyness and sociability. *Psychological Science, 10*, 316–320.

Schmidt, L.A., & Fox, N.A. (1994). Patterns of cortical electrophysiology and autonomic activity in adults' shyness and sociability. *Biological Psychology, 38*, 183–198.

Schmidt, L.A., & Fox, N.A. (1999). Conceptual, biological, and behavioral distinctions among different categories of shy children. In L.A. Schmidt & J. Schulkin (Eds.), *Extreme fear, shyness, and social phobia: Origins, biological mechanisms, and clinical outcomes* (pp. 47–66). New York: Oxford.

Schmidt, L.A., & Tasker, S.L. (2000). Childhood shyness: Determinants, development and "depathology." In W.R. Crozier (Ed.), *Shyness: Development, consolidation and change* (pp. 30–46). New York: Routledge.

Schneider, F., Weiss, U., Kessler, C., Muller-Gartner, H.-W., Posse, S., Salloum, J.B., Grodd, W., Himmelmann, F., Gaebel, W., & Birbaumer, N. (1999). Subcortical correlates of differential classical conditioning of aversive emotional reactions in social phobia. *Biological Psychiatry, 45*, 863–871.

Schneier, F., & Welkowitz, L.A. (1996). *The hidden face of shyness: Understanding and overcoming social anxiety.* New York: Avon.

Schneier, F.R., Johnson, J., Hornig, C.D., Liebowitz, M.R., & Weissman, M.M. (1992). Social phobia: Comorbidity and morbidity in an epidemiologic sample. *Archives of General Psychiatry, 49*, 282–288.

Schniering, C.A., Hudson, J.L., & Rapee, R.M. (2000). Issues in the diagnosis and assessment of anxiety disorders in children and adolescents. *Clinical Psychology Review, 20*, 453–478.

Schwartz, C.E., Snidman, N., & Kagan, J. (1999). Adolescent social anxiety as an outcome of inhibited temperament in childhood. *Journal of the American Academy of Child and Adolescent Psychiatry, 38*, 1008–1015.

Shaffer, D., Fisher, P., Dulcan, M.K., Davies, M., Piacentini, J., Schwab-Stone, M.E., Lahey, B.B., Bourdon, K., Jensen, P.S., Bird, H.R., Canino, G., & Regier, D.A.

(1996). The NIMH Diagnostic Interview for Children version 2.3 (DISC-2.3): Description, acceptability, prevalence rates, and performance in the MECA study. *Journal of the American Academy of Child and Adolescent Psychiatry, 35,* 865–877.

Shelton, K.K., Frick, P.J., & Wootten, J. (1996). Assessment of parenting practices in families of elementary school-age children. *Journal of Clinical Child Psychology, 25,* 317–329.

Silverman, W.K. (1994). Structured diagnostic interviews. In T.H. Ollendick, N.J. King, & W. Yule (Eds.), *International Handbook of Phobic and Anxiety Disorders in Children and Adolescents* (pp. 293–315). New York: Plenum.

Silverman, W.K., & Albano, A.M. (1996). *The Anxiety Disorders Interview Schedule for Children for DSM-IV, child and parent versions.* San Antonio, TX: Psychological Corporation.

Silverman, W.K., & Eisen, A.R. (1992). Age differences in the reliability of parent and child reports of child anxious symptomatology using a structured interview. *Journal of the American Academy of Child and Adolescent Psychiatry, 31,* 117–124.

Silverman, W.K., & Eisen, A.R. (1993). Overanxious disorder in children. In R.T. Ammerman & M. Hersen (Eds.), *Handbook of behavior therapy with children and adults: A developmental and longitudinal perspective* (pp. 189–201). Needham, MA: Allyn and Bacon.

Silverman, W.K., Ginsburg, G.S., & Goedhart, A.W. (1999). Factor structure of the childhood anxiety sensitivity index. *Behaviour Research and Therapy, 37,* 903–917.

Silverman, W.K., & Kurtines, W.M. (1996). *Anxiety and phobic disorders: A pragmatic approach.* New York: Plenum.

Silverman, W.K., Kurtines, W.M., Ginsburg, G.S., Weems, C.F., Lumpkin, P.W., & Carmichael, D.H. (1999a). Treating anxiety disorders in children with group cognitive-behavioral therapy: A randomized clinical trial. *Journal of Consulting and Clinical Psychology, 67,* 995–1003.

Silverman, W.K., Kurtines, W.M., Ginsburg, G.S., Weems, C.F., Rabian, B., & Serafini, L.T. (1999b). Contingency management, self-control, and education support in the treatment of childhood phobic disorders: A randomized clinical trial. *Journal of Consulting and Clinical Psychology, 67,* 675–687.

Silverman, W.K., La Greca, A.M., & Wasserstein, S. (1995). What do children worry about?: Worries and their relationship to anxiety. *Child Development, 66,* 671–686.

Silverman, W.K., & Nelles, W.B. (1988). The Anxiety Disorders Interview Schedule for Children. *Journal of the American Academy of Child and Adolescent Psychiatry, 27,* 772–778.

Silverman, W.K., & Rabian, B. (1993). Simple phobias. *Child and Adolescent Psychiatric Clinics of North America, 2,* 603–622.

Silverman, W.K., & Rabian, B. (1995). Test-retest reliability of the DSM-III-R childhood anxiety disorders symptoms using the Anxiety Disorders Interview Schedule for Children. *Journal of Anxiety Disorders, 9,* 139–150.

Silverman, W.K., Saavedra, L.M., & Pina, A.A. (2001). Test-retest reliability of anxiety symptoms and diagnoses with the Anxiety Disorders Interview Schedule for DSM-IV: Child and Parent Versions. *Journal of the American Academy of Child and Adolescent Psychiatry, 40*, 937–944.

Silverman, W.K., & Treffers, P.D.A. (2001). *Anxiety disorders in children and adolescents: Research, assessment and intervention*. New York: Cambridge University Press.

Silverman, W.K., & Weems, C.F. (1999). Anxiety sensitivity in children. In S. Taylor (Ed.), *Anxiety sensitivity: Theory, research and treatment of the fear of anxiety* (pp. 239–268). Hillsdale, NJ: Erlbaum.

Simonian, S.J., Beidel, D.C., Turner, S.M., Berkes, J.L., & Long, J.H. (2001). Recognition of facial affect by children and adolescents diagnosed with social phobia. *Child Psychiatry and Human Development, 32*, 137–145.

Skinner, H.A., Steinhauer, P.D., & Santa-Barbara, J. (1995). *Family Assessment Measure, Version III (FAM-III)*. North Tonawanda, NY: Multi-Health Systems.

Skre, I., Onstad, S., Torgersen, S., Lygren, S., & Kringlen, E. (1993). A twin study of DSM-III-R anxiety disorders. *Acta Psychiatrica Scandanavia, 88*, 85–92.

Smari, J., Petursdottir, G., & Porsteindottir, V. (2001). Social anxiety and depression in adolescents in relation to perceived competence and situational appraisal. *Journal of Adolescence, 24*, 199–207.

Smith, P.K., Eaton, L., & Hindmarch, A. (1982). How one-year-olds respond to strangers: A two-person situation. *Journal of Genetic Psychology, 140*, 147–148.

Sonntag, H., Wittchen, H.-U., Hofler, M., Kessler, R.C., & Stein, M.B. (2000). Are social fears and DSM-IV social anxiety disorder associated with smoking and nicotine dependence in adolescents and young adults? *European Psychiatry, 15*, 67–74.

Southam-Gerow, M.A., & Kendall, P.C. (2000). A preliminary study of the emotion understanding of youths referred for treatment of anxiety disorders. *Journal of Clinical Child Psychology, 29*, 319–327.

Southam-Gerow, M.A., Kendall, P.C., & Weersing, V.W. (2001). Examining outcome variability: Correlates of treatment response in a child and adolescent anxiety clinic. *Journal of Clinical Child Psychology, 30*, 422–436.

Spence, S.H. (1994). Preventative strategies. In T.H. Ollendick, N.J. King, & W. Yule (Eds.), *International Handbook of Phobic and Anxiety Disorders in Children and Adolescents* (pp. 453–474). New York: Plenum.

Spence, S.H. (2001). Prevention strategies. In M.W. Vasey & M.R. Dadds (Eds.), *The developmental psychopathology of anxiety* (pp. 325–351). New York: Oxford University Press.

Spence, S.H., Barrett, P.M., & Turner, C.M. (2003). Psychometric properties of the Spence Children's Anxiety Scale with young adolescents. *Journal of Anxiety Disorders, 17*, 605–625.

Spence, S.H., Donovan, C., & Brechman-Toussaint, M. (1999). Social skills, social outcomes, and cognitive features of childhood social phobia. *Journal of Abnormal Psychology, 108*, 211–221.

Spence, S.H., Donovan, C., & Brechman-Toussaint, M. (2000). The treatment of childhood social phobia: The effectiveness of a social skills training-based, cognitive-behavioural intervention, with and without parental involvement. *Journal of Child Psychology and Psychiatry, 41*, 713–726.

Spielberger, C.D. (1973). *Manual for the State-Trait Anxiety Inventory for Children*. Palo Alto, CA: Consulting Psychologists Press.

Sprafkin, J., Gadow, K.D., Salisbury, H., Schneider, J., & Loney, J. (2002). Further evidence of reliability and validity of the Child Symptom Inventory-4: Parent checklist in clinically referred boys. *Journal of Clinical Child and Adolescent Psychology, 31*, 513–524.

Stableford, W. (1979). Parental treatment of a child's noise phobia. *Journal of Behavior Therapy and Experimental Psychiatry, 10*, 159–160.

Stabler, B., Clopper, R.R., Siegel, P.T., Nicholas, L.M., Silva, S.G., Tancer, M.E., & Underwood, L.E. (1996). Links between growth hormone deficiency, adaptation and social phobia. *Hormone Research, 45*, 30–33.

Stabler, B., Clopper, R.R., Siegel, P.T., Stoppani, C., Compton, P.G., & Underwood, L.E. (1994). Academic achievement and psychological adjustment in short children. *Journal of Developmental and Behavioral Pediatrics, 15*, 1–6.

Stein, D.J., & Matsunaga, H. (2001). Cross-cultural aspects of social anxiety disorder. *Psychiatric Clinics of North America, 24*, 773–782.

Stein, M.B., Asmundson, G.J.G., & Chartier, M. (1994). Autonomic responsivity in generalized social phobia. *Journal of Affective Disorders, 31*, 211–221.

Stein, M.B., Chartier, M.J., Hazen, A.L., Kozak, M.L., Tancer, M.E., Lander, S., Furer, P., Chubaty, D., & Walker, J.R. (1998). A direct-interview family study of generalized social phobia. *American Journal of Psychiatry, 155*, 90–97.

Stein, M.B., Chartier, M.J., Kozak, M.V., King, N., & Kennedy, J.L. (1998). Genetic linkage to the serotonin transporter protein and $5HT_{2A}$ receptor genes excluded in generalized social phobia. *Psychiatry Research, 81*, 283–291.

Stein, M.B., Chartier, M.J., Lizak, M.V., & Jang, K.L. (2001). Familial aggregation of anxiety-related quantitative traits in generalized social phobia: Clues to understanding "disorder" heritability? *American Journal of Medical Genetics, 105*, 79–83.

Stein, M.B., Chavira, D.A., & Jang, K.L. (2001). Bringing up bashful baby: Developmental pathways to social phobia. *Psychiatric Clinics of North America, 24*, 661–675.

Stein, M.B., Jang, K.L., & Livesley, W.J. (1999). Heritability of anxiety sensitivity: A twin study. *American Journal of Psychiatry, 156*, 246–251.

Stein, M.B., Jang, K.L., & Livesley, W.J. (2002). Heritability of social anxiety-related concerns and personality characteristics: A twin study. *Journal of Nervous and Mental Disease, 190*, 219–224.

Steinhausen, H., & Juzi, C. (1996). Elective mutism: An analysis of 100 cases. *Journal of the American Academy of Child and Adolescent Psychiatry, 35*, 606–614.

Stemberger, R.T., Turner, S.M., Beidel, D.C., & Calhoun, K.S. (1995). Social phobia: An analysis of possible developmental factors. *Journal of Abnormal Psychology, 104*, 526–531.

Stopa, L., & Clark, D.M. (1993). Cognitive processes in social phobia. *Behaviour Research and Therapy, 31*, 255–267.

Stopa, L., & Clark, D.M. (2000). Social phobia and interpretation of social events. *Behaviour Research and Therapy, 38*, 273–283.

Storch, E.A., Masia-Warner, C., Dent, H.C., Roberti, J.W., & Fisher, P.H. (2004). Psychometric evaluation of the Social Anxiety Scale for Adolescents and the Social Phobia and Anxiety Inventory for Children: Construct validity and normative data. *Journal of Anxiety Disorders, 18*, 665–679.

Strauss, C.C., Frame, C.L., & Forehand, R. (1987). Psychosocial impairment associated with anxiety in children. *Journal of Clinical Child Psychology, 16*, 235–239.

Strauss, C.C., & Last, C.G. (1993). Social and simple phobias in children. *Journal of Anxiety Disorders, 7*, 141–152.

Strauss, C.C., Lahey, B.B., Frick, P., Frame, C.L., & Hynd, G.W. (1988). Peer social status of children with anxiety disorders. *Journal of Consulting and Clinical Psychology, 56*, 137–141.

Strauss, C.C., Lease, C.A., Kazdin, A.E., Dulcan, M.K., & Last, C.G. (1989). Multimethod assessment of the social competence of children with anxiety disorders. *Journal of Clinical Child Psychology, 18*, 184–189.

Strauss, J., Birmaher, B., Bridge, J., Axelson, D., Chiappetta, L., Brent, D., & Ryan, N. (2000). Anxiety disorders in suicidal youth. *Canadian Journal of Psychiatry, 45*, 739–745.

Sweeney, L., & Rapee, R.M. (2001). Social phobia. In C.A. Essau & F. Petermann (Eds.), *Anxiety disorders in children and adolescents: Epidemiology, risk factors and treatment* (pp. 163–192). New York: Brunner-Routledge.

Tancer, M.E., & Uhde, T.W. (2002). Pathogenesis of social phobia. In D.J. Stein & E. Hollander (Eds.), *Textbook of anxiety disorders* (pp. 301–308). Washington, DC: American Psychiatric Publishing.

Thyer, B.A., Parrish, R.T., Curtis, G.C., Nesse, R.M., & Cameron, O.G. (1985). Ages of onset of DSM-III anxiety disorders. *Comprehensive Psychiatry, 26*, 113–122.

Tillfors, M., Furmark, T., Ekselius, L., & Fredrikson, M. (2001). Social phobia and avoidant personality disorder as related to parental history of social anxiety: A general population study. *Behaviour Research and Therapy, 39*, 289–298.

Toren, P., Wolmer, L., Rosental, B., Eldar, S., Koren, S., Lask, M., Weizman, R., & Laor, N. (2000). Case series: Brief parent-child group therapy for childhood anxiety disorders using a manual-based cognitive-behavioral technique. *Journal of the American Academy of Child and Adolescent Psychiatry, 39*, 1309–1312.

Torgersen, S. (1983). Genetic factors in anxiety disorders. *Archives of General Psychiatry, 40*, 1085–1089.

Treadwell, K.R.H., Flannery-Schroeder, E.C., & Kendall, P.C. (1995). Ethnicity and gender in relation to adaptive functioning, diagnostic status, and treatment outcome in children from an anxiety clinic. *Journal of Anxiety Disorders, 9*, 373–384.

Tseng, W., Asai, M., Kitanishi, K., McLaughlin, D.G., & Kyomen, H. (1992). Diagnostic patterns of social phobia: Comparison in Tokyo and Hawaii. *Journal of Nervous and Mental Disease, 180*, 380–385.

Tupler, L.A., Davidson, J.R.T., Smith, R.D., Lazeyras, F., Charles, H.C., & Krishnan, K.R.R. (1997). A repeat proton magnetic resonance spectroscopy study in social phobia. *Biological Psychiatry, 42*, 419–424.

Turner, C.M., & Barrett, P.M. (2003). Does age play a role in the structure of anxiety and depression in children and youths? An investigation of the tripartite model in three age cohorts. *Journal of Consulting and Clinical Psychology, 71,* 826–833.

Turner, S.M., Beidel, D.C., & Costello, A. (1987). Psychopathology in the offspring of anxiety disorders patients. *Journal of Consulting and Clinical Psychology, 55,* 229–235.

Turner, S.M., Beidel, D.C., Dancu, C.V., & Keys, D.J. (1986). Psychopathology of social phobia and comparison to avoidant personality disorder. *Journal of Abnormal Psychology, 95,* 389–394.

Turner, S.M., Beidel, D.C., Dancu, C.V., & Stanley, M.A. (1989). An empirically derived inventory to measure social fears and anxiety: The Social Phobia and Anxiety Inventory. *Psychological Assessment, 1,* 35–40.

Turner, S.M., Beidel, D.C., & Epstein, L.H. (1991). Vulnerability and risk for anxiety disorders. *Journal of Anxiety Disorders, 5,* 151–166.

Turner, S.M., Beidel, D.C., & Townsley, R.M. (1990). Social phobia: Relationship to shyness. *Behaviour Research and Therapy, 28,* 497–505.

Turner, S.M., Beidel, D.C., & Townsley, R.M. (1992). Social phobia: A comparison of specific and generalized subtypes and avoidant personality disorder. *Journal of Abnormal Psychology, 101,* 326–331.

Vaal, J.J. (1973). Applying contingency contracting to a school phobic: A case study. *Journal of Behavior Therapy and Experimental Psychiatry, 4,* 371–373.

Van Ameringen, M., Mancini, C., Farvolden, P., & Oakman, J. (1999). Pharmacotherapy for social phobia: What works, what might work, and what does not work at all. *CNS Spectrums, 4,* 61–68.

Van IJzendoorn, M.H., & Bakermans-Kranenburg, M.J. (1996). Attachment representations in mothers, fathers, adolescents, and clinical groups: A meta-analytic search for normative data. *Journal of Consulting and Clinical Psychology, 64,* 8–21.

Vasey, M.W. (1995). Social anxiety disorders. In A.R. Eisen, C.A. Kearney, & C.E. Schaefer (Eds.), *Clinical handbook of anxiety disorders in children and adolescents* (pp. 131–168). Northvale, NJ: Aronson.

Vasey, M.W., Crnic, K.A., & Carter, W.G. (1994). Worry in childhood: A developmental perspective. *Cognitive Therapy and Research, 18,* 529–549.

Vasey, M.W., & Dadds, M.R. (2001). An introduction to the developmental psychopathology of anxiety. In M.W. Vasey & M.R. Dadds (Eds.), *The developmental psychopathology of anxiety* (pp. 3–42). New York: Oxford University Press.

Vasey, M.W., Daleiden, E.L., Williams, L.L., & Brown, L.M. (1995). Biased attention in childhood anxiety disorders: A preliminary study. *Journal of Abnormal Child Psychology, 23,* 267–279.

Vasey, M.W., Dalgleish, T., & Silverman, W.K. (2003). Research on information-processing factors in child and adolescent psychopathology: A critical commentary. *Journal of Clinical Child and Adolescent Psychology, 32,* 81–93.

Vasey, M.W., El-Hag, N., & Daleiden, E.L. (1996). Anxiety and the processing of emotionally threatening stimuli: Distinctive patterns of selective attention among high- and low-test-anxious children. *Child Development, 67,* 1173–1185.

Vasey, M.W., & McLeod, C. (2001). Information-processing factors in childhood anxiety: A review and developmental perspective. In M.W. Vasey & M.R. Dadds (Eds.), *The developmental psychopathology of anxiety* (pp. 253–277). New York: Oxford University Press.

Vecchio, J.L., & Kearney, C.A. (2005). Selective mutism in children: Comparison to children with and without anxiety disorders. *Journal of Psychopathology and Behavioral Assessment, 27*, 31–37.

Velting, O.N., & Albano, A.M. (2001). Current trends in the understanding and treatment of social phobia in youth. *Journal of Child Psychology and Psychiatry, 42*, 127–140.

Verduin, T.L., & Kendall, P.C. (2003). Differential occurrence of comorbidity within childhood anxiety disorders. *Journal of Clinical Child and Adolescent Psychology, 32*, 290–295.

Verhulst, F.C., van der Ende, J., Ferdinand, R.F., & Kasius, M.C. (1997). The prevalence of DSM-III-R diagnoses in a national sample of Dutch adolescents. *Archives of General Psychiatry, 54*, 329–336.

Vernberg, E.M., Abwender, D.A., Ewell, K.K., & Beery, S.H. (1992). Social anxiety and peer relationships in early adolescence: A prospective analysis. *Journal of Clinical Child Psychology, 21*, 189–196.

Walters, K.S., & Inderbitzen, H.M. (1998). Social anxiety and peer relations among adolescents: Testing a psychobiological model. *Journal of Anxiety Disorders, 12*, 183–198.

Warren, S.L., Huston, L., Egeland, B., & Sroufe, L.A. (1997). Child and adolescent anxiety disorders and early attachment. *Journal of the American Academy of Child and Adolescent Psychiatry, 36*, 637–644.

Warren, S.L., Schmitz, S., & Emde, R.N. (1999). Behavioral genetic analyses of self-reported anxiety at 7 years of age. *Journal of the American Academy of Child and Adolescent Psychiatry, 38*, 1403–1408.

Watson, D., & Friend, R. (1969). Measurement of social-evaluative anxiety. *Journal of Consulting and Clinical Psychology, 33*, 448–457.

Weinshenker, N.J., Goldenberg, I., Rogers, M.P., Goisman, R.M., Warshaw, M.G., Fierman, E.J., Vasile, R.G., & Keller, M.B. (1996/1997). Profile of a large sample of patients with social phobia: Comparisons between generalized and specific social phobia. *Depression and Anxiety, 4*, 209–216.

Weisz, J.R., Suwanlert, S., Chaiyasit, W., Weiss, B., Achenbach, T.M., & Walter, B.R. (1987). Epidemiology of behavioral and emotional problems among Thai and American children. *Journal of the American Academy of Child and Adolescent Psychiatry, 26*, 890–897.

Welner, Z., Reich, W., Herjanic, B., Jung, K.G., & Amado, H. (1987). Reliability, validity, and parent-child agreement studies of the Diagnostic Interview for Children and Adolescents (DICA). *Journal of the American Academy of Child and Adolescent Psychiatry, 26*, 649–653.

Widiger, T.A. (1992). Generalized social phobia versus avoidant personality disorder: A commentary on three studies. *Journal of Abnormal Psychology, 101*, 340–343.

Wilkes, T.C.R., Belsher, G., Rush, A.J., Frank, E., & Associates. (1994). *Cognitive therapy for depressed adolescents*. New York: Guilford.

Wittchen, H.-U., & Beloch, E. (1996). The impact of social phobia on quality of life. *International Clinical Psychopharmacology, 11*, 15–23.

Wittchen, H.-U., Essau, C.A., von Zerssen, D., Krieg, J.-C., & Zaudig, M. (1992). Lifetime and six-month prevalence of mental disorders in the Munich follow-up study. *European Archives of Psychiatry and Clinical Neuroscience, 241*, 247–258.

Wittchen, H.-U., & Fehm, L. (2001). Epidemiology, patterns of comorbidity, and associated disabilities of social phobia. *Psychiatric Clinics of North America, 24*, 617–641.

Wittchen, H.-U., Fuetsch, M., Sonntag, H., Muller, N., & Liebowitz, M. (2000). Disability and quality of life in pure and comorbid social phobia: Findings from a controlled study. *European Psychiatry, 15*, 46–58.

Wittchen, H.-U., Nelson, C.B., & Lachner, G. (1998). Prevalence of mental disorders and psychosocial impairments in adolescents and young adults. *Psychological Medicine, 28*, 109–126.

Wittchen, H.-U., Stein, M.B., & Kessler, R.C. (1999). Social fears and social phobia in a community sample of adolescents and young adults: Prevalence, risk factors and co-morbidity. *Psychological Medicine, 29*, 309–323.

Wolpe, J. (1990). *The practice of behavior therapy* (4th. ed.). New York: Pergamon.

Wood, J.J., Piacentini, J.C., Bergman, L., McCracken, J., & Barrios, V. (2002). Concurrent validity of the anxiety disorders section of the Anxiety Disorders Interview Schedule for DSM-IV: Child and Parent Versions. *Journal of Clinical Child and Adolescent Psychology, 31*, 335–342.

Woodruff-Borden, J., Morrow, C., Bourland, S., & Cambron, S. (2002). The behavior of anxious parents: Examining mechanisms of transmission of anxiety from parent to child. *Journal of Clinical Child and Adolescent Psychology, 31*, 364–374.

Woodward, L.J., & Fergusson, D.M. (2001). Life course outcomes of young people with anxiety disorders in adolescence. *Journal of the American Academy of Child and Adolescent Psychiatry, 40*, 1086–1093.

Woody, S.R., Chambless, D.L., & Glass, C.R. (1997). Self-focused attention in the treatment of social phobia. *Behaviour Research and Therapy, 35*, 117–129.

World Health Organisation. (1994). *Pocket guide to the ICD-10 classification of mental and behavioural disorders*. Washington, DC: American Psychiatric Press.

Yang, B., Ollendick, T.H., Dong, Q., Xia, Y., & Lin, L. (1995). Only children and children with siblings in the People's Republic of China: Levels of fear, anxiety, and depression. *Child Development, 66*, 1301–1311.

Yeganeh, R., Beidel, D.C., Turner, S.M., Pina, A.A., & Silverman, W.K. (2003). Clinical distinctions between selective mutism and social phobia: An investigation of childhood psychopathology. *Journal of the American Academy of Child and Adolescent Psychiatry, 42*, 1069–1075.

Zatz, S., & Chassin, L. (1983). Cognitions of test-anxious children. *Journal of Consulting and Clinical Psychology, 51*, 526–534.

Zatz, S., & Chassin, L. (1985). Cognitions of test-anxious children under naturalistic test-taking conditions. *Journal of Consulting and Clinical Psychology, 53*, 393–401.

Zimbardo, P.G. (1977). *Shyness: What it is, what to do about it*. Reading, MA: Addison-Wesley.

Zimbardo, P.G. (1982). Shyness and the stresses of the human connection. In L. Goldberger & S. Breznitz (Eds.), *Handbook of stress: Theoretical and clinical aspects* (pp. 466–481). New York: Free Press.

Zimbardo, P.G., & Radl, S.L. (1981). *The shy child: A parent's guide to preventing and overcoming shyness from infancy to adulthood*. New York: McGraw-Hill.

SUBJECT INDEX